The Secret History of Freemasonry

The Secret History of Freemasonry

Its Origins and Connection to the Knights Templar

PAUL NAUDON

Translated by Jon Graham

Inner Traditions
Rochester, Vermont

Inner Traditions
One Park Street
Rochester, Vermont 05767
www.InnerTraditions.com

Originally published in French under the title *Les origins de la Franc-Maçonnerie: Le sacré et le métier* by Éditions Dervy, 34, boulevard Edgar Quinet, 75014 Paris

First U.S. edition published in 2005 by Inner Traditions

Library of Congress Cataloging-in-Publication Data
Naudon, Paul.
 [Origins de la franc-maçonnerie. English]
 The secret history of freemasonry : its origins and connection to the Knights Templar / Paul Naudon ; translated by Jon Graham.— 1st U.S. ed.
  p. cm.
 "Originally published in French under the title Les origins de la franc-maçonnerie: le sacré et le metier by Éditions Dervy . . . Paris"—T.p. verso.
 Includes index.
 ISBN 1-59477-028-X (pbk.)
 1. Freemasonry—History. 2. Freemasons—History. 3. Templars—History. 4. Building guilds—History. I. Title.
 HS403.N3413 2005
 366'.1'09—dc22
                                                                    2004029773

Printed and bound in the United States by Lake Book Manufacturing, Inc.

10 9 8 7 6 5 4 3

Text design by Virginia L. Scott Bowman
Text layout by Priscilla Baker
This book was typeset in Sabon, with Chevalier as a display typeface

Contents

Part 2. From the Art of Building to the Art of Thinking

Preface

I state with all modesty, and without presuming to underestimate the value of preceding works on the subject, that to date there has been no truly scientific history of the origins of Freemasonry and that such a study is totally justified.

A number of valuable works on the history of Freemasonry have in fact been published since the appearance of the grand lodges at the beginning of the seventeenth century. Indeed, they have flourished in such number since the end of the Second World War that we can now hail the birth of a new discipline, which we might call *masonology*.

Nevertheless, operative freemasonry, which preceded this modern Freemasonry* and which is its source, has not been the beneficiary of such extensive examination. Those who have dealt with the origins of

---

* [The term *operative freemasonry* as used throughout this book refers to freemasonry in its original form, as represented by brotherhoods of builders. It is opposed in this study by the term *speculative Freemasonry,* having to do with those organizations that emerged in the seventeenth century divorced from the worker and the meaning of his tradition and made up of "accepted" Masons. Throughout this book and especially in part 2, the author strives to make a strong distinction between speculative Freemasonry and the operative freemasonry that is its origin and between more or less "accepted" Masons and those craftsmen—masons—who actually practiced the building crafts. To make these distinctions clearer, an upper case *F* and *M* are used to distinguish speculative and modern Freemasonry and Freemasons/Masons and a lower case *f* and *m* are used to refer to operative or original freemasonry/masonry and freemasons/masons. —*Editor*]

the order—for how can anyone claim to discuss this subject without touching upon this question?—have largely contributed insights only to the various fragmentary aspects their individual studies may have addressed. Far too often these studies have consisted of only an isolated, contemporary, and literal reading of documents with which most students of this subject are already familiar. Symbolism, which is the capital rule of Freemasonry, has often been either systematically overlooked or cursorily addressed on the broader historical plane. Some scholars have even believed Freemasonry's symbolism and history to be two separate domains, while others, conversely, have confused symbolism and history, boiling down both to a single reduction and seeking to deduce the meaning of one from the other. The veil formed by these symbols—words, figures, and signs— has concealed the structures and realities from them.

We must hasten to pay a well-deserved homage to this research, however, specifically to the remarkable works published since 1886 by the London Study Lodge Quatuor Coronati no. 2076, which has brought to light a significant number of old, specifically British documents. Myriad brilliant authors have applied themselves to the presentation and analysis of these texts, including R. F. Gould, D. Knoop, G. P. Jones, D. Hamer, Lionel Vibert, F. L. Pick, G. N. Knight. Harry Carr, and John Hamil. Their works are quite valuable for their probity, the precision of their notes, and their observations relevant to the factual study of the beginnings of Freemasonry in Great Britain.

This intellectual harvest has encouraged me to intensify the search for a way to better situate the masonic institution and its origins in their general historical and structural context, especially given that the facts related to the institution are inseparable from the social context, mindsets, and motivations surrounding it. Further, while modern Freemasonry has grown directly from an exclusively British framework, its origins and development extend far beyond Great Britain and that nation's history in both time and space, a fact that deserves some exploration.

My investigations on this subject have been quite extensive. I have made a point of attending to findings made in earlier works, incorporating those opinions whose premises were supported with proof. Research based on historical sources in all their complexity has been my chief concern. Quite often this research has led me to subject areas that might seem quite foreign to the topic at hand, such as archaeology, ethnography, sociology, law, and political economics. History, however, is traced not only through documents, but also through reconstructing the institutions, mores, and lifestyles in the past. The historical method is, by necessity, multidisciplinary in its theories and hypotheses. Nothing can be examined in complete isolation, *in abstracto*. Life is unity within diversity. I have consistently sought to gather what was scattered in order to reconstruct a living past and, consequently, one that is as close as possible to reality and truth.

Setting off on my journey objectively and without any preconceived notions, I have had to surrender to the evidence showing that certain opinions expressed in what are accepted as fundamental works on Freemasonry are actually lacking any basis of support.

Conversely, the same rectitude of thought and judgment led me to the opposite conclusion: that certain legends whose credibility had been greatly shaken among positivist minds were, in truth, based on sound arguments. This is especially the case for the Templar origins of Freemasonry. It should be clearly stated, though, that this does not mean I believe modern "speculative" Freemasonry is a direct survival of this vanished Order.

For their ceaseless understanding, kindness, and strong encouragement, I thank all those in the wide variety of fields I have explored in the undertaking of this book. I give my acknowledgment and thanks to all those who gave me their assistance or showed interest in the work I was doing. Certainly I am aware of the gaps that remain in this product. My ambition is to inspire further study in this fascinating subject that remains in large part unexplored.

Introduction

Behold the days come, oracle of the Eternal . . . I will set
my law within them and write it on their hearts . . .
Behold the days come that city shall be built.

To find the origins of Freemasonry, it is important first to isolate its original characteristics, which can be found in the institutions from which it appears to have emerged:

1. It was a professional builders—or, more precisely, construction—organization; the long-ago vocation of mason does not correspond directly to the modern specialization, but included an extensive knowledge of architecture. The organization was represented hierarchically.
2. The organization extended beyond a strictly professional framework. Its members considered themselves brothers and provided mutual assistance.
3. The association, in both its operations and assistance, followed traditional rites. Members were accepted into it through an initiation and the brothers were united by sacred practices that were illustrative of an asceticism, an indispensable condition for the realization of the work.
4. The association accepted members who were not practitioners of the trade.
5. The association displayed and highlighted its character of universalism.

This study of Freemasonry looks at both its specific history and the influences and events that have left their imprint over time on its formation and evolution. As such, it includes an examination of various spheres—social, juridical, religious, and philosophical—that have conditioned these events.

From a chronological perspective, the most certain sources of Freemasonry have emerged as the following:

1. The Roman *collegia,* the remnants of which remained in the West following invasions and survived in the East as institutions discovered by the Crusaders at the end of the eleventh century.
2. The ecclesiastical associations of builders formed by the bishops of the early Middle Ages, especially the Benedictines, the Cistercians, and the Templars.
3. Trade-based freemasonry, which was born under the aegis of these associations and followed the form of lay brotherhoods or guilds.

The history of Freemasonry and its origins will form the first part of this book. In the second part, we will study the evolution of the professional organization; its purposes, both operational and speculative; its initiatory and spiritualist nature; its gradual transformation from an organization of those who worked in the art of building to those who engaged in a *stricto sensu* art of thinking and living; and the creation of modern Freemasonry under the influences of and in circumstances connected to British history.

The greatest common denominator that we can distinguish across the centuries, truly the millennia, is the coexistence and interdependence of masonic objectives and a sense of the sacred. In fact, it is the sacred that is the effective and ultimate cause of these objectives, however different from one another they may appear in the various stages of their evolution. This is an exemplary illustration of an important truth: Faith lives only through works and works are worth only the faith that moves them.

PART 1

The Origins of Freemasonry from Ancient Times to the Middle Ages

1

The Ancient Corporations: Colleges of Builders in Rome

The Religious Character of the Ancient Corporations

The corporative organization of labor goes back to distant antiquity, and associations of builders are among the most ancient. When humans abandoned the nomadic lifestyle, they formed builders associations to erect durable shelters, protective ramparts, and temples in which to worship their gods. Architecture became an art—a difficult one demanding unique empirical knowledge prior to the development of the exact sciences. In some ways builders created the first aristocracy of jealous exclusivity whose services were indispensable to the gradually forming states. The association proved necessary because isolated individuals were incapable of erecting large structures by themselves and because this work required extensive general, technical, and artistic knowledge. Here it is necessary to make an important, preliminary observation if we truly wish to understand the history of labor and trades: First and foremost, this association always had a religious basis.

For the people of antiquity, every action of life was commingled with religion. Humans considered themselves the playthings of higher powers without whose help it was impossible to succeed at anything. Work was notably invested with a sacred nature. Oswald Wirth, in *Les Mystères de l'Art Royal,* translated this religious sentiment with great skill:

The hunter sacrificed to the guardian spirit of the animal he sought to kill, just as prior to chopping down a tree, the carpenter won the approval of the hamadryad. The quarryman, in turn, would have felt he had committed a sacrilege if he began cutting into rock without beforehand obtaining the consent of Mother Earth, whom he was mutilating. This is not the entire story, because avoidance of inspiring the hatred of a deity corresponds only to the negative side of worship by the professions. For his labor to be successful, the worker additionally had to ensure the positive support of the gods who dispensed the talents required. A pact was therefore necessary: By devoting himself body and soul to the service of the deity of the particular profession, the artisan would bilaterally contract sacred obligations, because by fervently striving to do his best in the domain of art, he compelled the god of his trade to come to his aid . . . So a union was therefore effected between the humble mortal and the god who worked through him, using him as an intermediary, therefore deifying the human through work . . . Each trade exalted its tutelary deity . . . Rich in imagination, the ancients were able to poeticize the actions of daily life and give their professional occupations a celestial aura. Thus were born the mysteries of the different trades.[1]

The cult of the ancient builders must have been of a distinct scope, for the noblest object of their labor was the construction of temples in which the gods were worshipped. In addition, human dwellings had religious significance. Rituals were an indispensable part of their construction. Among the Romans the home was the temple of the *lares* gods. This was true for all ancient peoples and still survives in the traditional societies of the East. "The dwelling was not an object, a 'machine to inhabit': It was the Universe that man built in imitation of God's exemplary creation, the cosmogony."[2] The home was not merely a geometrical space; it was an existential and sacred place.

When trade associations were indispensable, as was the case with those of the builders in ancient times, they were of a sacerdotal nature. Among the Egyptians, the priest embodied a special branch of human knowledge. Each grade put its students through a predetermined series of studies specific to the art or science that it professed. In addition, for each novitiate degree, students were subjected to trials of initiation the purpose of which was to ensure them a vocation and which added to the mysteries whose teaching was hidden from the public. It must be assumed that architecture, like all other sciences, was taught in secret. Louis Hautcoeur writes:

> The first architects known in Egypt, in Asia Minor, performed sacred duties independent from their role as builders . . . Imhotep, who built the first large stone complex in Saqqarah, was counselor to the pharaoh Sozer (circa 3800 B.C.), but was also priest of the god Amun. Sennemut, architect of Queen Hatseput, was the head of the prophets of Monthu in Armant and controller of the gardens and domains of Amun. Dherti was the director of buildings and a high priest. In the Louvre there are seated statues of Goudea, who was both a *patesi,* meaning a governor representing the gods, and an architect. . . . The architects seem to have been inspired by the gods they served.[3]

The Books of I Kings (5:13 ff and 7:13, 14) and II Chronicles (2:14 and 4:11) inform us that in Judea during the construction of the Temple of Jerusalem, under the direction of master builder Hiram of Tyre and Adoniram, Solomon had 70,000 men to carry loads and 80,000 to carve the stones from the mountains, not to mention those who had managed each job, who numbered about 3,300 and gave orders to the workers. Though we have no actual historical information on the subject, this story reveals that among the artisans busy on the construction of the temple there was a professional hierarchy and an organization, if not a corporation.

In Greece, professional organizations were known as *hetarias.* One of the laws of Solon (593 B.C.), the text of which was preserved for us by Gaius in his *De Collegiis et corporibus* (Digest), allowed the various colleges or hetarias of Athens to make rules for themselves freely, provided none of these rules went against the laws of the state.

Although the sacred nature of the builders appears to have become somewhat blurred among the Greeks, it survived all the same, notably in the legends concerning architect kings such as Dadaelus, Trophonius, and Agamedes. A typical example is that of the priests of Dionysius or Bacchus. They were the first to erect theaters in Greece and to institute dramatic representations principally linked to worship of the god. The architects responsible for the construction of these buildings maintained a priesthood through initiation; they were called Dionysian workers or Dionysiasts. We know through Strabo and Aulu-Gelle that the Dionysiasts' organization in Teos was assigned to them as a residence by the kings of Pergama around 300 B.C. They had a specific initiation as well as words and signs by which they recognized one another and were divided into separate communities called synods, colleges, or societies. Each of these communities was under the direction of a teacher and chairmen or supervisors who were elected annually. In their secret ceremonies the Dionysians made symbolic use of the tools of their trade. At certain times they threw banquets during which the most skilled workers were awarded prizes. The richer members gave help and assistance to the indigent and the sick. In Greece the Dionysians were organized in the same way, and Solon's legislation gave them some special privileges.[4]

It is important to note that banquets have held a religious and sacred significance from the time of greatest antiquity. Even the members of primitive clans gathered together to eat the sacred animal. "They communed," Durkheim wrote, "with the sacred principle that dwelled within it and they assimilated it . . . The purpose of sacrificial banquets was to bring about communion of the believer and his god in one flesh in order to knit between them a bond of kinship." Thus we may say that dietary communion was one of the earliest forms of religion.[5]

The Roman Collegia

It is supremely important to establish the connection between operative freemasonry and the *collegia artificum et fabrorum* of Rome, for the collegia exerted a major influence over trade brotherhoods of the Middle Ages, which more or less directly descended from them.

According to Plutarch, colleges of artisans were founded in Rome by King Numa Pompilius around 715 B.C. Plutarch cites nine colleges, including that of the carpenters, but says nothing about masons.[6] This is explained by the fact that Roman society did not then acknowledge a very extensive division and specialization of labor. As an example of the sociological law of the development of human societies, the Homeric era recognized only four specialized trades: woodworking—that is to say, the building of houses (so there can be no question of masons); metalworking; certified leatherworking; and clayworking (making vases and pottery). Going through the centuries, we find house builders falling under the term *carpenters*.

Yet the oldest code of laws to have come down to us, the Babylonian Code of Hammurabi discovered in Susa and dating back to about 2000 B.C., reveals even in its time a certain division in the art of building. It mentions architects, carpenters, stonecutters, masons, and bricklayers, and building seems to have been the only art to have contained this degree of specialization.[7]

The Roman collegia formed one of the essential parts of the constitution attributed to King Servius Tullius (578–534 B.C.), which remained in force until 241 B.C. This constitution is characterized by a system of organization according to *centuries*. It cites three collegia, each of which formed one century: the *tignarii* (carpenters and, consequently, home builders), the *oerarii* (workers in bronze or copper), and the *tibicines* (flute players) or *cornicines* (trumpeteers). Titus-Livy and Cicero ranked carpenters in the first and most fortunate class of citizens, consisting of 98 centuries (9,800 carpenters) and holding a majority in the *comices*.* The other two collegia also belonged to the first class of citizens. These three colleges of privileged artisans, endowed with political prerogatives and made up of a number of state bodies, were called upon to render the greatest service to a people who lived in an almost perpetual state of war. Were they not soldiers almost as much as they were artisans, these oerarii who forged shields and weapons, these cornicines whose martial fanfares called the Roman hosts to combat, and especially these tignarii who built, repaired, and, if necessary, maneuvered the engines of destruction such as ballista and catapults

---

* [This Roman term designates an elective or legislative assembly of the people. — *Trans.*]

and who built the fortified walls and camps and rebuilt, always better than before, what the combatants had destroyed? Weren't the Roman legions builders as much as they were soldiers? Servius Tullius himself commanded two centuries of workers as men at arms under the title of military companies.[8]

Sometime between 67 B.C. and 64 B.C., the Julia Law abolished a certain number of collegia and *sodalita* (associations founded on a solidarity of interests) because of the abuses that had accompanied their meddling with the *comitia,* namely the corruption of bureaucrats and the purchase of votes. The Julia Law, however, did exempt the college of *tenuiores,* or artisans who were purely professional. There were a number of these for the tignarii. The collegia that survived were subject to more rigorous regulation (one banquet a month at most and administrative oversight). Most important, they were made more subordinate to the state, something that did not hinder their development. Quite the contrary: Under Alexander Severus (208–235 B.C.), there were thirty-two collegia.

By this time the collegia had become essential state institutions wed to strong municipal organization. During the third century these institutions preserved their traditional importance but lost much of their former independence. They became cogs in the imperial administration, albeit the most important cogs, for they were in direct contact with the population.

With the empire now an absolute monarchy, the governmental authority was gradually assuming the task of assuring not only law and order, but material prosperity as well. To do this, it set up a vast system of social classes in such a way that all the services necessary to survival and living had sufficient personnel. The utmost effort was made to maintain the individual authority of each man in his duty or profession, which is how the collegia happened to be called upon to play a role of primary importance in this system. We will see how the lesson of this absolute and centralizing administration based on municipal organization and professional groups eventually inspired European sovereigns in their fight against feudalism and in their quest to strengthen their authority at the time of the Crusades, when they found Roman social institutions still in place in the East.

The Principal Collegia

In the latter days of the Roman empire, Christian influences brought about both a decline in slavery and the development of free labor. This labor remained completely organized under the corporative form of the collegia and each professional was compelled to join the college of his trade. The institution realized the height of its development in the fourth century.[9]

At this time a distinction was made between public and private colleges. Public colleges included all the professions that were indispensable to sustaining the people: arms manufacture, horse breeding, public transportation *(naviculars)*, bakers, butchers, manufacturers and suppliers of basic construction materials such as bricks and lumber. These trades were regarded as public services. Their members called themselves not collegiati but *corporati* and, if it was necessary, they were recruited from among the ranks of the condemned. Any individuals involved in these services remained so their entire lives and at no time had the right to sell their work.

The other professions made up the private colleges, which were actually semi-public bodies. These included mainly the *dendrophori* and tignarii, artisans specializing in woodwork. The college of the tignarii, homebuilders, remained hugely important and was widespread throughout the empire. Among the other colleges were the *argentarii* (bankers), the *lapidarii* and *marmorii* (various categories of stone and marble workers), the *centonarii* (garment manufacturers), the *negotiares vini* (wine merchants) and the *medici* (doctors) and *professori* (teachers).

Generally speaking, the state granted each collegium a monopoly on its trade. The members enjoyed certain advantages. For instance, they were exempt from certain taxes and from being drafted for labor. It was forbidden, however, for collegiates to change professions under pain of surrendering all their property to the collegium. They could sell their real estate and their slaves only to their colleagues. Moreover, membership in a collegium was hereditary. If a member died with no heir capable of taking his place in the profession, then the collegium would inherit his assets.

The Legal Organization of the Collegium

A collegium could exist only if it had been authorized. While members could freely question its statutes, provided they did not contravene public order, these statutes had to be monitored and sanctioned by the state, which gave them the force of obligation.

For each collegium a general list *(album)* of the membership, or *collegiate,* was kept. Above the simple collegiate were the magistrates of the corporation, elected by their peers: the *decurions* (heads of ten member groups), *curators, procurators, syndics,* and *questeurs* (judges of the corporation instituted by Alexander Severus). The effective leaders of the corporation, the *duumviri, quinquennali,* and *magisti,* sat above these various magistrates. Each college also included honorary members who made offerings and patrons *(patroni),* prominent figures who interceded with the authorities on behalf of the college.

The organization of the college appears to have been quite democratic. A common house *(schola* or *maceria)* was assigned for assemblies and the installation of the college's departments. It normally had a *tetrastyle* (a four-sided portico) on which the college rules were posted. The *arca* or cashbox of the community was kept there. It was in the schola, before altars or images of the gods, that sacrifices were preformed and where artisans of the same craft or the enthusiasts of a cult would join together in pious solidarity on certain days. One of the principal rites was the *repas* presided over by a *magister coenoe.* There can be no doubt that these meals had religious meaning, at least originally. Their degeneration into something lesser did not occur until later and was one reason why the Julia Law (67–64 B.C.) limited their number.

Professional Worship in the Collegia and the Conversion to Christianity

We now return to the fundamental nature of ancient trades. Originally, as was the case in other cultures, the laws and institutions of Roman society were essentially based on religion. This was also true for the collegia, whose activity was dominated by professional worship.

It was natural—and indispensable—for each Roman collegium to have its tutelary deities, just as every family had its *lares* (household gods). It was in this celebration of common worship that the affiliated members recognized each other—often through the employ of gestures, signs, and ritual touch that had a sacred and psychological, perhaps even physiological, aspect. These signs also became the means used by members to recognize their colleagues, thereby guaranteeing the sanctity of craft secrets and protecting them from the profane. This necessity must have made itself felt in the collegia of builders who followed the legions on their campaigns.

A collegium's divine protectors could be chosen by the order from almost anywhere. Often a college chose a god whose attributions were related to the daily labor of its members (for example, Sylvanus, god of woods, for the *dendrophori,* or wood carvers). In other cases it might choose a deceased emperor or even a foreign deity. We know that the Romans often adopted the gods of other peoples. We can surmise what deity the Roman tignarii, or carpenters, chose for themselves by looking at a stone discovered in 1725 in Chichester, England, that bears the dedication (52 A.D.) of a temple to Minerva, goddess of wisdom, and Neptune, god of the sea. The latter may well have been invoked both for the protection of the tignarii, who frequently had to cross the Channel, and for the construction of boats.[10] A similar inscription discovered in Nice-Cimiez shows the lapidarii making a vow to Hercules, their tutelary deity.*

It is also likely that the worship of Roman builders had experienced the influence of foreign peoples because of the itinerant nature of these artisans and the fact that the Romans benefited from the architectural knowledge of the Greeks, who in turn had been influenced by the Persians, Egyptians, and Syrians. In fact, the influence of the Syrians must have been considerable following their significant immigration into the Roman Empire, to Rome particularly, during the later years of its existence. "It was especially in the first century that the Syrian exercised his activities, charged with almost all the minor crafts . . . The Syrus (Oriental in the broad sense of the term) entered everywhere, introducing with him the tongue and mores of his country."[11] Indeed,

---

* For more on the symbolic myth of Hercules and its connection with builders, see my book *Les Loges de Saint-Jean* (Paris: Éditions Dervy, 1995), 71 ff.

the best propagators of Christianity in the working classes were the Syrians. "Christianity in the third and fourth centuries was preeminently the religion of Syria. After Palestine, Syria played the greatest role in its foundation."[12]

The community of worship and more or less religious or ritual practices had the natural effect of strengthening the ties bonding the faithful. A kind of solidarity compelled members of the same collegium to lend help and assistance to each other when life's circumstances so dictated. One of Trajan's letters responding to Pliny in 93 A.D. establishes that the *eranos* (association) of Amisus, a free city of Bithynia, concerned itself with, among other things, easing the misery of its poor members.

Like some inscriptions, certain texts from the Theodosian Code (a 483 A.D. compilation of earlier texts) reveal the germination of several of the charitable institutions that spread so widely during the Middle Ages. Law 5, for instance—*de pistoribus*—offers the example of a kind of adoption performed by craftsmen of certain collegia if a colleague left any orphans upon his death. As a testament to the collegiates' relationship and the charity it inspired, these colleagues are described as brothers *(fratibus suis)* in an inscription of the collegium of Velabre from the time before Christianity.

At the death of one of its members, the collegium could be counted on to step in to ensure honorable obsequy and to oversee the fulfillment of the prescribed rites. Among the Romans, the sepulcher, intimately connected to the *sacra gentilitia,* or family rites, held great importance. People wanted assurance that they would not be tossed into one of the atrocious mass graves common to that era and that their college would see to their funeral arrangements. Those who were buried together contracted a kind of intimate fraternity and kinship.[13]

The sacred character attached to labor continued with the rise of Christianity and in fact was reinvigorated and rejuvenated by the new religion, which enabled labor subsequently to acquire an even higher value. This effect, which is often overlooked, is of the utmost importance, for it appears in all the social and political upheavals that have taken place throughout the history of labor. Throughout the centuries the Church unfailingly proclaimed and continually developed this principle: Labor is the image of Divine Creation.

The influence of the Church was first felt on the ethical plane, resulting in the dignification of labor and the protection of the *humiliores* against the powerful in institutions. The earliest constitutions ordered that work be remunerated, and little by little slavery diminished and the fate of serfs gradually improved.

According to the Christian concept of labor, each trade was placed under the protection of a patron saint, who acted as an intercessor with the power on high. Over the centuries these saints became increasingly involved with people's everyday lives. But the relationship between artisan and the higher power extended much further than this. Christian religion teaches that we carry within us the divine virtues; we are, in effect, a temple for them. In following the exemplary life shown by Christ, we are able to attain perfection and, through the action of Christ within us, ensure that Christ lives. In our work we are thus a participant in the creative labor of God.

For more than a millennium, this Christian truth permeated more and more of human life. In the Middle Ages it became one of the principles of social organization. Even at the beginning of the fifteenth century, Fra Angelico's contemporaries would say that angels came down to paint his painting during the inspired slumber of this incomparable Dominican monk.

On the social and practical plane, it is not out of the question that traditional rites of the collegia survived during the time of the late Empire, despite the triumph of Christianity and its transformation into the state religion. With their initiatory and sacred value adapted to the new spirit of the age, these rites had in their favor the strength of popular custom and the people's interest in retaining them as signs of identification and professional secrets. It is generally thought that it was for reasons of this nature that early Christianity readily adopted pagan rituals, symbols, and even gods, whom it made into legendary saints. By giving these deities souls, they assured the perpetuation of the values the gods symbolically represented.*

---

* Baronius, *Annales* (XXXVI): "It was permissible for the Holy Church to appropriate rituals and ceremonies used by the pagans in their idolatrous worship because it regenerated them with its consecration." Saint Gregory did not wish to see these customs suppressed. "Purify the temples," he wrote to his missionaries, "but do not destroy them, for so long as the nation witnesses the survival of its former places of prayer, it will use

The Collegia of Craftsmen in Roman Gaul

Roman institutions were actually established quite easily in Gaul, as were the collegia. Specific traces of their existence have been detected in Nice Cimiez. Collegia were also quite numerous in Provence and the Narbonnaise, as well as in the Lugdunaise, where the collegia of the tignarii and the dendrophori, closely tied to municipal life, were located. A list of trade colleges existing before the fourth century mentions the presence of these institutions in Marseille, Aix, Arles, Vienne, Valence, Nîmes, Marbonne, and Lyon. Although the collegia appear to have had less success penetrating northern Gaul, it can be assumed that colleges of craftsmen were formed in the majority of the large towns in the region. In Paris, excavations beneath Notre Dame in 1715 unearthed an inscription dedicated to Jupiter by the *nautoe parisiaci*. It is likely important colleges of builders were also located in Lutece after Emperor Julian selected it for his dwelling and undertook important construction there that has survived into the present. These colleges must also have flourished in Treves, a rich Gallic capital; in Rhenanie, where Roman remnants are so numerous; and in the Duchy of Nassau.[14]

The Collegia in Great Britain

Given that modern Freemasonry can be traced directly to British origin, there is good reason to linger more extensively on the history of the collegia of builders in Great Britain.

Several brigades of construction workers stationed with the Roman legions in the countries bordering the Rhine were sent into Great Britain by Emperor Claudius in 43 A.D. to protect Romans from Scottish raids. Before their arrival, there were no towns or cities in this

them out of habit and you will win them all the easier to the worship of the true God." This same saint said, "The Bretons perform sacrifices and give feasts on certain days: Leave them their feasts; suppress only the sacrifices." We can conclude, with Eliphas Levi *(Histoire de la magie*, Éditions de la Maisnie, 1974): "Far from encouraging ancient superstitions . . . Christianity restored life and soul to the surviving symbols of universal beliefs." This explains how Celtic traditions maintained in Gaul were later to be found again in Romanesque art. See also M. Moreau, *La tradition celtique dans l'Art Roman* (Paris: Éditions Le Courrier du Livre, 1963) and Henri Hubert, *Les Celtes et l'expansion celtique jusqu'a l'époque de la Tène* (Paris: Albin Michel, 1950), 17–18.

country. The builders collegia were charged with the construction of camps for use by the legions. Gradually these military camps became outfitted with large buildings, baths, bridges, temples, and palaces. In all places where legions established permanent camps, these camps eventually became the core of more or less important cities, including York (the former Eboracum), which holds a prominent place in the history of Freemasonry. This was one of the first communities in Great Britain to gain significance and to be promoted to the rank of a Roman city.

Constant raiding from the mountains of Scotland forced the Romans to erect huge walls in the north of Britain on three separate occasions. The first great wall was constructed by order of the general Agricola in 90 A.D. The second was built under Emperor Hadrian in 120 A.D. Finally, the third was built from the Firth estuary to the river Clyde around 140 A.D., during the time of Anthony the Pious. Septimus Severus undertook construction of another wall farther north in the year 207, but we lack any precise information on on its building or whereabouts.

In 287 A.D., Carausius, commander of the Roman fleet stationed off the coast of Belgium, rebelled and took possession of Great Britain, where he declared himself independent of Rome and adopted the title of emperor. Fearing attack from Emperor Maximianus, he likely sought to earn the favor of the collegia, particularly the most important one, that of the builders. This is why in Veralum (the modern Saint Albans), where he resided, Carausius, through the mediation of the Roman knight Albanus and the Greek architect Amphibolus, confirmed to the corporations their ancient privileges conferred upon them by Numa Pompilius and Servius Tullius, who had formed them. Not only would he have abrogated the restrictions that had been enforced since the Julia Law, but he would also have added the right of special jurisdiction.

Freed from the power of the emperors, Carausius used his wealth to increase the well-being of the country. He especially kept the collegia busy with the construction of public buildings worthy of competing with those of other imperial residences. Following the death of Carausius, who was assassinated in 293 A.D., vice-emperor Constantius I (Chlorus), chosen by Maximanius and given governorship of Gaul and Great Britain, took possession of the latter province and established his residence in Eboracum (York). In 305 he became emperor following the abdication of Maximanius, but died in 306 during a campaign against the Picts.

He was succeeded by his son, Constantine I. Putting an end to the persecution of Christians, Constantine declared himself their protector. After his victory over his rival, Licinus, he himself converted to Christianity, which he made the state religion. During the next century Christianity spread throughout Great Britain and the Scots and Picts continued to harass the Romans, who, finding themselves attacked from all sides, left this land at the beginning of the fifth century. At this same time, almost the whole of Europe succumbed to the attacks of barbarians.

2

The Collegia and the
Barbarian Invasions

What happened to the collegia, particularly the organization of builders, when the Western Empire collapsed under repeated waves of invasion? The fate of Roman institutions varied by region. Obviously, they survived in those countries that were not occupied by conquering forces, which is how, in those parts of Italy that remained "Roman" (those transferred to the protection of the Eastern Empire and Byzantium—notably Ravenna, Rome, and Venice) the collegia continued to develop in the form of *scholoe* or *scuole* (schools). In the region of Gaul, Roman influence continued to be strongly felt in the kingdoms of the Visigoths and the Burgundians. They managed to survive to a much lesser extent in the kingdom of the Franks. In Great Britain, it does not appear that Roman institutions survived the invasions of the Picts, the Angles, and the Saxons. We will now look more closely at the situation in each of these areas.

The Fate of the Collegia in the Frankish Kingdom

We know that the Franks first penetrated Gaul as *foederati* (Frankish mercenaries) in service to Rome and that they contributed to the protection of the country against the Vandals and the Huns. It was with the aid of the Franks that the Roman general Aetius fought Attila in 451 on the Catalaunic Fields near Châlons. But this accord, born of a common danger, was temporary. The Franks, both Ripuarians (who lived south of the Rhine) and Salians (who settled north of the Rhine), gradually infiltrated from the Paris basin to take a predominant position in northern and eastern Gaul. In 464 the Ripuarians occupied the diocese of Treves once and for all. Following this time and lasting more than a century, Christian inscriptions disappeared in this diocese, a certain sign that the Christian—in other words, Roman—populace had been decimated, forced into exile, or reduced to the condition of Germanic serfs known as *lites*. From this point on we can no longer find any trace in these Ripurian-ruled lands of the collegia that had built the monuments in the Gallic capital of Treves.

But in the regions subject to the authority of the Salian Franks, of whom Clovis became king in 481, it seems that the Gallo-Romans retained their property and civil rights. Albert Esmein proposes the theory that during the Frankish era, corporations of craftsmen and especially merchants survived, no doubt freer than before, maintained by their members' common interest. In support of his opinion he cites an allusion made by Gregory of Tours in the sixth century concerning the kingdom of Austrasia.* This text may not be so definitive, however. The Gallo-Romans' loss of some freedoms in these regions during the rule of Clovis, even when subsequently recovered, casts doubt on the possibility of a complete legal continuity of the collegia.

Additional notable facts provided by Gregory of Tours, however, lead to a more subtle view of matters. While the Roman institution of the collegium disappeared, it is quite possible that remnants survived long afterward. It is probable that builders from the collegia found shelter, work, and protection with the bishops. Until at least 600 A.D., all

---

* A. Esmein, *Histoire du droit français*, 4th ed. (Paris: Librairie du Recueil Sirey, 1892), 291. Esmein cites the following text from Gregory of Tours (*Hist. Francorum*, III, 34), the address of a bishop to Austrasian king Theodebert (sixth century): "Rogmo, si pietas tua habet aliquid de pecunia, nobis commodes . . . cumque hi negucium exercentes responsum in civitate nostra, sicut reliquae habent, praestiterint, pecuniam tuam cum usuries legitimis reddimus."

bishops of Gaul, even in the Frankish areas, were Gallo-Romans. It is likely that some of these were remarkable builders who were actually aided by the Frankish kings. In 472, through the efforts of Perpetue, or Parpet of Tours, a first-class basilica, the most beautiful in the West, was completed to house the tomb of Saint Martin. A century later in Paris, Chidebert I (d. 558) kept masons busy on the magnificent Saint Vincent Church (now Saint Germain des Près). In Nantes, the bishop Felix (550–583) focused his concern on useful public works such as roadways, bridges, and canals, and consecrated a cathedral that is said to have been as beautiful as Saint Martin Basilica. In his city and diocese, Gregory of Tours built several churches, notably Saint Maurice Cathedral, which was consecrated around 580.[1] All this attests to the survival of not only Roman traditions, but also important associations of builders, artists, and specialists.

The Fate of the Collegia among the Visigoths and Burgundians

Roman institutions persisted to a great extent in the kingdoms of the Burgundians and the Visigoths, who had established themselves in the empire as foederati and *hospites* (billeted mercenaries). Roman laws continued to apply to Gallo-Roman citizens in these lands. In fact, Visgoth and Burgunidan kings had compilations of Roman law drafted for the use of barbarian judges responsible for adjudicating among Gallo-Romans. These were the *lex romana visigothorum* or the Breviary of Alaric (505–506) and the *lex romana burgundionum* from the same era.

This situation did not change when Clovis, in 507, with the help of the Burgundians, fought the Arian Visigoths in Vouillé, resulting in his annexation of Aquitaine and Languedoc minus the Duchy of Septimania, which, under the hegemony of Narbonne, would remain Visigothic for two more centuries. Despite Clovis's victory, the Breviary of Alaric continued to be applied. Its clauses remained in practice and contributed to the formation of the law set down in central France, where it supplanted the lex romana burgundionum.

The province of Auvergne remained the most Roman in tradition. For centuries it had been the religious center of Gaul. From the fifth century on, churches (several of which are noteworthy) multiplied there under the influence of Christianity. The Visigoths, who were in the Narbonnaise from 413 or 414, did not succeed in conquering Auvergne until 475, by which time they had become more than half Romanized. The Franks did not become masters of this area until the expedition of Thierry I in 531. Following the death of Clotaire in 561, the region returned to the control of the Austrasian kings and, as a result, from 566 to 613 it was under the domination of the daughter of a Visigoth king. Queen Brunehaut shared her family's predilection for Latin culture. In the sixth century Auvergne still possessed its own senate and Gallo-Roman bishops continued to hold sway there until the reign of Pippin the Short. Though this king trampled and ravaged Auvergne during his bitter struggle against Aquitaine, Auvergne still had the dual advantages of the spirit of its inhabitants, who were tenacious, organized, and level-headed, and its geographic position far from major roads. More than any other region, Auvergne was protected from distant influences and infiltrations.

Roman institutions were also strongly maintained in the territory of the Burgundians after it was annexed by the Franks in 533. In fact, the Gombetta Law (517), which applied to Burgundians (whereas the lex romana burgundionum applied only to their Gallo-Roman subjects) was strongly influenced by Roman law.* In the Burgundian kingdom, we see educated families rising to assume the top posts of the state and supply the highest dignitaries of the Church. One example is Enius, also known as Mummolus, a general under King Gontran.

This survival of Gallo-Roman institutions in the Roman-influenced regions south of the Loire, in the Rhone and Saone Valley, and in Auvergne in particular, allows us to presume that the collegia survived in these areas. We can find proof of this in the buildings erected in these regions at that time and in the celebrity and influence of some of their architects.

---

* Research has supplied evidence of the persistence of Roman legal precepts in the social life of southern Gaul (Narbonnaise and Aquitaine) until the end of the seventh century. See M. Rouche, *L'Aquitaine des Visigoths aux Arabes (418–781)* (Lille: 1977); E. Magnou-Nortier, *La Société laïque et l'Eglise dans la province ecclésiastique de Narbonne (VIIIe–Xie siècles)* (Toulouse: 1974); and M. Banniard, *Le Haut Moyen Age Occidental* (Paris: Éditions Seuil, 1980).

One such building is the cathedral built in Clermont under the aegis of Bishop Namatius some time around 450 or 460 A.D. It's "blueprints" can be seen today, carved on the walls of its eastern apse, precursors of those that would be in great vogue starting in the eleventh century. During the following century, Agricola, bishop of Châlon sur Saone (532–580), had a number of buildings erected in this city, including houses and a church supported by columns and decorated with colored marble and mosaic paintings.

The Gallo-Romans were not the only ones who were skilled at building, however. The barbarians also distinguished themselves in the art of building, a significant fact:

> Toward 475 a governor of Auvergne saw to the building of Saint Julien de Brioude, with its superb columns, on the orders of King Euric. It eventually became a popular pilgrimage site. Around 530–535, the terrible Clotaire employed Goth architects to build the Church of the Holy Apostles (Saint Ouen) in Rouen. This work was described as admirable by the people of the time. Under the reign of Clotaire's son, Launebode, the governor of Toulouse, the former Visigoth capital, guided the construction of a church dedicated to Saint Saturnien. According to the poet Fortunatus, this project was attended to by more talent than a Roman outside of Italy would display. A large portion of the eastern ramparts of Carcassone are attributed to the Visigoths for very plausible reasons. And finally, there are Saint Marcel near Chalon and Saint Martin of Autun, two important buildings connected to the memory of King Gontran and Queen Brunhilde.[2]

The last of the Gallo-Roman provincial leaders may well have been a bishop of Cahors, Saint Didier or Géry, who died in 654. He won fame as a builder and was regarded by his contemporaries as having rediscovered the ancient mechanical system for producing large cut stones, which had been abandoned during the final years of the empire. In addition to his cathedral, he repaired or built part of the ramparts of Cahors, erected bridges across the Lot River, and built an Episcopal palace and various religious establishments.

The knowledge and reputation of the Gallo-Roman builders was such that their influence extended outside Gaul. According to Bede, in the year 675 Bishop Benoit of Weymouth in England was forced to go to France to find builders capable of building in the Roman style.[3] Toward the end of the seventh century and the beginning of the eighth, Anglo-Saxons went to foreign lands, primarily Rome and France, to recruit those skilled in the art of building: masons, glass workers, and other craftsmen.[4] If we assume that this art of building *more Romanum* was indeed preserved in France, and that artists and workers were there in great number and enjoyed great renown, then we can deduce that Goth architects had Roman teachers and that associations still existed that had inherited the traditions of the Roman collegia. It is also worth nothing that the influence of these associations occurred in an era contemporary with that of Charles Martel, who, as legends in France and England have it and as we shall see, played a prominent role in the formation of Freemasonry.

It is necessary, however, to stress that Gallo-Roman and Goth art of that time had evolved. The basilicas of Gaul did in fact differ from those of Rome in that Goths and Visigoths introduced Eastern influences, particularly those from Egypt, Palestine, Syria, and Sassanid Persia. In the fifth and sixth centuries

> The whole of Gaul was penetrated by Asia . . . the Gauls were in constant relation with the remote Orient that fascinated them so much . . . The Eastern monasteries then enjoyed a singular power of seduction . . . Honorat had lived with the cenobites of the East before gathering his first disciples together on the isle of the Lerins. We might conjecture that certain architectural forms had been transmitted from East to West through the intermediary of monks.[5]

We should also note that the Goth builders utilized triangles, interlacing, strapwork, and snakes as their primary decorative motifs. Here again ancient Eastern influences can be seen at work, an observation that is especially interesting when applied to the history of masonic symbolism.

The question arises as to what legal form builders associations assumed in the Visigoth and Burgundian kingdoms. In the absence of texts we are forced to envision the most plausible hypothesis. We can theorize that these associations were nothing more or less than Roman collegia adapted to new circumstances. Put forth by A. Esmein, this notion, which remains a doubtful explanation for those associations in the Frankish regions, does appear acceptable for the regions south of the Loire, where Roman institutions persevered.

These collegia, or at least their remnants, probably continued at least until the seventh century. At that time they were forced if not to disappear, then at least to transform. Even in lands where Roman law survived, however, it is not possible to speak of collegia in the strict sense of the term, for we must take into account the social, economic, and political evolution that led to the formation of feudal society. In the feudal world, individuals and groups must be envisioned in light of the bonds of suzerainty and vassalage that characterized the society of that time. There was no legal framework permitting the existence of autonomous professional associations. More important, individual freedom no longer guaranteed the work of the independent craftsman. An individual could become only a serf. The remnants of the collegia no longer offered any refuge except that provided by the bishops, who remained builders, and they were integrated primarily into monasteries, which were multiplying throughout the Christian world.

The bishop's authority or conventual grip extended even into the cities. Withdrawing into themselves in response to the shock of invasions, cities had become veritable fortresses almost everywhere. The possessions of the Church expanded there until the secular populace became a minority and urban life took on an increasingly clerical nature.[6] All of these factors explain the formation of the monastic associations, which we will look at in chapter 3.

The Fate of the Collegia in Italy

In 493 the Ostrogoths became masters of all Italy. They maintained Roman laws there just as did the Visigoths and the Burgundians in their kingdoms. But when it came to the question of adaptation, the

Ostrogoths went even further. Not only did they leave the Romans their own laws, but also King Theodoric subjected his barbarian subjects to the force of Roman law at the beginning of the sixth century. This case of assimilation by barbarian conquerors remains unique.

The reign of the Ostrogoths was temporary. In 554, Narses, Justinian's lieutenant, succeeded in driving them out of Italy. This liberation, however, was equally ephemeral. In 568, other Germans, the Lombards or Longobards, invaded the peninsula. The kingdom they founded lasted until it was destroyed in turn by Charlemagne in 774. Their conquest in 568 was not complete, however. Several regions of Italy escaped, including Rome, Ravenna, Venice and the south, and remained legally attached to Byzantium. Before studying the fate and evolution of the collegia that continued to exist in those parts of Italy that remained free, as well as the collegia in the Eastern Empire, we need to look at what happened to them in the Lombard kingdom. This region has left behind the memory of renowned architects, the comacine masters.

The Comacine Masters

The Lombard kingdom was divided into three classes: free men; *aldions,* or those who were semi-free, protected, and represented by their superiors; and serfs, who were completely under their superiors' subjugation. As in other countries occupied by the barbarians, Roman laws could have continued to be in effect for Roman subjects in the Lombard region, but the Edict of Rotharis abolished these laws in 643.[7] Articles 143 and 144 of this edict were dedicated to master masons, known as *magistri comacini* (masters of Como). It recognized their right to stipulate contracts and salaries, a right that belonged only to free men. We can therefore see that in 739 a certain *magister comacinus* named Rodpert gave up one of his businesses without the intervention of any superior,[8] despite the fact that Law 253 of the Rotharis Code forbade aldions from selling the smallest plot of land without permission of their superior. It seems, then, that Rodpert enjoyed total freedom.

We possess another document that is relevant to the magistri comacini, King Liutprand's (712–744) *Memoratorium* in eight articles.

This text underscores the importance of these master masons. It commands the magister who leaves his land, whatever the nature of the job, to return there within three years, and if illness makes it impossible for him to comply, then at the very least he must send news. If he fails to comply with this legal obligation, his property is transferred to his family or, if he has no family, to the Royal Court, as though he were dead. It so happens that Law 224 in the Rotharis Code stipulates that the goods of the free man who dies leaving no heir are bequeathed only to the Royal Court, so it is quite clear that in King Liutprand's mind, the traveling magister comacinus was considered a free man, entirely his own master.*

The question that arises is whether these magistri comacini—who were free men, unlike other craftsmen classified as serfs—were grouped in a corporation similar to a collegium. Without hesitation we can answer in the affirmative. First, it is quite likely that the maintenance of a particular tradition and art during several centuries assumes some kind of permanent organization. Second, we have an eleventh-century Lombard text that its last editor entitled *Instituta regalia et ministerial Cameroe Regnum Longobardorum et Honorantioe Civitatis Papioe.*[9] This text reveals that long before the communal movement of "trades," there existed in Pavia *ministeria* similar to the collegia of the late empire. Composed of free men, these ministeria enjoyed an absolute monopoly. Of course, this text makes no mention of ministeria of masons. It appears only to focus on the collegia we have described as "public colleges." Still, it shows nothing less than that the Roman institution of the *collegia opificum* had traveled through the entire Lombard era and that continuity exists between these associations and the corporations of the Middle Ages.[10]

The importance attached by the Rotharis and Liutprand laws to the magistri comacini allow us to believe that the Lombards permitted

---

* These authentic documents are well known to legal historians but are apparently unknown to historians of Freemasonry such as Knoop and Jones (*Genesis of Freemasonry,* Quator Coronati Lodge No. 2076, 1978, 60–61). In their opinion, the word *comacinus* does not derive at all from Como, but from the English co-mason! This logic reveals how circumspect the use of earlier works can be. For more on the comacins, see M. Salmi, *Maestri comacini e maestri lombardi* Palladio: 1938).

these professional groups to survive. As their name allows us to presume, it seems that their principal seat was in the town of Como, which must have been granted certain privileges, no doubt the same enjoyed by a sanctuary.

The comacine masters were recognized as particularly skilled architects. They contributed a great deal to the gradual development of architecture in northern Italy over the course of the seventh, eighth, and ninth centuries. Nevertheless, their art hardly evolved at all. Their churches were faithful copies of the Roman basilica, testament to the workers' knowledge of traditional rules. They did introduce into their ornamentation, however, all kinds of animals and motifs derived from Byzantine and Eastern sources, proof of their contacts with the Roman collegia and the Byzantine regions of Italy. They made particular use of the endless cord, woven into complicated designs and known as the comacine knot. The *houppe dentelée* [serrated tassel] of the Freemasons is strangely reminiscent of this decorative element. The comacines did not, however, take advantage of other Byzantine teachings in the art of building.

The Collegia in Regions of Italy Free from Lombard Rule

In those regions on the Italian peninsula that were dependencies of the Eastern Empire, Roman laws remained in effect. Craftsmen were still trained in collegia and were governed as they had always been. In time, the name *collegia* was changed to scholoe or scuole (schools), but the system and its workings did not undergo any substantial changes. In Ravenna, capital of the Exarchat, the charters of the tenth and eleventh centuries mention schools of merchants, butchers, and fishermen; and in the reformed statutes of the city (1213–1253) there is mention of all the other trades in general, in particular the schools of house roofers and the *magistri lignaminum,* or builders, as very ancient institutions worthy of great protection.[11] That Roman laws always governed these schools is proof of the survival of the institution of the collegia through the ups and downs of the centuries. The same may also be noted regarding the craftsmen of Venice, a city that never fell into the hands of the Lombards.[12]

In Rome the spirit of association was quite commonplace. The entire populace was divided into schools according to social status, nationality, duties, and professions. Each school had its own insignia, patron, statutes, offices, and assigned duties in the public demonstrations of devotion and rejoicing. These associations were not organized solely to advance the progress of arts and trades, but also to encourage piety. Each had their own church in which to hold gatherings, common burial grounds, and the responsibility to fulfill certain duties in processions, station displays, and other solemnities and festivals. In compensation, they received remuneration twice annually, at Easter and Christmas. For example, the masons of Saint Peters received eight *solidi provisini* and the masons of other schools received five.[13] The schools also offered charity and assistance in a variety of ways.

Eventually, Roman schools of builders attained such prosperity that they were able to send a good number of their masters elsewhere, especially to England, as we shall see.

The Fate of the Collegia in Great Britain

Following the invasions of the Picts, the Angles, and the Saxons, Roman institutions collapsed in Great Britain. It is likely that the collegia, which had been so important, were not able to survive this upheaval intact. Their influence, however, could not disappear completely. It was preserved within the sect of the Culdees, or Colidees.

The Culdees originally consisted of a community of Celtic Christians who, in order to better propagate their religion among the people of the North, retained in their doctrine a familiar simplicity and loyalty to autochthonous traditions that made it understandable and accessible to all. Their name seems to be the result of a merger of two Latin words, *colitores* and *Dei,* which together mean Servants of God.

These Culdees would have infused their doctrine into the collegia that had been in existence from the time of Carausius to the final departure of the Romans. After the disappearance of the collegia following Britain's invasions, these Christians were forced to seek refuge in Wales, the Orkneys, Scotland, and especially Ireland, countries that had never experienced Roman occupation and that medieval authors often referred to together as Little Scotland, Scottia Minor.

The Culdees were the source of Celtic or "Scottish" art. A distinctive and unique style rather than the survival of Roman techniques is what is most visible in their work.

In the transmission of Roman traditions it is important to underscore the action of Saint Augustine, or Austin, during the second evangelization of England, which was started by his impetus. This country's architectural art then underwent a period of very obvious influence of the Roman collegia, now scholoe, and that of the architectural associations that survived in Gaul under the Goths.

Roman architects and workers built the monasteries and churches founded by Saint Augustine and also built the cathedral of York, which was erected at the command of Edwin, the first king of Northumbria, who converted to Christianity in 627. Saint Wilfried built the famous Saint Andrew's Cathedral in Hexham (completed in 674)* and founded those of Ripon and Hagulstead among others, but it was Rome that provided the blueprints and workers to perform the labor. Saint Benoît Biscop, a Benedictine monk of Lerins who made the journey to Rome five times, constructed the monastery of Wearmouth *more Romanum* in 675. To do this, he visited Gaul in search of builders and glassworkers whose art was unknown in England. It was the *opere Romanum* (Roman work) that raised the ancient church of Canterbury. The raids of the Danish having ravaged and pillaged most of the churches in the towns, the powerful and victorious king Alfred seeded the country with fortified castles, rebuilt London, and erected churches everywhere, importing designs and workers from Rome (880–900). The repeated summons from Great Britain for builders from Rome and the continent point to the fact that architecture was a lost art in Britain and that there was little trace of the collegia left there. It has been established, however, that from the eighth century on, under the influence of the Roman scholoe, there were a large number of builders in Great Britain. In fact, in 716, when Saint Boniface, the English Bishop who succeeded Saint

---

* The surviving description of this cathedral seems to suggest some resemblance to Saint Vital of Ravenna. Cf. Ramée, *Histoire générale de l'Architecture* (Paris: Aymot, 1860), 1055.

Willibrord, went to continue his conversion of the Hessians, Frisians, Saxons, and Bavarians, he erected churches with journeymen from England.[14]

Maintaining and Spreading the Collegia in the Eastern Empire

The heart of Roman civilization found itself shifted to the East once Emperor Constantine, in 330, transferred the capital of the empire to Byzantium, which took the name Constantinople. In 395, at the death of Theodosius, the empire was divided in half and Constantinople became the capital of the Eastern Empire. Rome was hence primed for invasion and ruin. Those parts of the Western Empire that did manage to escape barbarian invasion fell under the authority of the Eastern Empire and formed the Exarchat, with Ravenna as its capital.

The Eastern Empire became the keeper of Greco-Roman secular traditions. It was also—perhaps even more than Rome—the seat of Christendom, for which, after all, it had been the cradle. Located at the gates to Asia, it could easily receive the teachings of the old Eastern civilizations that Sassinaid Persia had harvested and reformatted into audacious and scholarly inventions cast in gripping phrases. Byzantium and Alexandria, the other spiritual capital of Christianity (before it fell into Arab hands in 640), were the natural vessels of these brilliant civilizations.

Philosophical thought flowered during this time into great syncretic Neoplatonic and Hermetic theories. It was also the acme of Roman law, the complete development of which took place in the sixth century under Emperor Justinian. Roman institutions experienced their fullest development at this time. The collegia were no exception, becoming some of the principal cogs of Byzantine life. Religious at their foundations, these collegia had to transform their pious practices under Christianity's influence, but it is very likely that they preserved their rites and symbols, principally those connected to their operational secrets. Symbols remain but their interpretations change: This is a law of evolution. Nor is it to be doubted that Eastern influences were at work in this area as they were in others. In fact, they became so imbedded that several centuries later, the Crusaders had trouble recognizing their own religion among the various Christian sects of Asia Minor.

Architecture also transformed at this time. The curved shapes of circular churches replaced the straight lines of the Roman basilica, and eventually the domes, each more audacious than the one built before, took on an appearance that indicated their architects had found models among the Persian Seleucca and Ctesiphon. This period marked the birth of Byzantine art, a synthesis of Greco-Latin art and the teachings of Asia Minor, Egypt, and Syria, which themselves were descended from Persia. The same synthesis that took place in art and architecture also affected philosophy. Under the influence of the collegia, Byzantine art spread throughout the empire. There was an Asia Minor school of Byzantine art (the churches of Ephesus, Sardes, and Philadelphia in the fifth century), a Syrian Byzantine art (the cathedrals of Basra and Ezra in the sixth century), and a Byzantine art of Egypt. The most powerful marvel of this architecture is Santa Sophia of Constantinople, which was built from 532 to 537 by Anthenius of Tralles and Isidorus of Miletus. Never had the genius of Rome and the East been combined in a more amazing and harmonious whole.

Byzantine builders at this same time erected churches in Thessalonica, Parenzo, and Ravenna, the city where the collegia endured, and followed this with a prodigious blossoming of monuments that spread throughout the entire empire: the Byzantine palaces of the ninth, tenth, and eleventh centuries and the churches of Constantinople, Thessalonica, and Greece built in the tenth and eleventh centuries. Because the Byzantine capital was located at the center of the civilized world, Byzantine art could not help but wield great influence both far and wide. It was this art that left its imprint on the oldest structures of Christian Russia, such as Saint Sophia in Kiev (eleventh century). Armenia and Georgia also have an abundance of Byzantine buildings. The Arabs of Syria and Spain and the Christians of the West also experienced this influence. During the eleventh and twelfth centuries, the scholoe of the builders of Venice, which was entirely Greek with respect to mores, built a cathedral in the purest Byzantine style in honor of Saint Mark. Works that are admirable testaments to Byzantine art can also be found in central Italy and Sicily, and in France, in the area of the former Visigoth kingdom, we find the example of Saint Front of Perigueux.

In the kingdom of the Franks, where the art of building had disappeared, Frankish kings, as we have seen, resorted to hiring Visigoth architects. Later, Charlemagne was struck with admiration for Italian monuments, which aroused his desire to have similar buildings erected in his own country, but a dearth of workers forced him to seek assistance from the Italians and the Byzantines. In 796, when he undertook the construction of the admirably designed Basilica of the Holy Mother of God in Aix la Chapelle (Aachen), history informs us that he gathered together for this labor master workers and laborers *(magistros et opifices)* who had the greatest renown "this side of the sea" and placed at their head the extremely skilled Ansigis, abbot of the abbey of Fontanelles (abbey of Saint Wandrille).[15] The same text tells us that among the most expert workers who were laboring on the cathedral and buildings of Aix la Chapelle there were also serfs who had been sent by their lieges. We should note this opposition between the masters and workers from "this side of the sea," who were free and no doubt products of a Byzantine college, and the autochthonous workers of servile status—proof that no association of free builders existed in the Frankish kingdom.

Notre-Dame of Aix la Chapelle is modeled on Italo-Byzantine structures. The role played by the Greeks in its construction is reported by a fourteenth-century author who informs us that Bishop Meinwerk of Paderborn (d. 1036) had a chapel erected in the style of a similar, older monument that he claimed Charlemagne had ordered Greek craftsmen to construct *per operarios groecos*.[16]

According to the *Chronicle of Leon of Ostia* (III, 29), Didier, abbot of Monte Cassino, ordered from Constantinople at great expense masters in the art of mosaic and hired them to decorate the church. He also desired that some of the inhabitants of the monastery would take pains to learn that art, which was almost lost in Italy.

So during the first half of the Middle Ages, Byzantium generally paved the way for art for the rest of Europe. Romanesque architecture itself may owe more to Byzantine art than is commonly believed. The principal Romanesque innovation was the covering of the church nave with a vault instead of a framework. Is this not a Byzantine influence? Those who spread this influence were the members of the collegia of builders, keepers of the secrets of the original collegia in Rome that were subsequently enriched with Eastern traditions. It was the lessons provided by these Byzantine collegia that formed the basis of the indigenous schools in various parts of the empire. Outside the Byzantine empire, this influence is particularly noticeable in the regions where similar builder's associations existed: the Middle East; the parts of Italy not under Lombard control;* and those former kingdoms of the Burgundians and Visigoths in which Roman institutions had not disappeared. We will soon see how it was in these same regions that Romanesque art first bloomed.

Finally, there is one important fact that produced its own ramifications: The still-thriving Byzantine collegia, with their traditions, rites, and symbols, were later discovered by the Arabs and the Crusaders, a discovery that both turned to their own advantage.

---

* We have seen how the art of the magistri comacini betrayed a Byzantine influence, but this is secondary. It is not visible in the art of building itself, which remained Roman and did not evolve, but is apparent in ornamentation (e.g., in the comacine knot).

3

Ecclesiastical and Monastic Associations

Ecclesiastical associations, primarily monastic organizations, are of twofold interest in the study of the origins of professional building organizations. First, they contributed—and this is critical—to the preservation and transmission of the traditions and secrets of the collegia that had been more or less overwhelmed by the barbarian invasions, then legally dissolved by the formation of feudal society. Second, the monastery schools trained the lay masters, who, starting in the twelfth century, took over the brotherhoods of builders jointly with the ecclesiastical masters. These brotherhoods were precursors to later trade guilds and corporations; they were able to be transformed into these new structures when social evolution offered a legal framework that supported this change.

The history of monastic associations is primarily linked to that of two religious orders: the Benedictine Order and its various persuasions (Cluny and Cîteaux), and the Templar Order. The role of the Benedictines was especially prominent up to the twelfth century. They can be credited with not only the propagation of Romanesque art but also the birth of Gothic art. As for the Templars, initially students of the Benedictines, with whom they always maintained a connection, their activity extended well beyond the time of the monastic associations. From the twelfth century on they were involved with the organization of lay communities of builders that enjoyed specific franchises, earning them the name *francs métiers* (free craftsmen; see chapter 6).

In this chapter we will study these monastic associations specifically. The role of the Templars, which appears to be closely tied to the birth of operative freemasonry, will be developed in chapters 5–7.

The Formation of Ecclesiastical and Monastic Associations in the Goth Regions and Their Extension into the North

We have seen how in England and the Frankish kingdoms the advocates of Christianity appealed to the Roman collegia and their remnants in the Visigoth regions. This was widespread due to the fact that members of the collegia were regarded as the best artisans for propagating the faith by erecting churches in all areas where Christianity had spread. When their existence became incompatible with the state of the society, however, it was around the Church that new groups of builders began to form. As a self-contained body, the Church had retained its own rights. It remained subject to Roman laws. At this time, the Church did not merely represent a belief and a form of worship; it also constituted a political organization. As a veritable state, it exercised all the attributes of one and extended its authority over all Christian countries. Its legal and institutional rights, combined with the zeal of faith, explain how the Church became a pole of social and political attraction. As Etienne Gilson rightly argued, the Roman Empire was dead, but the Church saved its culture from destruction and then imposed it upon the peoples of the West.

This universal role of the Church and the relative security it provided were much more in evidence in and applicable to the great religious orders than to the bishops, who were more often compelled to confront temporal requirements and whose nominal authority stopped at the borders of their dioceses.

The builders from the collegia, who, as we have seen, found refuge with the bishops, discovered themselves to be bound simply by close personal ties to these prelates. This was not the case with those members of the collegia who were integrated into monasteries. While their former status had vanished, they were better able to survive corporatively, preserving their practices and traditions and even their rites and secrets, which allowed them to form veritable schools whose influence often radiated quite far.

The expansion of monachism appeared in the East toward the end of the third century. In the West it dates from the time of Jean Cassien (d. 432), founder of two monasteries in Marseilles; Saint Cesaire (470–543), a monk of Lerins, then bishop of Arles, who set down a rule for the monasteries of his regions; and especially Saint Benoit (480–547), abbot of Vicovaro and founder of Monte Cassino, whose rule was imported into Gaul by his disciple, Saint Maur.

The development of monasteries in sixth century Gaul, which generally followed the rule of Saint Benoit, gradually moved from the center of the country to the north. At that time, either bishops or kings founded them. Monks were always lay individuals.

During the seventh century, the high nobility (dukes and counts) multiplied their founding of monasteries. A regular clergy to attend them appeared by order of Pope Gregory I, with abbots serving as their heads despite the opposition of the bishops. Many abbeys, which had become quite wealthy, were the greatest landowners in the kingdom. In Paris, the domain of Saint Germain des Prés covered 50,000 hectares and numbered some 25,000 inhabitants.

Population centers grew around the monasteries as people settled near them in search of both protection and the possibility of a livelihood. Agriculture and all trades were practiced there and builders were numerous, working primarily for the monks. In this world where social and legal constraints imposed immobility and attachment to a fief, the status of the Church allowed an escape from this servitude. For builders it included a precious right, one that was indispensable to the practice of their trade: the right of circulation, the freedom to travel.

The most famous of the ecclesiastical architects of the Merovingian era, for his science and his virtue, both connected to his education and his role in the monastic movement, is Saint Eloi. He was born in 588 in Cadillac, near Limoges, where he took lessons from a teacher named Abbon. He then moved to the kingdom of the Franks, where he became the minister of King Dagobert. He designed the blueprints for several churches and monasteries (Solagnac Monastery near Limoges, a convent for nuns, and Saint Paul and Saint Martial Churches in Paris). His name is especially prominent in connection with the famous abbey of Saint Denis (631–637). He also created superb works in gold and silver.

In eighth-century Spain, in monasteries founded by the architect and mason Saint Fructueux, there were masters who taught theory and, if need be, directed construction. Special compartments were assigned to the art of decoration.[1]

During the darkest hours of the Middle Ages, the monastery of Saint Gall in what is now Switzerland distinguished itself by the skilled teachers who flourished there. It was this monastery that produced the monks Tutillon, Notker, Adalberne, and Durand of Utrecht.

We must pause here for an observation: Our investigation relates essentially to religious architecture, but what of civil construction? It should be noted that during these centuries there was a considerable slowdown in the construction of significant buildings. Ordinary houses were built of wood, cob, and mortar made from straw and clay. From the seventh to the tenth centuries, there was a need to erect castles, large constructions indeed. Of course, in those years some building specialists, architects and sculptors still existed, but they were few in number and were largely itinerants. Bound to a noble, king, or archbishop, they were "lent" by their patron to individuals requiring their services.

Therefore, as noted earlier, a number of architecture schools whose masters moved north to ply their trades were located in the former kingdoms of the Goths and Burgundians, where many Roman institutions endured; we have already stressed how this region preserved the art of building passed down by the collegia. There is perhaps no reason to seek elsewhere for the origin of the architectural term *Gothic*. Today this word defines a very specific building style. It is thought that the Renaissance Italians originally used it in complete derision. In reality, the term goes back to a much earlier time. It can be found in the writings of Fridegode, a historian who wrote in Latin in 950. Fridegode said, in speaking of the Saint Ouen Church of Rouen,* that it was built

---

* As we have seen, this was built by "Goth" architects.

in quarried stone with a kind of magnificence in the Gothic manner: "muro opere quadris lapidibus, manu gothica . . . olim nobiliter constructa."[2] The word *Gothic* continued to be used subsequently to label what we now call Romanesque art, which was later distinguished from the new, ogival ribbed style by names such as Old Gothic and New Gothic. These terms indicate with extreme precision the origin of these styles and the relationship that exists between them. In fact, it is a mistake to oppose the two.

Romanesque Art and Monastic Associations

Romanesque art of the Old Gothic style was born after the year 1000 in regions south of the Loire—the former Gothic Gaul. It seems fairly well established that the oldest Romanesque school was that of Auvergne. Romanesque architecture is Roman architecture that has been refined and "finished": "While a time of decadence saw a retreat from Roman art, a more progressive era returned to it, but it was a free Roman art that had been emancipated from the yoke of entablature. The Romanesque style was regarded as a self-evident innovation by the Roman as well as the Gothic."[3]

Romanesque art has been labeled monastic art in opposition to the Gothic, a secular art. It is an undeniable fact that the propagation of Romanesque art was the work of monastic associations, particularly the Benedictines. But there were no builders outside of these associations. Later we will consider more closely how Gothic art emerged and spread.

The Order of Saint Benoit first contributed to the spread of the art of building through its preeminent role in the propagation of the sciences. Until the tenth century, churches were primarily built of wood. The art or science of framework construction, although complicated, is still less difficult than that of cutting and constructing with stone. The progress of this latter method brought about the overall advancement of architecture. Stonecutting in fact leads to statics, the science of balance, and mathematics is the basic element of this discipline.

Toward the end of the tenth century, a man renowned for his position, character, and worth, the Benedictine Gerbert (a native of Aurillac and, under the name of Sylvester, the first French pope) brought about great progress in science and mathematics through his broad knowledge, which contributed greatly to architecture's ability both to embellish and to be lighter and bolder. Gerbert had studied architecture with the Arabs of Spain in Cordoba and Grenada and brought what he had learned to his own country, where he entrusted its teaching and practice to the ecclesiastical schools. Gerbert himself taught in Reims and his knowledge spread rapidly.

Abbot de Fleury, Fulbert (founder of the theological school of Chartres), and Béranger (creator of the schools of Tours and Angers) continued Gerbert's work. Lanfranc, who moved to France from Pavia, established a monastic school at the Bec Abbey in Normandy, which became the seat of a renaissance in the sciences and the arts. An era of excitement in the minds of people began at this time, which far from being hostile to the arts, only gave added impetus to them, especially to architecture. The reading of Aristotle's metaphysics, also brought back from Spain by Gerbert, initiated Christians into the Pythagorean symbolism of numbers. Thus the symbolism of numbers and dimensions in churches dates from this time.

The Benedictine Order to which Romanesque art owes the greatest debt is definitely that of Cluny. During the twelfth century the abbey of Cluny was the center and regulator of civilization. Solely from an architectural standpoint, the Cluny monks carried their art as far as the East. The churches they erected in Jerusalem and elsewhere in the Holy Land during the time of the First Crusade were Burgundian. In this land of great relics and Byzantine art, France remained naively faithful to its genius. Though the Knights Templar contributed most to the spread of Eastern influences on an operational level, the Benedictines were subject to the influence of these regions, and the Romanesque style does indeed have a Byzantine feel.

The statutes from the Cluny monastery are divided into two books. The second volume contains the rules to be followed in founding and constructing new abbeys. According to the legislator, among the compartments that the body of the abbey contains, there should be a house 45 feet long by 30 feet wide designated to be the dwelling of all those who toil on behalf of the monks. There should be another building

125 feet long by 25 feet wide intended for the goldsmiths, inlayers, marbleworkers, and other artisans.

The magnificence of Clunisian churches, including excesses of decorative art that lacked any symbolic meaning, shocked Saint Bernard (1090–1152) early on. This sensitive soul, enamored of inner perfection, felt it was a betrayal of the gospels to give any sops to the senses. In reforming the order of Saint Benoit, he imposed on the architects of his order a principle of total simplicity. Thus the monks of Cîteaux, faithful to the spirit of the great reformer, spread an austere and bare style of art throughout Europe. These strict, plain churches are not sad, however, for they hold a kind of mathematical beauty that comes from the harmony of their proportions.

The prodigious and symbolic art of light was not produced until the bays of churches were cunningly pierced in coordination with the proper orientations of the entire structure. Favorable to contemplation, these resulting buildings defy time. This stripped down but suggestive and magisterial layout marvelously assists the sensibility to share in the comprehension of the liturgy. The physical sensations awakened in these structures also awaken the soul turned toward God.

Gothic Art as an Evolution from the Romanesque

It is important to understand that Gothic art does not oppose Romanesque art; instead it has evolved from it. Nor did it spring from the imagination of a single master; it was the gradual and slow work of collective faculties who ripened their concept little by little, through implementing and modifying it.

The Gothic style supplied the solution to a technical problem that had arisen for Romanesque architects: The weight of the vault forced them to give their buildings squat proportions. This problem "inspired them to perfect their balance system, which was how they were led to the discovery of a system of intercrossed buttresses that would carry the vault while disguising its weight; the Gothic cathedral continues and completes the Romanesque church."[4]

The distinctive feature of Gothic art is essentially the use of intersecting ribbed arches that support the vault like a kind of armature based at the tops of the supports.

> In the art of building, this feature constitutes the great discovery of the system of active stability resulting from the use of paired vaults, like that inaugurated by the Romans, as opposed to the system of inert stability, which emerged from the use of heavy materials and monolithic beds without the lateral thrusts used by the Greeks and Egyptians. The discovery of this miraculous artifice was not at all the result of luck; it could have emerged only from profound causes, a kind of imperious necessity, and a series of trials and errors.[5]

In actuality there is an art of transition characteristic of that period of time marking the passage from the Roman and Romanesque groined vault to the vault constructed from the crossed ribs and broken arches associated with flying buttress. This transition occurred only in France, the country where Gothic architecture was born. In the other schools during this intermediary period there were only blends—"Romano-Gothic" monuments.

It is an error to regard the broken arch or tiers-point as a characteristic innovation of the Gothic style, however. Ancient Persia, the Orient (mainly Armenia), and Muslim Spain knew it before the West did. The pilgrims of the end of the ninth century, the Crusaders of 1099, or those who had fought against the Moors of Cordoba in the Iberian peninsula were able to propagate it on their return. "It was accepted by Roman architects not as a thing of beauty but as a necessity. The broken-arch vault in fact had a weaker thrust than the groined vault."[6]

Because there was technically no opposition of Gothic art and Romanesque art, there was no opposition of Gothic artists and Romanesque artists.

> The antitheses, in their seductive clarity, are a danger of erudition, which they compromise in seeking to overly simplify everything. Few of these are more subject to caution than the double antitheses creating an absolute opposition, an incompatibility, and antagonism

between Gothic and Romanesque art, between secular architects and monks, the latter authors and stubborn preservers of Romanesque style, the former revolutionaries of the ogival style.*

In fact, there were secular Romanesque architects, such as Walter Coorland, a native Englishman, who provided in the second quarter of the eleventh century the blueprints for Saint Hilaire in Poitiers. Others include Benoît, architect of Saint Eutropes de Saintes around 1075; Gislevert, who worked on Saint Ouen in Rouen around 1100; Jean, a bourgeois of Saint Quentin in 1113; and Gervais, who built a cathedral in Béziers in the second half of the twelfth century.

In any case, what is at play here is a partial approach to the facts. In medieval society, whether twelfth or thirteenth century, Romanesque or Gothic, art in both its concept and creation was religious at heart. It expressed only the directives of the Church, which gave long and detailed guidelines for artists and their works, priests, and liturgists. Nothing was left to the artists except for their skill and ability to execute.

To dispel any misunderstandings that may linger, it should be emphasized that the Benedictines at Cluny and Cîteaux were by and large the source of the Gothic style. One author, alluding to the roughly 350 monasteries that made up the religious community of Cîteaux in the middle of the twelfth century, suggested that "thanks to their colonization practices . . . they were the first missionaries of Gothic art. In architectural technique if not in decor, though, the two branches of the order were quite opposite. The Cistercians, however, who came later, played the main role in the propagation of the Gothic style. They did for Gothic architecture what the monks of Cluny had done for the Romanesque.†

It is in Norman territory at the end of the eleventh century where we must search for the first manifestation of the French ogival rib. The aisle of the Anglo-Norman cathedral of Durham, dated convincingly to

---

* Anthyme Saint-Paul, *Histoire monumentale de la France* (Paris: Éditions Hachette, 1932), 89. We cannot stress too strongly the inexactitude of this legend, still commonly accepted by some Freemasons, such as L. Lachat, who view these Gothic cathedral builders as the precursors of freethinkers and anticlericalists.

† Ibid., 241. For more on the Cistercian influence on the continuity between the Romanesque and the Gothic, see also Henri Focillon, *Art d'Occident,* vol. 2 (Paris: Librairie Armand Colin, 1971), 56 ff.

some time between 1093 and 1104, presents it in a form that reveals a mastery of the procedure, implying earlier experiments.

Among the most ancient attempts of currently existing paired vaults, especially praiseworthy are the capitulary of Jumièges (1101) and the venerable apse of the church of Morienval (Oise), which dates from around 1125 and which is the rudimentary prototype of the Gothic style. As for monuments of the transition, we can cite the ancient Saint Benoit Chapel in the Lerin Abbey and the choir of Saint Martin des Champs in Paris, which was a priory of the Cluny Order.

The oldest of the Gothic monuments marking the end of the transition is the choir of the Benedictine church of Saint Denis, begun in 1129 under the impetus of Abbot Suger. Consecrated in 1144,

> . . . it was the first building in which the new system appeared in all the potentiality of its consequences, in the juvenile vigor of its methods, in the conviction of its ambition. Its inauguration—celebrated in the presence of a throng of bishops and high dignitaries from the four corners of France, a large number of foreign prelates, and the king himself—was the ostensible and echoing sign of a major architectural event, the departure point for an enthusiasm that would prove irresistible.[7]

Among the monks who were the first Gothic architects, we can cite Hilduar and Giraud, first mentioned around 1160, the former for the choir he designed at Saint Peters in Chartres, the latter for his nave at Saint-Benoit sur Loire. The Cistercians, too, played an important role. They were the first to spread the knowledge of Gothic art throughout Italy, Germany, and the Scandinavian countries. And we cannot overlook the Templars, students of the Benedictines, among the architects of the Romanesque-to-Gothic transition. Their church on Fleet Street in London (1165), more or less influenced by the Templar Church in Paris, is in fact one of the more unusual buildings from this transitional period.

We can see, then, that there was no gap existing between Romanesque (or Old Gothic) art and the New Gothic. One flowed out of the other and the secret of the ribbed vault was perhaps invented by the same masters who had spread the Romanesque vault, just as the

Romanesque vault was a return of the Roman, influenced by the Byzantine style. Gothic and Romanesque also coexisted chronologically. The first applications of the ogival rib, in Durham and Saint Denis, were coincident with the golden age of Romanesque art, a period to which the great cathedrals of the second half of the twelfth century still belong.

Some still see significance in the geographical rift between the two styles. Romanesque churches are the exception rather than the rule north of the Loire, in those regions where the Gothic style first made its appearance. There are concrete reasons for the fact that the Romanesque style spread only south of the Loire: the continuation of Roman institutions and traditions in the south, the remnants of the collegia that existed there, and the possibility of builders creating associations allied with monasteries. Perhaps the best proof may be found in Auvergne, the last of the Roman provinces and the one that remained faithful to the genius of Rome for the longest time. It is precisely here that the greatest Byzantine influence can be seen and it is here, at Limoges, that we can discover the traces of a seventh-century architectural school. The Romanesque school of Auvergne is one of the oldest and most characteristic of its kind.

While churches covered all the lands south of the Loire, they were noticeably scarce in the north. It was impossible for the art of building to spread in the north. We have seen how Roman institutions came to grief in the Frankish kingdom. In addition, the capitularies of the Carolingian kings and even the Church stood in opposition to associations and guilds. Building there began to blossom only when, in conjunction with the evolution of mores and customs, new forms of association became possible, exemplified by brotherhoods that included both clerics and laypeople as their members. In northern regions, where architecture changed slowly, artists continued to perfect Romanesque art and did not cross through it, so to speak. From this we should not conclude that the "crossed rib" and Gothic architecture that appeared in the Ile de France region was the spontaneous creation of that area's genius.

In looking at the existence and growth of architectural schools, we should pay specific attention to Lombardy in Italy. We have seen how this region, notably the area of Como, managed to maintain a Roman tradition with associations of free builders despite the upheavals of history. A veritable school of architecture took form in Lombardy, with its principal constructions existing in Como, Milan, Pavia, and Parma. It was a singularly influential force. The Rhine school owes much to it (Spire, Worms, Mayence) and its influence can likewise be seen in France in the areas of upper Provence and Languedoc

The structures of this Lombard school betrayed for a long time its imitation of the fifth-century Latin basilica. The lessons of Byzantine architecture, however, although close at hand, did not make themselves felt in Lombard construction; the political separation between the barbarous world of the Lombards and the Byzantine world of Venice and Ravenna was simply too great. But at the end of the eleventh and throughout the twelfth centuries there appeared vaulting that, unlike the round-rib vaulting found in France, was made up of square ribs that formed beneath the vault they held up—suggesting a large, branched archaic cross. An interesting French example of this structure, undoubtedly of Lombard origin, is the ogival square crossing erected in 1178 on each of the transepts of the ancient cathedral of Maguelone, in the Hérault. Another is the large, square-ribbed crossing on the porch of Moissac.

This Lombard ribbed crossing is fairly contemporay with or appeared even a little earlier than the ribbed crossing found in the structures of northern France. But because the two styles are completely different, neither one can be regarded as the precursor to the other. Perhaps they may be viewed as the results of similar research and trial and error. Perhaps the crossed ribs had been envisioned by the Romans and employed later by the Lombards. Although Lombard builders knew of this style at the end of the eleventh century, however, and even exported it, it must be pointed out that its use remained a limited construction procedure for them. Thus we cannot see in it the principle of a new architecture and get a sense of its power and prodigious future.*

---

* The same could be said of Armenian construction. As the first Christianized region of the East, it was subject to the strong influence of Rome and Byzantium. The use of square crossed ribs, as in the Lombard model, appeared there at the end of the tenth century in the fullness of its architectural function. It is not impossible that the West was familiar with it at this time. It would have adapted it to its principles and existing architectural styles. Here again, we can assume the role of monks in its propagation—cf. H. Focillon, *Art d'Occident, Le Moyen Age Roman,* vol. 1 (Paris: Librairie Arand Colin, 1971), 117 ff.

Though we are discussing cross-ribbed architecture in terms of two different schools, we should take care not to oppose or even separate them. Their relation is much like that of the Romanesque and Gothic styles. Here we must acknowledge again that the initiative for realizing and executing works was not connected solely to the imagination and talent of artists. The Benedictines and Cistercians were generally the master builders and overseers of all work in religious buildings. It was on their orders and directives and through their coordination that different kinds of expertise were utilized as determined by place and circumstance. It is thus both an exaggeration and a limitation to classify architectural art simply according to geographical locale and time period.

The Fratres Pontifices

During the Middle Ages the erection of civic structures—bridges, in particular—for public use was considered a work equal in piety to the building of churches. Religious institutions were formed with this purpose in mind, some of which have remained famous, like the Hospitaller congregations of the Fratres Pontifices.[8] These monks of the Benedictine Order were involved particularly with the construction of bridges and roadways, as well as with the defense of travelers against the assaults of criminals, noble or common, who infested the roads at this time. The Hospitallers were established in Avignon in 1177. Saint Bénézet, who left his name on the bridge made famous by song,* was one of the most renowned of these pontiff friars. The construction of regional bridges such as those of Bompas (which earned a congratulatory bull from Pope Clement III in 1189 and franchises from the counts of Toulouse in 1203 and 1237), Lourmarin, Malemort (the name of which brings to mind the dangers faced by travelers crossing the Durance), Mirabeau, and Pont Saint Esprit is attributed to them.

"In 1277 the community of Bompas, whose prior was one

---

* [This refers to the bridge of Avignon. —*Trans.*]

Raymond Alfantim, delegated one of its members, Pierre de Régésio, to go to the Holy See to request that it join with the Templar Order. Giraud, bishop of Cavaillon, after having given his assent to this request, rescinded his decision and asked Pope Nicolas III to unite the Brothers of Bompas with the Hospitallers of Saint John of Jerusalem, which was done."[9] At this time the Templars also concerned themselves with the establishment and maintenance of roads and the construction of bridges and hospices.

Over the course of three or four centuries, the Fratres Pontifices were responsible for the construction of almost all the bridges of Provence, Languedoc, Auvergne, Brittany, Lorraine, and the Lyon region, as well as those of Ratisbonne, Dresden, Luzern, and Prague. They were considered a religious order but accepted laypeople into their ranks. As the result of a decree enacted in 1469, individuals belonging to the order were conferred the status of tradesmen. The Fratres Pontifices also existed in Lucca, Italy, where they remained until 1590. The head of the order had the title *magister* meaning "master." Jean de Medici was the master of the order in 1562.

Monastic Associations in Great Britain and Ireland, Including the Culdees

Benedictines spread throughout Great Britain under the impetus of the monk Austin or Augustine, who came from the monastery in Lerins. This English apostle became the first bishop of Canterbury in 596. In England, as on the Continent, the creation of builders associations allied with monasteries was becoming quite commonplace. Saint Augustine himself left behind a reputation as a great architect.

What exactly were the relations between the continental Benedictines, who had traveled to Britain across the English Channel, and the native Culdees, who had remained on their home soil and were very much attached to their own traditions? Are there really grounds for maintaining, as has always been done, the existence of a specifically Culdeen art and architecture that would have greatly influenced the Benedictines and their monastic brotherhoods of builders?

As far as this primary role played by the Culdees is concerned, it is important to separate what is certain or at least probable from what is most likely legend and exaggeration.

First, let us look at the specific religious elements of Culdee belief. The Culdees followed a rite that was different from but not fundamentally at odds with the Roman rite. There are six particular points on which the two differ: the date when Easter is celebrated, the importance of the tonsure, the Episcopal consecration, baptism, the use of the Gaelic language, and the marriage of priests. There was no truly doctrinal divergence or heresy on the part of the Culdees, but they maintained a spirit of independence that could and did inspire conflict. As an example, after Benedictine monks in 710 succeeded in converting the Pictish king Nectan to the Roman rite, the king then commanded the monks of Iona to adopt the Roman date for Easter and the Roman tonsure. They refused, however, and were forced to leave their monastery and scatter throughout the mountains.

Through their actions, two men—often confused with one another—have come to epitomize this Celtic Christian community: Saint Columba (known in Ireland as Columkill) and Saint Columban.

Saint Columba (521?–597) was the founder of the monastery of Derry and, in 563, of the monastery on the isle of Iona, which he transformed into the center of Irish Christianity and the brotherhood of the Culdees. His missionaries evangelized as far afield as Iceland and Feroe and were responsible for restoring the Christian religion in Britain.

Saint Columban (540–615), one of the fathers of the Culdeen Church, preached the Christian gospel to the Picts and the Scots. Later, in the company of twelve monks, he arrived in France, where he founded the Luxeil Abbey. In 613 he also established the monastery of Bobbio in Italy, where he died. Columban wrote a monastic rule urging asceticism. He declared the preeminence of the Roman pontiff, but not his authority. "The pope," he wrote, "is not someone who holds the keys to absolute truth and whose words carry the seal of the Holy Ghost. He is a bishop, a weak man whom one can advise and rebuke. Above the authority of Rome there is the authority of the truth."

The Culdees were connected with King Athelstan, who played a large role in the legendary history of Freemasonry. In 936 this king, in his march against the Scots, made a stop in York, where he found the

Culdeens officiating as the clergy of Saint Peter's Cathedral. He asked that they pray for his victory and consequently, on his return from a victorious campaign, gave them a special donation or tithe on wheat throughout the entire diocese to aid them in their pious and charitable works.

Their history also tells how Edwin, Athelstan's son, gave York a masonic charter in 926. This Celtic or Scottish (in the broad sense) Rite, pronounced by the Synod of Cashel, persisted until 1172, the date when Henry II had gained enough power to enforce its condemnation.

Certainly the contributions of Celtic Christians were significant. Historians have often stressed the importance of Celtic art in the early Middle Ages. Architecture, carving, and the application of metals onto objects of worship were among the practices at that time. Because they are so widely reproduced, the best-known Celtic works of the time remain the illuminated manuscripts that traveling Irish monks, the *peregrini Scoti,* transported throughout Europe.[10]

With respect to architecture specifically, Dom Fernand Cabrol, in his *Dictionnaire d'archéologie chrétienne* (Paris: Letouzy, 1924), in the article entitled "Art celtique," provides a thorough list of the buildings constructed by the disciples of Saint Columban, such as the first abbeys of Jumièges and Saint Wandrille. In general, however, this aspect of Celtic art, far from denoting progress, seems instead to represent a backward or decadent technique. Culdeen architecture testifies to the inadequate mastery of Roman traditions by the Celts. The particularly local character of these structures may be seen as evidence of an incomplete science. For a long time the Culdees built only in wood. They decried the use of stone in construction as being Gallic or Roman, though this disdain of stone may have had no other cause than their own inability to utilize it competently. In addition to the divergence of the Culdeen and Roman rites, lack of skill with stone was very likely the reason that compelled seventh-century missionaries to select the Roman scholoe as their source for qualified workers.

In the eighth century, the Venerable Bede recorded in his *Historia Ecclesiastica* that Nectan, king of the Picts, who had converted to the Roman rite, no longer wanted wooden churches like those built by Celtic architects. He asked the abbot Geolfrid (an Anglo-Saxon who also followed the Roman rite) to send him architects to build a church in the style of the Romans.

Culdeen influence is much more noteworthy in ornamental art, mainly in sculpture, many examples of which have survived into the present. This art greatly contributed to the transmission of ancestral Celtic symbolism to Romanesque art, where its presence is quite visible.

Romanesque art brings us up to the eleventh century. But with respect to earlier centuries, there is little remaining architecture by which we can judge the Culdeen influence. Nevertheless, it must be acknowledged that the Culdees had acquired some renown in this field, as demonstrated by the expressions used to characterize their works or those that followed their style: *more Scotto,* or "according to the Scottish Rite"; *opus Scotturum,* or "the work of the Scots"; and even *juxta morem Hibernioe nationis,* or "according to the custom of the Irish nation."

Most important, these phrases and the other remnants we have looked at in this chapter attest to the survival of organized building associations with traditional roots through the centuries of barbarian dominance.

4

Secular Brotherhoods: The Germanic and Anglo-Saxon Guilds

In examining the rise of secular brotherhoods and guilds in the Middle Ages, we move into the realm of new associations in which professional objectives became predominant and secular elements became oriented in a technical direction.

The Secular Brotherhoods

The first secular brotherhoods appeared in the middle of the twelfth century. Their appearance is connected to two interdependent factors: the enthusiasm of faith and the communal movement.

Born from vast religious and social upheavals that were then taking place, the brotherhoods first assembled with a general common purpose of uniting all people from all trades. As their goals became more precise, they became more specialized in the professional sphere, gathering together individuals of the same profession, starting with tradesmen, then craftsmen.

We can see in the general features of these brotherhoods the social context from which they sprang and the changes society was undergoing.

Key among these was the emancipation of the serfs, who made up the bulk of the populace. Triggered in the eleventh century by precepts of the Church, this emancipation was given a general impetus by the Crusades at the beginning of the twelfth century, but the specific motives for this action in the domains of kings, dukes, counts, and barons, as well as in the realms of bishops and abbots of monasteries throughout Europe, was an enthusiasm for Christian sentiment and the necessity of finding ways to meet expenses generated from waging the Holy War: The richest of the serfs could buy their freedom and continue to pay rent to the nobles, their former masters, who could then use this money to organize their expeditions to the East.

The effects of this movement varied depending upon the region. In France, serfdom disappeared utterly from the lands of the West (Brittany, Normandy, and Anjou). On the other hand, it remained quite active in southwest France and the Languedoc. In northern and eastern France, serfdom continued to affect almost the entire rural populace, whereas the incidence of serfdom in the Ile de France region was quite variable. Even where it did exist, however, the conditions of serfdom were no longer what they had been. In the ninth and tenth centuries, they were very near those of slavery, but in the thirteenth century serfdom affected entire segments of the population and was characterized by responsibilities that benefited the serf's sovereign lord. This kind of serfdom did not definitively vanish until the time of the French Revolution.

The Crusades, concurrent with this broad serfdom, engendered a commercial cosmopolitanism that encouraged the development of a class of merchants and a kind of social and cultural intermixing, which brought about a rebirth of ideas that we will explore in more detail later.

These phenomena set off a powerful movement toward the formation of associations with the specific purposes of defense, protection, and independence. These led first to the immigration of tradesmen toward towns, then to the development of cities, and eventually to the emancipation of these areas, which put the finishing touches on the emancipation of individuals. A veritable urban revolution was underway. Life, activities, and knowledge that had found refuge for centuries around monasteries and castles was now concentrated in cities. This regrouping of the populace in fact inspired the formation of law, municipal bodies, universities, brotherhoods, and guilds to respond to new economic, social, cultural, and political needs and aspirations.

In France, north of the Loire River, the most remarkable and elo-quent illustration of this enormous evolution is apparent in the con-struction of cathedrals and churches. In this era, religious sentiment asserted itself and was symbolized in monuments that also reflected the life and soul of the Middle Ages. These works were executed by thou-sands of volunteers sharing the same piety and persevering together in a common effort, which strengthened the ideas of union and solidarity.

Next in significance to all the merchants and artisans who ensured the necessities of subsistence and daily life were masons and workers who built the large churches and who founded brotherhoods that were both mystical and corporate in nature. It was in Saint Denis between 1130 and 1140, then in Chartres in 1145, that we can first detect the organization of these popular brotherhoods. In Chartres, history has preserved the name of one of the most skilled of the secular architects, Beranger, who worked on the cathedral and died in 1180. The example of the faithful church builders of Saint Denis and Chartres was immediately copied at the abbey of Saint Pierre sur Dives (Calvados) and, soon after, throughout Ile de France and Normandy. The cathedrals of Strasbourg, Laon, Noyon, Senlis, and Soissons were cradles of similar associations, whose members were both ardent Christians and artists beyond compare.

In a letter of 1140 addressed by the abbot Aymon to the masons of Tuttebury in England, we have testimonies of the bursts of faith that animated these men.* This piece of correspondence provides us with

---

* *Hist. Litt. de la France par les Religieux Benedictines,* vol. 12 (Paris: M. Paulin, 1865–1866), 356; Mabillon, *Ann. Benedict.,* vol. 128, (Paris: Billaine, 1668–1701), n. 67. It should be noted that the English legend places among the ancestors of the order a cer-tain Aymon, son of Hiram, who was the greatest of master masons. Should we view as a coincidence the fact that the elements of the legend of Hiram are also present in the earlier *chanson de geste,* "The Four Sons of Aymon"? In this text we see Renaud de Montauban, who, after following a life that has been hardly edifying and wishing to atone for his sins, hires on to the construction of the cathedral of Cologne. His uncommon strength and dex-terity create a situation about which all the masters argue. But then his fellow workers become alarmed and find common cause: They fear he will spoil their trade. They plot to knock him over the head with a hammer when he is not looking and then put his body in a sack, and throw it into the Rhine. At the time they customarily eat, when "the master masons and the top workers" leave the construction site to go to *osteaux* (vespers), they put their plan into operation. Their crime does not remain a secret for long, however. The fish in the Rhine, gathered together by a miracle, push up the body, now lit by three tapers. The murderers, in complete confusions, have no alternative but to make penitence.

some very valuable clues: It seems that any individual, regardless of personal status, could become a member of one of these brotherhoods. At this time, there was one in every diocese of Normandy. An individual of proven virtue stood at the head of each one and the Most Holy Virgin was selected as the patron saint of each. In order to be accepted it was necessary for an individual to meet three conditions: sacramental confession, the fulfillment of whatever penitence was imposed following this confession, and reconciliation with any personal enemies. When word went out about a new church to be built, the brotherhoods traveled in groups to the designated site. Their first concern was to form a wall with the carts that had carried them there, and then settle inside as if it were a spiritual campground. There they spent the first night, singing hymns in the light cast by hundreds of torches. Once they had begun work, there was not a single task, no matter how painful, to which they did not submit with good heart and unshakable steadfastness. During working hours, silence and order reigned, and the time of rest was devoted to prayer, charitable acts toward the sick, and pious discourse. Abbot Aymon began his letter like a man completely stupefied at the sight of so much abnegation among his colleagues. He described their manner of living as "a completely new kind of piety that is unknown to all the centuries."

Piety and fervor do not explain everything, however. These folk migrations and regroupings also implied economic, social, political, and juridical causes and effects. The construction of religious edifices is a phenomenon that cannot be separated from the general context in which it occurs.

Enthusiastically erected with extraordinary fervor, churches and cathedrals were not merely places of prayer. Built to the scale of their respective cities that were constructed and organized around them, people gathered there to argue freely about matters that concerned them. They were houses of the people placed under a benevolent and tutelary protection. As much if not more than the belfries, they were the centers and guarantors of freedom. Even political assemblies concerning the life of the kingdom were held at cathedrals, notably Notre Dame of Paris, as was the case in 1302 with the famous assembly of the General Estates. In a society dominated by the sacred, it was logical that the temple was, for all actions playing a determinative role in social life, the terrestrial reproduction of a transcendent model. The same was true in the traditional civilizations of ancient peoples.

Each of the brotherhoods to which Abbot Aymon refers was not yet strictly composed of artisans of one trade who had banded together to perform their profession. Instead, for work that was not planned in advance, brotherhoods were formed spontaneously on the construction sites themselves and were concerned with numerous activities. In their composition they were often temporary or itinerant associations. Specialization and regionalization took place as the populace became fixed in cities and as the cities organized around their growing populations.

As we consider their formation, some important questions arise regarding these brotherhoods: Where did their peerless artisans and artists come from, especially in the specialized trades of construction, sculpture, decoration, and glasswork? Where and from whom had they received their training that allowed them to achieve such heights in their work? It is obvious that the majority and the most skilled could only originally have been members of monastic associations. Who else indeed would have been able to pass on the torch that only those associated with monasteries had taken pains to keep alight?

The secularization of monastic associations had actually been underway for a long time in preparation for their transformation into independent brotherhoods when the social setting was ready to permit their existence. By virtue of the fact that the monastic schools had given people an education and training from which it had derived enormous profit, the monks gradually lost their monopoly on knowledge and art. These fields had become popularized; the lay master builders, who had learned their secrets and traditions from ecclesiastics, grew greater in number until they were soon the majority. According to Springer, out of 210 artists' names found in the period spanning the ninth to the twelfth century, there are 64 monks or clerics and 146 laypeople. To be more precise, there were 20 ecclesiastical architects, 19 ecclesiastical sculptors, and 26 ecclesiastical artists as opposed to 55 lay architects, 61 lay sculptors, and 32 lay painters.[1]

The fact remains, however, that quite often the entrepreneurs, directors of construction, and teaching masters were monks whose intellectual and religious influence incontestably dominated the master builders.

Jean d'Orbais, Villard de Honnecourt, and Pierre de Corbie were among those who had received their training in the school of the monks and as such, were heirs to the entire science of their teachers.

In sharing a similar origin in monastic associations, all the lay brotherhoods respected the same religious spirit and the same tradition. The professional rules were identical everywhere, often down to the last detail. The work left no room for innovation. Nevertheless, the status of these brotherhoods and the position of their members were often quite varied depending upon their training and the means by which they had become established. Evolution had led to adaptation of feudal law, but it had not altered the principles of this law.

The brotherhoods that had emerged directly from monastic associations and that remained in the abbey's domain remained subject to the sovereign jurisdiction of the abbey and often continued to benefit from great franchises and privileges issued by the Church. It is within these brotherhoods that we can see the birth of the *francs métiers* (free craftsmen) and freemasonry.

The "communal" brotherhoods, on the other hand, developed in the cities and became the cogs of their urban settings. Despite their autonomy, they were far from holding the same extensive franchises enjoyed by their monastic colleagues. The restrictions imposed upon them came either from the high lord and dispenser of justice, the city itself, or from the sovereign who took the bourgeoisie of the town under his protection in order to fend off feudal lords and under his tutelage so that they would serve his policies. In any event, the rights of these artisans never extended beyond city limits.

Yet within these limits, the franchises connected to the power and patronage of the Church were reduced to a singular degree. The local authority of the bishop and lay clergy generally replaced the spiritual and lordly supervision of the monks, which had served as a guarantee for territorial universalism.

Only later, in recollection of Roman law and the institutions of the Roman Empire and in order to strengthen absolute monarchy, would the royal powers in France and England attempt to group trades into their own communities that tended to extend over the whole of the nation and contribute to its unification.

The Guilds

The guild constituted a legal form of association that allowed manual laborers to form the kinds of autonomous groups that had been impossible to maintain in the West since the annihilation of the collegia.

Origins of the Guild

The etymology of the word *guild* has provided fuel for much debate. The term appears to derive either from the German verb *gelten* (to be worth) or the Anglo-Saxon *gylsa* (worship, sacrifice).

The institution seems to have a tie to one of the most ancient of German customs, that of *convivium*.[2] Tacitus had made note of the distinctive custom of the Germans to handle their most serious affairs at the table, during a time marked by the drinking of repeated toasts. Born amidst the clamor of blows and the sound of song were fraternities whose membership was made up of warriors who had drunk together from the cup *(Minne)* of friendship. A passage from the Icelandic *Gisla Saga* maintains that it is a duty to avenge fellow drinkers as if they were brothers. Also notable in this regard are texts in which colleagues *(Bruderschaft)* unite by blending their blood and drinking together. In the custom of convivium observed in the Roman collegia we find these same religious and sacred elements of meals eaten together.

It remains to be seen how and at what time the ideas connected to the convivium became more specific and eventually led to the formation of legitimately constituted societies. Various theories have been offered on the subject of the origin of guilds. For some, the guild owes its origin to the influence of Christian ideas and fraternity. For others, the guild was once the Roman collegia, specifically the kind imported by the apostles of the Christian faith into southern lands, where it was subsequently transformed. It is quite possible that these two hypotheses can be reconciled by the acceptance of a third factor: pagan traditions.

The coincidence of the first manifestations of the guild and the conquests of Christianity are especially notable in England. Christianity, which had been preached anew by Saint Augustine of Canterbury starting in 596, triumphed definitively in 655 with the victory of Bretwada Oswin, king of Northumbria, over the last pagan king of Mercia. By the beginning of the eighth century all of Great Britain was Christian. It just so happens that it is precisely at this same time that the laws of Ine, king of Wessex (688–725), mention guilds for the first time.

An important fact to note before we begin an overview of the three different categories into which guilds fell (religious or social, merchant, and craftsman) is that with the advent of these associations came the ability of women to gain membership in them.[3]

Religious or Social Guilds

The first guilds to appear were associations founded for the purpose of either mutual defense or religious association. This is the case for those cited in the laws of Ine from the end of the seventh century. The oldest mention on the Continent of the institution of the guild (which, as it so happens, forbade their organization) is in a capitulary issued by Charlemagne in the year 779. Despite this, there are sufficient grounds to deduce that guilds may have appeared initially on British soil.

The *judicia civitatis Londonioe,* redrafted under the reign of King Athelstan (895–940) make reference to this institution:

> Every month the members of the guild shall assemble for a feast in which their common interests, the observation of statutes and other similar matters shall be discussed. On the death of a member, each associate must offer a piece of good bread for the salvation of his soul and sing fifty psalms within a month's time. All participants in this league shall not give allegiance to any other; they are expected to make common cause of their affections and their hates and to avenge an insult given to one of their brothers as if it had been addressed to all.

It is interesting to find these indications concerning the guilds in a text dating from the time of King Athelstan, given that according to legend it is to the era ruled by this king that Freemasons attribute their oldest charter. It was in 926 in York that Edwin, adopted son of Athelstan, gave a charter to the masons. The oldest text attesting to the existence of this document, however, the *Cooke Manuscript** dates back only to

---

* This manuscript takes the name of its first publisher, Matthew Cooke.

the beginning of the fifteenth century. It is doubtful that the craftsman guild was formed in the tenth century.

While traces of religious and social guilds are quite ancient, their oldest known statutes—those of the guilds of Abbotsbury, Exeter, and Cambridge—date back only to the beginning of the eleventh century. These statutes offer an analogy to those described by the judicia: "Once a year in Abbotsbury and three times a year in Exeter, the member fellows will gather together to worship God and their patron saint. They will share a meal together, with one portion going to the poor. Mutual assistance will be given in the case of illness, fire, or during a journey; the insults given by one member to another will be punished; members will attend the funeral service of a deceased colleague."[4]

Social guilds can also be found in Germany, and "in Denmark they played an important role as demonstrated by this historic fact: Magnus, son of King Nicholas of Denmark, had killed Duke Canut Lavard, alderman or protector of the League of Sleswig, known as a *Hezlag* (oath-bound fraternity). In 1130 the king wished to visit Sleswig, and despite being defended by the *congildi*, he was massacred with his entire retinue."[5]

The statutes of the Danish guilds—especially those of Saint Kanut, Flensbourg, and Odense (which were written in 1200)—included clauses quite similar to those of the English guilds: right of entry, close solidarity, mandatory assistance to assemblies, a prohibition on interrupting a brother (Law 33 of Flensbourg), mutual assistance among brothers, and arbitration of other members in the event of a dispute among congildi.

In France social guilds appeared at almost the same time as their first appearance in Great Britain. The interdiction against them by Charlemagne's capitulary in 779 was copied in a number of other texts, including, in the ninth century, in a capitulary issued by Hincmar, bishop of Reims.*

In this regard, we can make a fairly broad observation: No association could exist at this time without authorization from the Church,

---

* According to some historians, the Council of Nantes condemned these guilds as early as 658, but the authenticity of the canons issued by this council is dubious.

which never missed an opportunity to clamp down on guilds, brother-hoods, and other associations whose purposes appeared to conflict with canonical laws. The interdictions that were promulgated for this reason (and which could target only specific cases) provide us with valuable information on certain kinds of associations. On January 30, 1189, the Council of Rouen banned the societies and brotherhoods of clergy and laypeople that swore an all-encompassing oath of aid and protection to each other that could lead them to take actions that ran counter to canonical law and that might even lead to perjury. A century and a half later, on June 18, 1326, the Council of Avignon condemned certain fra-ternities and brotherhoods. From this action we have learned that these societies possessed particular insignia and a special language and writ-ing with which members could recognize one another. The tenets of these groups obliged members to render to each other aid and protec-tion in all matters and suggested that those who broke this oath would incur punishment. With regard to leadership, they elected a master as well as associate leaders who took the titles of abbots and priors. These societies, composed of nobles, laypeople, and ecclesiastics, were con-demned by the council as having committed all manner of depredations against the life and property of their fellow citizens.[6]

There are no traces of guilds like these having existed in Great Britain during the Saxon period. Their history begins with the Norman Conquest, which was ensured by the Battle of Hastings in 1066.

Merchant Guilds and Artisan Guilds.

The merchant guild is mentioned for the first time in England in a char-ter granted to the bourgeois of Burford (1087–1107) and in Flanders in both a charter given by Count Baudoin and Countess Rachilde to the Guild of Valenciennes in 1167 and one from the twelfth century approving the statutes of the Guild of Saint Omer.* The primary pur-pose of these merchant guilds was to guarantee the protection of their members and their property.

---

* In his *Description des Pays-Bas* (Anvers: 1582) Guichardin claims to have seen docu-ments attesting that Flemish corporations were established as early as 865 by Baudoin, son of Arnould the Great. There are solid grounds for doubting this assertion.

The first artisan guilds or trade guilds (craft guilds) appeared in England and Normandy during the reign of Henry I (1100–1135). Similar guilds in Germany and the Scandinavian countries seem to date from the same era. These craft guilds (made up of bakers, carpenters and builders, tailors, weavers, and so on) were first started as associations for protection and mutual aid and gradually expanded until they became veritable professional corporations.

The origins of the craft guilds, as for the French brotherhoods, followed a line of descent—at least indirectly—from the collegia and monastic associations such as the Benedictines. Like their earlier counterparts, merchant and craft guilds were important cogs in the emancipation of cities. The case has even been made that municipal governing bodies and merchant guilds were one and the same from the very beginning. In fact, in the town of Saint Omer the merchant guild went on to become the commune.*

In the second half of the twelfth century, London may not yet have had a builders guild. In fact, we know that craftsmen and artists capable of building in stone were few in number in that city. In chapter 5 we will learn that in order to build their church on Fleet Street, the Templars had to import an architectural brotherhood from the Holy Land and thus may well have been responsible for the formation of the original masons guild in London.

The statutes of the earliest Germanic, English, and Scandinavian guilds include precious little information on their professional hierarchy. In the twelfth century in the Norwegian city of Bergen, however, there existed the classic tripartite division of *discipuli* (apprentices), *formuli* (journeymen), and *magistri* (masters). In part 2, we will look more closely at the English guilds as they existed in the fourteenth century.

---

* Esmein, *Histoire du droit françois*, 292–93. [A commune is equivalent to the English or American district. —*Trans.*]

5

The Crusades and the Templars

he eight Crusades, which took place from 1096 to 1291, had a profound social, economic, political, cultural, and religious effect on Western Europe. And from the beginning to the end of the Crusades, the Templars were among the Continent's most important and effective agents in all these areas of experience.

The Order of the Templars, derived from its true name, the Militia of the Temple, was created in Jerusalem in 1118 or 1119 by nine noblemen who were, as Guillaume de Tyr writes in his history of the Crusades, "distinguished and venerable men":* Hughes de Pains or Payens, their leader, who adopted the title of master of the Temple and who was customarily called grand master; Geoffroy de Saint-Omer;

---

* Guillaume de Tyr, *Histoire des Croisades,* vol. 2 (Paris: Éditions Guizot), 202. Guillaume was born in Jerusalem around 1130 and became counselor to Amaury of Jerusalem and tutor of his son Baudoin, royal chancellor in 1173, and archbishop in 1174. He fulfilled numerous missions and attended the Council of Latran in 1176. He died from poisoning in 1193. His testimony of the strong campaign against the Templars that was based on a conflict over ecclesiastical rights makes Guillaume's history of the Crusades particularly valuable. In his *Historia Orientalis* (written in the thirteenth century), Jacques de Vitry, bishop of Acre, who was closely aligned with the Templars, ceaselessly refers to Guillaume's book.

Paien or Payan de Montdidier; Archambaud de Saint-Armand or Saint-Aignan; André de Montbard, maternal uncle of Saint Bernard de Clairvaux; Godefroy; Gondemar; Roral or Roland; and Godefroy de Bissot or Bissor. In 1126 Hugues, count of Champagne and donor of Clairvaux, joined this number. Together they drew their authority from the patriarch Theocletes, sixty-seventh successor of the apostle John, for whom the Templars maintained, along with the Holy Virgin, a special worship. These men took the three vows of obedience, poverty, and chastity and swore an oath to do all in their power to safeguard the roads and protect pilgrims against the attacks of brigands and infidels.

Initially the Order, which at first followed the rule of Saint Augustine, did not expand greatly. In the ninth year of the order's existence, however, as Guillaume de Tyr notes, "during the council held in France at Troyes [in 1128], attended by the lord archbishops of Reims and Sens; their suffragans; the bishop of Albano, legate to the apostolic see; and the abbots of Citeaux, Clairvaux (Saint Bernard),* and Pontivy . . . a rule was instituted for the new knights." The chronicler adds,

> Their affairs had prospered so well that at this time they had in their monastery three hundred knights, more or less, all wearing the white robe,† not including the brother servants, whose number was almost infinite. It is said they own immense properties, on both sides of the sea and that there is not a single province in the Christian world that has not assigned some portion of its holdings to such an extent that their wealth is, on this we can be sure, equal to that of kings.

The Order of the Temple was able to establish itself and prosper not merely in the Holy Land, but in all regions of the Christian world during the same era that witnessed the appearance of brotherhoods and

---

* With the council's consent, Saint Bernard, responsible for writing the new rule of the Templars, would have delegated this task to Jean Michel (Jean Michaelensis). See also H. de Curzon, *La Regle du Temple* (Paris: 1886). It should be noted that the rule of the Temple had much in common with the rule of Citeaux.

† From 1146 on these robes were embellished with a red patty cross embroidered on the chest, which referenced the privilege bestowed upon them by Pope Eugene III on the authority of Bernard of Clairvaux. The servant brothers were clad in brown.

communities of builders. The primary question—one that has always been subject to controversy—is this: Did the Templars wield any influence over these brotherhoods and communities and, if so, what was the nature of this influence?

In this chapter we will examine:

1. The direct influence of the Templars on the art of the builders. In this sense they followed the example of religious communities such as the Benedictines and Cistercians.
2. The influence that the Eastern world—Byzantine and Islamic—exercised over Western civilization at the time of the Crusades and the primary role assumed by the Templars in this social and cultural influence, including the close ties they developed to Byzantine and Muslim guilds.
3. The Templars' specific involvement in the formation in Europe of professional communities, primarily those of builders, which includes our discovery of the source of the francs métiers in general and operative freemasonry in particular.

The Templars, Creators of the Brotherhoods of Builders

The Templars, protectors of the Holy Land and guardians of the faithful, were great builders of churches and fortified buildings.

The task they undertook in the areas of protection and defense evolved into a real need during the Crusades. The earliest Crusades had very few qualified workers at their disposal. In 1099, during the siege of Jerusalem, their efforts suffered particularly from the lack of equipment, war machines, and qualified workers.[1] In 1123, at the siege of Tyre, the Crusaders paid a king's ransom to an Armenian named Havedic to come build ballista for them.[2] On entering Tyre in 1124, the Christians greatly admired the fortifications, the solidity of the buildings and ramparts, the height of the towers, and the elegance of the port—proof that these kinds of works were novel to them and were regarded as revelations.[3] This is precisely the time when the Order of the Templars began to extend itself throughout the Holy Land with the building of fortresses, called *kraks,* which can still be admired today.

The first krak appears to have been built in 1141 in Ibelin, between Ascalon and Jaffa. Numerous workers participated in its construction, outfitting it with four towers just like the tower of the Templars in Paris.[4] This project was followed in 1142 by the krak of Moab, or the Stone of the Desert, in TransJordania;[5] in 1143, the fortress of Geth near Lydda; and in 1144, on the shining Mount or Hill near Ascalon, a high fortress that was flanked by four towers. The local people called this important construction the "white guard" and the Latins, citizens of the Latin states in the Holy Land, called it the "white workman's hut."[6]

In 1148, the Christians, especially the Templars, undertook the reconstruction of ancient Gaza. "With the buildings finished and well-kept, the Christians resolved unanimously to place the town and all the land surrounding it in care of the brothers of the Temple and granted it to them in perpetuity. The brothers, strong men who were valiant in battle, have to the present day preserved this trust with loyalty equal to their wisdom."[7]

The Templars fulfilled prominently and for all time this role of builders on behalf of the Crusaders. The importance of this was emphasized a century later, in 1240, during the construction of the castle of Safed on the instigation of the bishop of Marseilles, Benoit d'Alignan, who had gone to Acre to visit the Templar master Armand de Perigord and tell him that he must at any cost build the fortification in Safed. The master of the Temple, who was ill at the time, answered that he did not have any money. "Stay in bed," Benoit told him, "but tell your brothers that it is your desire that this construction be undertaken—I am convinced that the action you inspire from your bed will be greater than that of any army."[8] In fact, the fortress was rapidly erected under the direction of the Templar Raymond de Caro. It came to govern some 260 caserns and a rural populace of more then 10,000 and guaranteed the safety of the pilgrimage roads to Nazareth and other sanctuaries in Galilee.[9]

In 1243, following an accord reached with the malek of Damascus, the Franks took possession of the whole of Jerusalem, after which the Templars set about building a fortified castle there.[10]

The construction activities of the Templars were not confined to the Holy land, however. They erected churches and chapels throughout all of Christendom. During the time of the Council of Troyes, Hughes de Payens went to London to found the first Templar house at Holborn Bars, and during the second half of the twelfth century, the Templars built their famous chapel on Fleet Street on the banks of the Thames. In France, they had maintained an establishment in Paris since the reign of Louis VI the Fat, who died in 1137.

The Templars devoted themselves to the laying out and maintenance of roads and the construction of bridges and hospices, which responded to their mission of protecting and facilitating journeys of the faithful to the holy sites. According to F. T. B. Clavel's *Histoire pittoresque de la Franc-Maconnerie*:

> One of the routes of Spain that comes out of the Pyrenees goes through Roncevaux, and ends in Lower Navarre has retained the name of the Path of the Templars. It owed its construction to these knights, who, furthermore, protected travelers along its entire length. The Templars were given the task of maintaining the three Roman roads that existed beyond the Pyrenees. Also attributed to them is the building of most of the bridges, hospices, and hospitals from Rousillon all the way to Santiago of Compostella. One circumstance that should be noted, because it establishes the relationship this Order had with corporations of construction workers, is that the old churches in Italy that had once belonged to the Order traditionally retained the name churches *della massone* or *della maccione* [of the masons]." [11]

The Templars most certainly gained their earliest knowledge of architecture, and consequently its trade secrets, from the Benedictines and Cistercians.* In fact, we have already pointed out the Romanesque Cistercian style of the basilicas built by the Crusaders in the East.

The Templars behaved much as the monastic builders associations had, though their construction talent was displayed in venues beyond just churches intended to propagate the faith. The first concern of these "warrior monks" was the erection of construction that could be used

---

* The Templars recognized themselves as "brothers and companions" of the Cistercians, to whom they owed assistance and protection.

for purposes of attack and defense. Rather than being assumed by the knights, who were primarily soldiers, the role of architect must have fallen upon the chaplains, who were religious clerics, as well as upon actual specialists. Each Templar commandery, though under the orders of a single commander, was managed by a certain number of officers, one of whom was a master carpenter.[12]

In addition to their servant brothers, the Templars also employed Christian workers who were not officially members of the Order. These persons were sometimes Crusaders, but might also be local operatives, especially in northern Syria, where the Armenian and Syrian population had remained entirely Christian and welcomed the Crusaders as liberators.[13] According to the chronicles, these workers held free status, rather than that of serfs, and enjoyed consideration beyond that accorded the simple manual laborers.

Bernard the Treasurer, the continuer of Guillaume de Tyr, recounts how in 1198 when the Christians laid siege to Beirut, the Saracens "emptied the castle of women, children, and weakened individuals and sent as hostages to the land of the pagans the wives and children of all the slaves and a carpenter they held therein, so that these would not commit any treachery." Thanks to a ruse, this carpenter made it possible for the Crusaders to successfully capture the castle. Amaury, king of Jerusalem, "honored him greatly, giving to him and his heirs a large private income inside the castle and ensuring that his wife and children, who had been sent to the land of the pagans, were freed."[14] The useless precautions of the Saracens and the honors bestowed by King Amaury on this "carpenter" show that this title must have concerned a man of a certain high social standing, most likely a master builder.

Hugues Plagon, the second continuer of Guillaume de Tyr, writes that in 1253 the Saracens of Damascus came to Acre, destroyed Doc and Ricordane and captured Sidon, "and slew eight hundred men and more, and took prisoners, including masons as well as other folk, some four hundred persons."[15] This quote from a contemporary underscores the regard held for the masons on the part of the Crusaders. What might have been the nature of this true crafts community? Was it a monastic association formed by the Crusaders or an association of the type that then existed in the Byzantine and Islamic world?

The Influence of the Eastern World

Byzantine Influences

The Christians of the East, subjects of the Byzantine Empire, were still grouped in the ancient Roman collegia, keepers of the Greco-Latin traditions that had evolved through contact with the people of the East. These associations—particularly those of the builders, which had disappeared as legal entities in the West as a consequence of the barbarian invasions but of which traces and remnants still remained in the monastic associations—appeared to the Crusaders as signs of progress and dispensers of valuable teachings. The Byzantines were the first to educate the Crusaders in the art of constructing war machines. In 1137, during the siege—also a fratricide—of Antioch, Emperor John Comnenus employed "immense instruments of war, machines that hurled blocks of stone that were of enormous weight and size."[16] These machines were a novelty to the Crusaders, but beyond their service during battle, they could also be used to lift the stones necessary to construct churches and fortresses.

The Templars, the Crusaders' legion specializing in the building of military works, did not fail to absorb the lessons from the Byzantine collegia. Some in the Order, trained in the Cistercian school, were already of a mind to fraternize with the Eastern builders. Byzantine lessons gave them the knowledge to erect their defense works and kraks. "The Templars, always suspected of a leaning toward mysterious Eastern arts and heresies, took up the mantle of Justinian as represented by the degenerate fortresses in Northern Syria and, in simplifying it, served to amplify it."[17] When they set aside their arms and when truces in the fighting left them leisure time, the Templars, mindful of their religious vocation, turned to erecting churches dedicatd to the glory of the Lord. Like their Benedictine teachers, they first built in the Romanesque style, but here again Byzantium prevailed and Eastern churches often served as models for those of the Templars. This influence was extended to the construction of the Orders' commanderies in Europe and is especially visible in the shapes of the Templar chapels, which are either circular, such as those in Paris (the Rotunda), London (Fleet Street), and Tomar in Portugal, or polygonal, such as those in Segovia, Montmorillon, Laon, and Metz.[18]

Architectural details amount to merely one sign of Eastern influence. The rediscovery of the Byzantine world actually gave impetus to a broad and profound cultural and social movement. The contact with Byzantium established by the Crusades made it possible to rediscover the legal compilations, in all their originality and potency, that the emperor Justinian applied as the foundation for his empire. It was now possible to conduct a direct and detailed study of Roman law, both public and private, and Roman institutions. The Crusades thus revealed a vast new world rich in less tangible though enormously significant treasures.

Teachers soon carried into other lands this new understanding of Roman law. Schools focusing on its teachings were founded in Italy and France. This rebirth became one of the most important factors in the development of European civilization, not only resulting in a great influence on the development of private law, but also exercising a profound influence on public law and on the thought of Western nations. This, says A. Esmein, is a fact of the first order from both the political and scientific point of view.[19]

Legists of the time not only considered Roman law as the science and law of the past. They endeavored, with deep faith, to bring these laws back to life, to restore them to common practice in both institutional and private arenas. In France, especially, government and administrative personnel were soon recruited primarily from among these legists. This evolution reached its full flowering under Philip the Fair, when French legists strove to reformulate the power of the Roman emperor for the king's benefit. "The king of France is emperor in his kingdom," legal counselor Boutellier declared at that time. We should recall, however, that absolute imperial power was also based on the strong municipal organization that had been created and on the economic and social role of the collegia, both of which effected the policies of the king concerning cities and the trades. In fact, the Temple took part in this game—for its own benefit, of course—and though it contributed to the greatness of the Order, it ultimately abetted its downfall.

The Influence of the Muslim World

Crusaders and Templars, and through them the Western world, were subject to the overall influence of Byzantium and particularly that of its secular institutions, notably the collegia. But occurring at the same time was Islam's powerful ascendancy and its influence was as profound as that of the Byzantine Empire. Nor was it limited to the operative plane of construction. Born from a social and practical viewpoint, its effects overflowed widely into the speculative, intellectual, and spiritual domains until its message was propagated, just like that of Byzantium, throughout the entire Christian West.

It is important to note that there was never a constant state of warfare between the the Christian and Muslim camps. In fact, a strong, neighborly relationship was created between them. There were even alliances concluded between the two sides. The necessities of war led the Crusaders to profit from the divisions that existed among the "infidels" and to exploit the offices of one to combat the others—so much so, in fact, that the first lessons learned from the Muslims were primarily utilitarian and military.

From the very beginning of the First Crusade, the Franks reached a military understanding with the Fatimids of Egypt against their common enemy, the Turks. The Fatimids were far from viewing the Frankish invasion adversely because they deemed that it would stop the advance of the Turks in the direction of Egypt. Arab historian Ibn al-Athir accused the Fatimids of having summoned the Franks into Syria in order to use them as defense against the Turks. In 1099 the Crusaders signed an accord with the emir of Tripoli, Ibn Ammar, which stipulated that they would spare the city in return for the emir's delivery of three hundred pilgrims who had been held captive in his city; 15,000 bezants; and food, supplies, and guides. The emir even went so far as to promise the Crusaders that he would convert to Christianity.[20]

Other alliances were similarly concluded. In 1100 a veritable *modus vivendi*, both political and economic, was established between the Franks and the Arabs in Palestine. In 1102 the grand master of the Assassins (see page 74) sent an ambassador to Baldwin, King of Jerusalem.

In 1138 the Christians allied with the Turks of the kingdom of Damascus, which was ruled by Ainard. Together they subsequently set siege to Paneade. Turkish warriors, assisted by Turkish workers and carpenters, taught the Christians how to erect siege apparatuses and to assault the besieged site with machines called stone throwers.[21]

On the Christian side the Templars were always the most active artisans of these kinds of alliances. In 1129, the Templar grand master urged Baldwin II to come to an understanding with the Ismaili Abu Fewa. Under the terms of their agreement, Baldwin exchanged Tyre for Damascus. In fact, "for some eighty years, the Templars maintained close relations with the heads of the Ismaili sect."[22] Similarly, in 1136 the Templars of Saint John of Acre became friends with the Turkish capitain Unur.

In 1167, a peace treaty was concluded in Cairo between the Christians and the caliph of Egypt. The negotiators for the Crusaders were Hugues de Cesarée and Geoffroi, a Templar knight. The event was noted by Guillaume de Tyr, who recounts in dithyrambic style all the marvels that struck them with admiration in the capital of Egypt. During that same year, however, the Christians broke the peace treaty and invaded Egypt on the instigation of the Hospitaller Order. "The brothers of the Temple, whose grand master was then Bertrand de Blanquefort, wished to take no part in this expedition, saying that it was most unjust to wage war against a kingdom whose alliance was based on our good faith, and to misinterpret the tenor of a treaty and the sacred principles of law."[23]

In 1187, in order to obtain the surrender of Ascalon and other Christian strongholds, Saladin employed as negotiators his prisoners, Guy de Lusignan, king of Jerusalem, and Gerard de Ridefort, grand master of the Templars. Though these negotiations went nowhere, a short time later the grand master succeeded in having Gaza turned over to Saladin, who then freed his prisoners as a sign of thanks. While R. Grousset views this as a cynical transaction, perhaps this negotiation occurred in response to the needs of the day and from a desire to avoid the useless spilling of blood. The Greek Orthodox community of Jerusalem acted from a similar attitude, with a fortunate result: Saladin, once master of the kingdom of Jerusalem, behaved toward the city's Christian populace with feelings of loyalty, humanity, and chivalrous grace, which struck the Latin chroniclers with admiration.[24]

Bernard the Treasurer indicates in his chronicle that in 1198 the "Lord of the Assassins" (the Old Man of the Mountain) treated the Christians and their leader, Count Henri, as royalty. The same author informs us that in 1227 the sultan Coradin, at the time of his death, entrusted his land and children to a Spanish knight who was a Templar brother. "He was fully aware that this knight would faithfully protect his land. He had no desire to leave it to the Saracens, for he knew full well that they would entrust it to his brother, the Sultan of Babylon."*

It was through the intervention of the Templars in 1243 that the Christians were able to conclude an accord with the malek of Damascus and take possession of Jerusalem. In the following years, the Franks made an alliance with the malik of Homs, al-Mansour. The Templars made themselves noticeable by their eagerness to arrange this union. In fact, they celebrated in their strongholds to such an extent that Islamic prayers could be heard echoing beneath the roofs of their monasteries.[25] In 1247 the Templar grand master Guillaume de Sonnace got along so well with the Turkish emirs that a chronicler wrote: "The master of the Temple and the sultan of Egypt have made so strong a peace between them that they bled themselves together every two years in the same bowl."†

When the different branches of the military, governed mainly by common interests, gave way to a peaceful coexistence, the Christians found in the Muslim world a favorable milieu and climate. Claude Cahen, a specialist in Islamic studies, came to this conclusion in his summary work *Orient et Occident au temps des Croisades:* "The image of the Muslim world up until the eleventh century is that of a very

---

* Guillaume de Tyr, *Histoire des Croisades,* vol. 4, 243, 414. Geoffrey de Tyr, who was hostile toward the Templars, appears to have inflated the importance of the murder by a Templar of an envoy from the Old Man of the Mountain to King Amaury. It turns out that according to de Tyr himself this Templar, Gautier de Mesnil, had acted on his own. The grand master Eude de Saint-Armand did not refuse to punish him; instead he refused to surrender him to the king, making the argument that it was up to the sovereign order or the pope to judge him. How Grousset (*Histoire des Croisades,* vol. 2, 600), who is normally so perspicacious, could deduce from this murder that the Templars were the sworn enemies of the Ismailis is puzzling.

† Saint Louis refused to profit from these negotiations and sharply criticised Guillaume de Sonnace. This occurred during the Seventh Crusade (Boulenger, *La Vie de Saint Louis,* Paris: Gallimard, 1929, 101).

remarkable multifaith society that is politically dominated by Islam, but in which a large proportion of believers in other faiths manage to live without difficulty, in a kind of symbiosis for which we would search in vain to find an equivalent in other societies."

Islam opened for Christians numerous doors toward social understanding and harmony. On the Muslim side, the principle artisans of this action were the Ismaili sects, particularly the Karmates and the Assassins.

The Ismaliens were a bough of the Shiite branch of Islam. Karmate propaganda, born from Ismailism, took on the form of a large reform movement that was both social and religious in scope. From the ninth to eleventh centuries, this movement shook the Muslim world, including Syria, Persia, India, and especially Egypt, where it led to the installation of the Fatimid dynasty. It was in Egypt that a command center for the majority of Ismailian sects, the Dit ul Hikmat, was founded.

In the social sphere, Karmatism is characterized by the organization of labor and groups of workers into professional corporations (sinf; pl. asnaf), which seem to have been in existence since the tenth century and were connected with religious brotherhoods (tariqa; pl. turuq). It is important to note that the contemporary recollections of asnafs and turuq in Shiite sects emphasize both the spiritually and socially educational value of labor.[26] The hierarchical degrees—apprentice, worker, foreman, and master—were the rule, as were the obligation to mutual assistance and the initiatory oaths.[27] Trade secrets were gradually passed on to each grade in accordance with a legal custom (dustur), which was transmitted orally.

The kinship of these professional brotherhoods with the Christianized collegia of the late Roman empire is obvious. Among their members could be found not only Arabs but converts—mainly Christians and Jews. In lands that had become Muslim it seemed that there was some sort of transformation taking place in the various models of Latin and Byzantine institutions that had survived.

The Karmati movement, which is the source of these Muslim institutions, stands out both religiously and philosophically in its introduction to Islam of basic foreign assumptions—primarily those that were Hellenic, Neoplatonic, pseudo-Hermetic, and "Sabine." By spreading these elements through an esoteric method of initiation based on reason, tolerance, and equality, the Karmates facilitated ties among all races and castes.*

A conversion to Ismailism is the basis for the creation of the brotherhood of the Assassins: the conversion of its founder and first grand master, Hassan Sabah, a highly educated man who was a minister of the Sultan of Isfahan. He reformed Ismailism with a less flexible administration that provided him with a military organization.

The word *assassin* as applied to the brotherhood does not mean, as some have maintained, "eater of hashish." In reality, *assassin* is the plural form of the Arab word for guardian, *assas*. The Assassins or "Guardian Brothers were so named because the purpose of their order was the protection of the Holy Land, whose central orientation, the axis of the Spiritual World, was the mystic Mountain, which explains the title held by the grand master, the Sheik el Djebel," interpreted by the Europeans to mean the Old Man of the Mountain. (*Sheik* means "master," "teacher," or "head of a brotherhood" and "old man" as in a person worthy of respect.)[28]

The higher adepts within the Assassins devoted their time to the study of philosophy in the fortress of Alamut, which was located in a Persian domain. When the Mongols of Kubla Khan defeated the Assassins in the twelfth century, the victors found an immense library and an astronomical observatory there.

Outside of the Holy Land, there was another region where Christians had contact with Arab civilization and Ismailian sects in particular: Spain. In the eleventh and twelfth centuries, an Ismaili group similar to the Assassins, the Brothers of Purity, lived on the Iberian peninsula. We possess fifty-one treatises left by these brothers and know that their initiation consisted of four grades. The objective they pursued was the propagation of a philosophy inspired by that of Aristotle with Neoplatonic interpretations.

There is no need anymore to provide proof of the influence exercised by the Arab civilization over the Western world. We have already

---

* It should be noted that the Middle East, cradle of the Christian world, had long been disposed to the synthesis of religions and philosophies.

shown how such influence occurred well before the Crusades in the Holy Land. In fact, the very first Crusade was the eleventh century Crusade in Spain, the advance post of Christianity against the Muslim world. This effort was the work of the Benedictines of Cluny. The Crusades into Spain and the Middle East served to intensify and expand the propagation in the West of Arab influences triggered two centuries earlier by the initial contact between the two civilizations. These influences were especially attributable to the initiatory movements that maintained the best and most long-lasting relations with the Crusaders: those of the Karmates, Ismailians, Fatimids, Assassins, and Brothers of Purity. It was perfectly natural that spiritual and social interpenetration would be the outcome of the extensive relationship between the two cultures.

It is this extensive Arab influence, twin to that of the Byzantine world, that prompted the first cultural and philosophical renaissance that took place in the West during the twelfth and thirteenth centuries, especially in France. Along with the rebirth of the studies of Roman law, the royal role enjoyed by theology, which had ruled as sovereign over the world of ideas and provided society with it principal leaders, was strongly undermined. A new science was born that, rather than being fundamentally opposite to its theological predecessor, was instead independent of it. This was not the science of society such as the one the Romans had let loose. Despite the official resistance of the Church, this science was a synthesis, a joining: The great renown of the Roman empire, like the wisdom of Greece or Egypt, had never vanished from the memory of men. The Church was the direct heir to Rome and retained its dominance in this new world. But now next to the theologian stood the jurist, the philosopher, and the scholar. This conjugation, a return of authentic traditions, was the collective work of the Latins (Europeans or their descendants living in the Latin States in the Holy Land), the people of the East, and the Arabs.

We have seen a broad view of the role played by the Byzantine world in the growth of culture in the West. It was the Arabs, though, who reintroduced Aristotle in a form permeated with Neopythagorism and Neoplatonism. It was also the Arabs who passed on the knowledge of mathematics in general, particularly algebra and the works of Euclid.

Nor should we overlook the considerable influence of alchemy. This science, which took shape in the syncretic milieus of third-century Alexandria as a synthesis of Egyptian, Chaldean, Jewish, and Hellenic speculations and practices, evolved rapidly before entering Byzantium and from there the Arab world, notably in the Fatimid and Ismailian sects. It was among the Arabs in the thirteenth century that Arnaud de Villeneuve, Saint Thomas, Raymond Lulle, and Roger Bacon studied alchemy, which took on considerable importance in Europe during the fourteenth and fifteenth centuries. We should also note that its symbolism is closely tied to that of philosophy and construction.

In the architectural domain, European builders were subject to the direct influence of the Arab world. In fact, masons' marks, those symbolic markings left by European masons on all their work starting at the end of the twelfth century, had been in common use throughout the East since the remote past.[29]

Those in the East and Muslim Spain were familiar with the broken arch and the tiers point long before the Europeans. In some portions of France (especially in central France and the Midi region), in Spain (as seen in the portal of Santiago de Compostela and the San Pablo del Campo Cloister in Barcelona), and in Germany, (primarily along the banks of the Rhine), Romanesque buildings, some of which date to before the twelfth century, have architectonic forms borrowed from the Arabs. These forms, which are most often seen above compartments such as bays, doors, and windows, consist of several sections of circles combined in various ways. Examples are trefoil arches and arches with multifoil festoons and two-color archstones. The churches of Auvergne and of the Velay, particularly the apse and tribunes of Notre Dame du Port in Clermont Ferrand and the cloister, transept, and chapels of the cathedral Notre Dame du Puy, provide some characteristic examples that have inspired several imitations in the surrounding areas.* Other examples include the triforium of the meridional transept of the Cluny

---

* Bands, archivolts, *modillons à copeaus* [the console figures that have a design element, *copeaux*, resembling wood shavings], multifoil porches, and polychrome stonework give Notre Dame du Port and Notre Dame du Puy a resemblance to the mosque in Cordova, which left such a strong impression on Emile Malé (*Arts et Métiers du Moyen Age,* 33 ff).

Abbey; the bell tower, the tower of the crossing of the transept, the triforium of the nave, and the choir of the church of La Charité sur Loire, a former Cluny priory; the bell tower of the transept of Saint Philbert of Tournus; the apse and transept of the cathedral of Valence; the bell tower of Saint Peter's Basilica in Vienne; the nave of the church of Champagne (Ardèche); and the multifoil portals of numerous churches in the southern half of the former Bourges diocese. The same influences have also been detected in the dormitory of the convent of Saint Gereon in Cologne, in the church of Saint Quirin in Neuss, in the church of the Holy Apostles in Cologne and in many of the houses of this same city, and in the church of Limburg.[30] No less curious are the borders and frames that derive from Arabic letters and that even carry transcriptions in Kufic of passages of the Qur'an (which can be seen in Moissac, Puy, and Saint Guilhem le Desert in the Herault region).

Templars and Muslims

On the Christian side, the Benedictines and Templars played an important role in the propagation of these Muslim influences. Of course, the Templars, recipients of Arabic knowledge and culture, which they then passed on to others, did not necessarily explore these influences through high scientific and metaphysical speculation. They were primarily men of action, warriors and builders.* From their extensive relations with Ismailian sects and Arab corporations, the Templars were at least aware of and largely adopted—if only on an operative plane—certain Arab organization structures, rites, symbols, practices, and trade secrets. Many brother servants had already been initiated in their secular lives to similar operative rituals. They were particularly open to receiving this new contribution and transplanting it to the West, where the social fabric had become propitious for its introduction.

It is a fact that the architecture of the castles and fortified churches built by the Templars show clear evidence of ancient Arab lessons. "It

---

* The Templars were not completely uneducated, however. In one sermon, Jacques de Vitry speaks of "educated brothers who the commanders pointed in the direction of theological schools and secular studies" (Marion Melville, *La Vie des Templiers*, Paris: Gallimard, 1951, 175).

was in the east that the Crusaders learned from the Byzantines and the Arabs the art of fortifying a castle, a millenarian art in Asia that went all the way back to ancient Assyria."[31] The Templar master builders and workers had to have been in contact with their Assassin colleagues, who were also great builders. These Assassins, we are told by Guillaume de Tyr, possessed notably ten fortified castles in the province of Tyre.[32]

Going beyond simple architectural instruction, the influence of the Ismailians and the Assassins also left its mark on Templar ceremonies as well as on many of their customs. "Ismailism clearly seems to have been the practical model that the Templars adopted almost immediately after the formation of the Order, with respect to its hierarchy and the obedience to a grand master and commanders on whom the Order firmly established its discipline."[33] This hierarchy in fact was derived from the Pythagorians and the Egyptian mysteries. The same could also be said about other customs and symbols that the Assassins and Templars had in common. For example, couldn't the white garb of both the Assassins and the Templars be modeled on that of the disciples of Pythagoras?*

It is also acceptable to believe that outside the respective dogmas of Assassins and Templars there were flexible interpretations of ideas and doctrines. Members of the two groups managed to make the transition from one faith to to another: Muslims became Christians and Christians became Muslims without experiencing any disorientation. There were affiliations of Ismailians and Saracen rulers in the Temple and perhaps Templars among the Muslim brotherhoods. This becomes all the more likely given that the faith of Eastern Christians showed such distinctive features that it was almost impossible to discern any demarcations between these Christian sects and the derivatives of Islam. Both sides came closer to one shared ideal. The Fatimids of Cairo imagined the possibility of a peaceful universalism that was the rebirth of the thought of the pharaoh Amenhotep IV. The Templars echoed

---

* We should recall that the Essenes also dressed in white linen and practiced a form of solar worship. The uniform of the Assassins consisted of a white robe, red cap, belt, and boots. The Templars, at least the knights in the Order, wore a white robe with a red cross on the chest. White is the symbol of light and red is the symbol of fire.

them on this point by trying to establish cooperative relations between Easterners and Westerners united in the desire for universal peace.

Despite the considerable influence of the Arab world, however, there are no grounds for concluding that the Templar Order underwent a secret Islamization, even if only relatively, as some are prone to think. Quite a few of the more subtle aspects of Christianity that were not deemed suspect or condemnable before the Council of Trent became so afterward. Free thinking was not considered heresy during the Middle Ages, as can be shown by the fortunate Raymond Lulle. He spent time with Muslims, was influenced considerably by the Sufis, and sought, naturally outside of dogmas, to bring Muslims and Christians closer together. The Templars did the same. Among all the Crusaders they were the ones, writes Gerard de Nerval in *Les Illuminés,* who tried to realize the broadest alliance between Eastern ideas and those of Roman Christianity.

> The name the "Militia of Christ and the Temple of Solomon" that the Templars assumed immediately after the creation of their Order was evocative not only to Christians. While it recalled the Holy Sepulcher, it also recalled to Jews and Muslims the Temple of Solomon (Wisdom), which was furthermore reproduced on the seal of the grand master. A sacred sanctuary, it spoke simultaneously to the sons of Shem, Cham, and Japhet.[34]

So the reason for the condemnation of the Templars is not to be sought in a heretical deviation. In fact they were never condemned by the pope—who was satisfied with simply dissolving the Order—but by the temporal authority. Philip the Fair could not take action against the Templars, a sovereign and independent religious order, without a condemnation or dissolution of the Order by the Holy See. Dissolution was forthcoming from Rome in payment of a debt of gratitude owed the king of France. The action Philip the Fair took against the Templars had nothing to do with the struggle against heresy, a pretext, at any rate, that no one believed. Nor can the trial of the Templars be explained simply by the greed of the king. It certainly seems that the destruction of the Order in France was justified by reasons of national politics. It falls into the framework of the struggle, ongoing at the time, between the king and the feudal authorities. The Temple was in fact a sovereign entity of great power; its domains, great in number, with their own legal, political, and social armatures, formed autonomous enclaves inside the territory ruled by the crown. At the end of the thirteenth century, the Templars owned almost a third of Paris, a vast part of the city that escaped royal jurisdiction and authority. The jurist Guillaume de Nogaret was especially concerned with defense of the French monarchy. His purpose was the pursuit of national unity under the sole authority of the king. It is not possible to take seriously the accusations of heresy lodged against the Templars. It should certainly be acknowledged, however, that without the destruction, or at least the weakening, of the Holy Land's Latin states, whose great strength derived not only from their ties to the top feudal families, but also from their wealth, immense domains, perpetuity and mysterious prestige, and divine character that had no equal on earth, the French kingdom—that is, French unity—never would have prevailed. In short, it is acceptable that the destruction of the Order was legitimized by reasons of state; it was only the means used to accomplish this destruction that were iniquitous.

6

The Templars, the Francs Métiers, and Freemasonry

The Templars and
the Master Builders

When the Templars extended their commanderies into Europe with the help of their Christian worker assistants, they brought with them the traditional rites and secrets of the Byzantine collegia and the Muslim turuq, which had much in common. It is not rash to assert that the forms and ideas of these associations inspired and penetrated the "master associations" that were forming then and which the Templars used or guided for their constructions. These rites and customs combined with the remnants and symbols passed down by the brotherhoods of the early Middle Ages in regions where memories of Roman and ancient times had never entirely disappeared.

Given the number and importance of their building projects, it is most likely that the Templars played a prominent role in the formation of European "master associations." We know that the Templars, just like the Benedictines, employed many workers in their service in addition to their servant brothers, notably masons and carpenters. In each commandery, these builders were under the direction of an officer of the Temple, the *magister carpentarius*. This individual, a veritable architect, taught laborers working for the Order the art of building and geometry. Whether they were brother servants or lay workers, everyone contributed to the construction of Templar buildings; in short, they labored for the Temple. While remaining under Templar tutelage, however, these associations soon became more independent of the Order. They expanded their field of activity by working not only for the Templars but also for the inhabitants of their domains, which continued to develop in both population and wealth. The bond that tied operatives to the Temple was now simply one of a manorial order. In this insecure time, tradesmen flocked to the commanderies, where, in addition to its powerful protection, the Temple offered to operatives considerable advantages, including the right of asylum, the right of franchise, and fiscal privileges.

The Privileges of the Temple: Asylum and Franchise

Like the majority of religious orders, the Templars had the privilege of asylum, meaning that they could protect those individuals who sought refuge in their domains from any legal proceedings against them. One of the oldest legal documents that offers evidence of this is a papal bull from Innocent III dating from 1200 and stating that those who used violence against the colleagues and liegemen of the Temple who had entered into an area under God's truce as preached by the Church would be excommunicated.

"The Bible of the Lord of Berze," a poem composed during the early years of the thirteenth century, expresses it as follows:

> *Dare not strike one of its knights*
> *Its Sargents nor its squires*
> *Threaten not to slay them*
> *or to the Hospital he shall flee*
> *Or to the Temple, if he can manage to do so.*

The right of franchise was much more exceptional than the right of asylum. It is certain that the Benedictines, Cistercians, and Hospitallers of Saint John of Jerusalem offered an equal measure, at least originally.

This right of franchise allowed any craftsman to exercise any craft or commerce within the domain of the Temple, despite any rules or regulations promulgated by the sovereign authority of the nation or the city. The inhabitants of the Templar commanderies were also exempted from the majority of tariffs and taxes imposed by the king, the lord of the area, or the municipality. In Paris this is how they were able to avoid the tallage, the *corvee,** and a very unpopular kind of servitude, the watch, something in which the bourgeois residents of Paris were compelled to participate. The trades that benefited from such franchises were known as the *francs métiers* [free craftsmen].

Francs Métiers and Freemasonry

It is perhaps within these privileged francs métiers that we should place the origin of operative or traditional freemasonry. Apparently, the term *freemason* was imported from England. In that country there are texts from 1376 and 1396 in which the word *ffremasons* or *ffreemaseons* appears for the first time. In reality, however, the English had borrowed the term from the French language, as is evidenced by its etymology. We should not forget that under the Norman monarchs and for three centuries following William the Conqueror's victory at Hastings in 1066, the official language of England was French. The oldest statutes of English workers to have come down to us (from 1351 and 1356) were still written in French. Throughout the Middle Ages on into the Renaissance, French was also the international language of crafts and the esoteric language that craftsmen used. Thus it is in France where we actually must look to find the origin of this term.[1]

In the Middle Ages the word *franc* served not only to qualify what was free—in opposition to that which was servile—and what bore the mark of purity and high quality, but it also and more specifically designated every individual or property that was exempt from manorial servitudes and laws. Thus a *franc-alleu* was a land completely owned as property and owing no lord any right, faith, homage, or investiture. Opposite the franc-alleu were the servile status and the fief that made

---

* [*Corvee* is the unpaid labor owed by peasants and bourgeois to their sovereign lord. —*Trans.*]

its owner or lord a vassal to a suzerain. At the beginning of the four-teenth century, Boutillier wrote in his *Somme rurale* (1, 84): "[T]o hold as a franc-alleu is to hold land from God alone and owe neither cens, allowance, debts, service, nor any fee; the tenant holds the land freely from God." In the sixteenth century the legal counselor Guy Coquille pro-claimed, "The franc-alleu is called free because it is not in the sphere of any landed lord's influence." Among the different kinds of franc-alleu there was the *franche-aumone,* a land donated to the Church free of any charge. Because this property ceased to be feudally dependent upon a lord, its transfer could be made without the lord's consent.

With respect to individuals, a *franc homme* or *franc hons* [free man] was not only the opposite of a serf but also the opposite of a vil-lain.[1] This latter was free, but lived as the dependent of a lord. The free man, although a commoner, escaped this state of dependency. The term is found in Beaumanoir's *Coutume du Pantagrue:* "A franc hons who is not a gentleman". . . In the prologue to the fourth book of *Pantagruel,* Rabelais speaks of *francs gontiers.* These individuals were most likely peasants benefiting from specific franchises.

Free Archers were an order of soldiers who were only to serve dur-ing times of war and were created for that purpose by Charles VII in 1448:

> This ruler [Charles VII] commanded that the most reliable inhabi-tant in each parish of the kingdom be elected for training in the bow, and that this individual also be under the obligation to fur-nish a crew . . . Each of the Archers would receive 4 pounds a month when serving in war . . . But they enjoyed a general exemp-tion from all manner of taxes or fees. It is for this reason that they were known as Free Archers.[2]

The inhabitants of towns and cities who had obtained charters of exemption were called the bourgeois—in other words, free men. They were, however, distinguished from the *francs bourgeois* "who did not have to pay and did not pay any to the lord for any bourgeois right, and were free and quit of him," to use the terms employed by the *Coutume de Berry.* In Paris the bourgeoisie owed the king both the tallage and corvee; to the municipal authorities they were compelled to give time in service of the watch. The Parisian francs bourgeois, some of whom left their name to a street that still exists today,* were exempt from all taxes and unpaid service.†

The tallage was actually a tax on revenue. It earned its name from the notches or cuts made into the pieces of wood that served as receipts for paid debts. Originally it was due to the suzerain lord, but later it was owed to the king. Tallage did not exist in the Templar commanderies.

The watch, a Roman institution introduced early on in Gaul, was responsible for the surveillance of the city while it slept. In 595 King Clotaire II had established the rules for its practice, but Henry II suppressed this police service. It was reorganized by Saint Louis in 1254, and again by John II in 1364 and Francois I in 1540, but was eliminated in 1559 by Henry II. Mandatory for all individuals to participate in until the age of sixty, the bourgeois watch had become the function of guards known as the *assis* [seated ones], who were assigned specific posts. Comprising almost sixty men, they met every three weeks. The royal watch, another company maintained by the king, made daily rounds. Both watches were under the sole command of the Knight of the Watch. Only those living in the domain under the control of the Temple were not compelled to fulfill this watch service.

As for those who pursued various crafts and trades, in the rural areas they were either serfs or villains, while in the towns they held the status of bourgeoisie. Free craftsmen, however, meaning either villains or bourgeois, did not perform their trade under similar conditions everywhere. As a general rule, the artisan owed taxes and allowances to the king or lord. In Paris, at the time the crafts were organized during the reign of Saint Louis, the artisan was subject to community regulation. Quite often entrance into a craft was not free; it was necessary to purchase this right from the king. Just as the bourgeoisie, artisans were

---

* [It is located in the Marais district of Paris. —*Trans.*]

† It should be noted that the rue Francs Bourgeois was located in the censive district and was under the jurisdiction of the Temple. Maps from the time of Louis XIV show the existence of another rue Francs Bourgeois located on the left bank (today it forms the upper part of rue Monsieur le Prince). See also Lefeuve, *Histoire de Paris, rue par rue, maison par maison*, vol. 5 (Paris: C. Reinwald, 1875), 244.

also obligated to the responsibilities (the watch and so forth) demanded of them by the city.

Along with the trades performed by free men were the free and exempted crafts performed by *francs métiers,* meaning those entirely free and exempt from the majority of taxes and mandatory services. In Flanders, a land where the Templars had established some of their first and most important commanderies, the four cities of Bruges, Gand, Audenarde, and Alost, where crafts operated in franchise, were metonymically known as the "four free crafts."* One canton [administrative district] in Bruges long retained the name of Franc and in 1579 it still included a jurisdiction called the Chambre du Franc de Bruges.[3]

The terminology relating to the franchises of crafts and free crafts stands out in Etienne Boileau's *Livre des Métiers* (1268). As we shall see, the texts it codifies apply only in the case of the royal provostship, meaning a unique part of Paris where free crafts were the exception. Thus, when speaking of pewtersmiths, Boileau writes, "Whosoever desires to be a potter in pewter in Paris can do so freely so long as he does good and loyal work." The same expression can be found referring to some forty other crafts, among which are cutlers, silver- and goldsmiths, smelters, tapestry makers, dyers, clothes tailors, image makers, lantern makers, button makers, saddlers, hatters, and bowers (or the makers of bows and arbalests). In their edition of the *Livre des Métiers,* Lespinasse and Bonnardot write: "To be freely master of a craft is to have the right to set up an establishment and take on apprentices."[4]

For the duke of Levis Mirepoix of the French Academy, craftsmen who exercised freely in this way fell under the category of francs métiers. "Within the crafts," he writes, "some individuals are 'francs,' meaning that the only requirement is that they show suitable proof of their ability to become a master. Others purchased at a set price the right to perform their trade, with this fee being determined by regulations or by the lord who allegedly holds the ownership of the craft in question."[5]

This does not correspond entirely to the definition of *franc métiers*

---

* La Curne de Saint Palaye, *Dict. hist. de l'ancien langage français* (1879), who quotes here a text by Froissart. In the ancient custom of Alost we find the expression *francs bateliers* [free boatmen].

such as it appeared in the *Livre des Métiers*. In the cases in which the craft was exercised freely, the exemptions from which the craft benefited remained relative. The term *franc métier* implies in fact much more extensive franchises. For the provost of Paris, as Lespinasse and Bonnardot indicate, it concerns freely exercised trades that exempted these craftspeople from the watch and special fees.[6] The *Livre des Métiers* expressly cites only two cases of this nature: crafts that are attached to the service of either the Church or the nobility, such as crystal engravers and hatters working with flowers.

> Title XXX. On Crystal Engravers. I. Whosoever desires can be a crystal engraver in Paris . . . he can establish a trade and has what is necessary, as such he will open in accordance with the customs of the craft. . . . XIV. The crystal engraver owes to the King the tallage and others owed by his fellow bourgeois. But the watch he will pay never, nor sally forth when the King is overseas; neither will he pay or owe tax, as they deem fit, for their craft is free,* as such he owes nothing from buying nor selling. Neither toll nor home tax owes he in any land of the things of his trade, as their craft belongs forwith to the honoring of the Holy Church and the high homes. Title XC. Flower Hatters. I. Who so desireth to be a Hatter of flowers can be so freely so far as he knows the craft and he has the wherewithal. VII. No hatters of flowers are compelled to fulfill watch service, because their craft is free and was established to serve the gentlefolk.

In Paris, with respect to the royal provostship, the mortarers and stonecutters were regarded as free in the sense that they were exempt from various compulsory duties, mainly the watch. But masons, plasterers, and carpenters did not enjoy this exemption; therefore they were not francs métiers.

In their most extensive acceptance, the free crafts appear to have had their origin in the jurisdiction of abbeys and religious orders, a fact

---

* It should be noted that in such cases the franchise does not provide complete exemption, for the craftsman must still pay the tallage.

that has often been overlooked given that many French authors (such as Martin Saint Leon, Olivier Martin, and E. Coornaert) generally studied only the corporate regime of the oath-bound and regulated crafts. Certain English authors, however, such G. W. Speth and Lionel Vibert, noted the distinction among crafts on this point. Speth writes: "The masons were free of restrictions, free of the ordinances of corporations, for the same reason that their employers were not citizens . . . but ecclesiastics who lived outside the cities and were their own masters."*

In his splendid book *Les Chantiers des Cathedrales,* Pierre du Colombier pertinently raises this question:

> How were religious or feudal ties compatible with the migratory nature of the manual laborers who worked on the cathedrals? Not only were these manual laborers free, but in a good number of cases we have proof that they were independent; they were not bound to the corporative organization of the towns where they were employed. While French documents are not very explicit in this regard, the German ones are much more detailed. Quarrels were common between the city workers and those of the cathedral in fourteenth-century Strasbourg. Should this lead to the conclusion that the cathedral builders had their own organization?

We should recall that at the time craft communities were being formed, brotherhoods existing under the protection of monasteries transformed quite naturally into lay brotherhoods whose sole tie with the abbeys remained a feudal bond. But these brotherhoods, whose economic and social evolution had transformed them into distinct and autonomous entities from the monastery, nevertheless continued to enjoy exemptions from the Church from which they had emerged and which remained the sole institution to which they remained subordi-

---

* G. W. Speth, "Free and Freemasonry: A Tentative Inquiry," *Ars Quatour Coronatorum* (1897). L. Vibert, *La Franc-Maçonnerie avant l'existence des Grandes Loges* (Paris: Gloton, 1950), 36. "The oldest free masons were free of any company or any kind of guild," writes Bernard E. Jones, who does not specify, however, that such an exemption could result only from affiliation with the Church ("Le mot 'Franc' dans Franc-Maçon," *Le Symbolism,* July/August, 1954, 340).

nate. On the one hand, they were free of all bonds of subordination with respect to the local lord, the city, or even the king. On the other hand, the members of these brotherhoods, placed under the protection of the Church and, more precisely, under an order possessing all the rights of higher and lower justice, benefited from the valuable privilege of being able to circulate and find welcome in other abbeys and houses belonging to the same order, and even other orders.

It is therefore easy to understand how these craftsmen who were dependent on ecclesiastical jurisdictions—particularly those who moved most often, such as masons and boatmen—could be labeled as francs when compared to the craftsmen of other lords or of the cities. These latter, even when free, could acquire exemptions only from their lord high justice. Their rights existed only on the sufferance of this lord and their freedom did not extend beyond the city limits. In addition, as we have seen, often the autonomy of the city and the guilds it housed within its walls entailed particularly burdensome responsibilities and duties. Finally, it frequently happened that the craftsmen of the towns and cities could be freed of their ties to their lord only with the support of the king; they would be released from the tutelage of one only by placing themselves under that of another. It is true the king's was ordinarily less heavy because he was a more remote presence, but this does not mean that the bourgeoisie of the king did not subsequently seek with any less energy to emancipate themselves from his control.

The king, however, especially in England, sometimes conferred more or less extensive exemption to certain crafts, granting them charters that encompassed all members of the same craft throughout the entire kingdom and subjected them to the same regulations. In the fourteenth century, this was the case for the weavers, and it is possible that the Company of the Masons of London enjoyed certain privileges outside the city, among them more or less acknowledged suzerainty over all other guilds forming part of this trade.[7] English masonry was then known as *franc-maçonnerie*, but the term at this time had a much more extensive acceptance than its original meaning.

At the time when crafts communities were initially being formed, the first religious order whose abbeys gave birth to free communities was that of the Benedictines, who for centuries oversaw the art of construction. This role and its effects on social organization were already in decline when existing monastic brotherhoods began transforming into secular confederations. The number of craftsmen, especially builders, diminished considerably near Benedictine abbeys. As we have seen, craft associations enjoyed specific exemptions in Benedictine jurisdiction. Thus in Paris we have Saint Germain des Pres, Saint Martin des Champs, Saint Eloi (Saint Maur), and Saint Magloire. Yet it does not appear that a large number of lay craftsmen benefited from this, for proof has been offered showing that the Benedictine censive districts remained sparsely populated for long periods of time.

The religious order that appears most prominently at the origin of the francs métiers is that of the Templars, a fact that has largely gone unnoticed.* In the jurisdiction of its commanderies, free craft was the rule, just as the bourgeois residents of Templar-controlled areas were free bourgeois. In the cities where the Templars had establishments, a distinction can be made in the same craft between the "franc" craftsman (who were free and enjoying certain exemptions) living in the Templar's domain, and artists who were merely free who worked in other quarters and were subject to royal and manorial charges and taxes as well as to their own trade regulations. This was the case in Paris with respect to the masons. Clearly in this distinction between "franc" craftsmen and free artists, we can seek the origin of the term *francs-maçon (franc-maçonnerie),* for with this term, the noun that labeled and distinguished the worker eventually became one with the name it qualified, quite opposite to a simple free mason who did not enjoy the benefits of any exemptions.

It can also be said that because of the spiritual and temporal autonomy and authority of the Temple, as well as that of a large number of its commanderies spread throughout the land, the *francs-maçons* and all other free, exempt craftsmen in Templar jurisdiction could move about freely. They enjoyed freedom of passage and were confident both of receiving assistance and protection everywhere and of their right to settle in one location and find work there.

---

* Abbe Auber sensed this and drew some tendentious conclusions from it in his small tract, *Francs-Maçons du Moyen Age* (Tours: 1874).

The European Mastery Associations and the Templars

The exemptions and privileges that craftsmen benefited from in Templar commanderies were particularly propitious for increasing the Order's influence and popularity. In the troubled times of the twelfth and thirteenth centuries, when the craftsmen and bourgeois of the cities sought protection for themselves and their properties by freeing themselves from their cities' control, the Temple offered them not only asylum but also the model of a free professional organization. The status of the inhabitants of commanderies could only inspire those outside to benefit from the same rights and to obtain their recognition—if need be, by force—from the lords.

There is no doubt that under these conditions the Templars exercised, directly or indirectly, an important influence on the formation of craft communities. This is not to say that the activity of the Templars and the example they set was the sole origin of guilds and mastery associations, whose creation was largely a response to profound political, economic, and social needs. But the Templars and their franchises, while they may not have been the primary cause, were at least a determinative cause.

It is striking to observe that the first crafts guilds appeared at the time and in the regions when and where the Templars were first in action and founded their earliest establishments. Such a parallel goes beyond simple coincidence and any gratuitous hypothesis to attribute the formation of these mastery associations to the Order.

From the start of their existence as an order, the Templars held large domains in Flanders, Hainaut, Artois, and Picardy as a result of donations made by the first knights Templar such as Geoffroi de Saint Omer. This was how such large commanderies like those of Ypres, Tournai, Bruges, Loverval, Moustier sur Sambre, Mesmin les Mons, Chantraine, Aires sur la Lys, Bailes, Arras, Abbeville, Saint Quentin, Laon, and so forth, were created so quickly between 1130 and 1140. The Templars owned a significant number of domains in these regions and their activity here was intense. The construction of all major monuments in Picardy has been attributed to them.

It is precisely in these northern provinces that the first professional guilds made their appearance in the second half of the twelfth century

(Valenciennes, 1167; Saint Omer, 1200). In fact, as we saw earlier, the importance of the francs métiers was so great in Flanders that the four cities of Bruges, Audenarde, Gand, and Alost were called the "four francs métiers." The exercise of crafts in franchise was no doubt unknown in the West before the Templars introduced the free forms of craft associations that they had created earlier in the Holy Land based on Byzantine or Muslim models. It could be said that under the Templar influence, Flanders became the cradle for the franc métiers. This explains and provides justification for the theory, presented by some other authors, that freemasonry was created by the Templars in the kingdom of Jerusalem and imported from there into Flanders and Hainaut and England as well.

In England the Order received large donations, notably from King Henry I, and Hughes de Payans visited the country personally to found a new province.[8] In London in 1154, when the commander of the Temple of London undertook construction of the Fleet Street chapel, he had at his disposal an architectural association that had come from the Holy Land—proof that few workers in the English capital at that time had the qualifications necessary to realize this work successfully, and that no community of masons existed there at that time. This builders' association from the Middle East remained in the English capital under Templar guidance until 1199.[9] During this time it may have become the constitutional core of the Company of Masons of London. This transformation, which coincided with the social and political evolution of that time, was achieved when the association became important enough to escape Templar tutelage and find in the guild the legally autonomous structure its members were seeking. Indeed, the Company of Masons of London appears to date from the beginning of the thirteenth century.[10]

The likelihood of this influence of the Templars in England is all the stronger when we consider that the Order was the beneficiary of the English kings' personal trust. Bernard Le Tresorier informs us that King Henry kept a treasury in the Temple to which he sent large sums. The prestige of the Templars was especially great under the reign of Richard the Lionheart (1189–1199). When he took possession of the island of Cypress following his crusade with King Philip Augustus of France, he commanded the Templars to guard it. After the capture of Saint John of Acre on July 12, 1191, Richard was given lodging in the house of the Templars, whereas the king of France was garrisoned in the castle. The chronicle of Bernard the Treasurer also informs us that Richard the Lionheart often took counsel from the Templars.* Further, according to Guillaume de Tyr, the occasion of Richard's truce with Saladin on August 10, 1192 inspired the following:

When the king of England had made a truce with the Saracens, he made ready his ships, to have his vessels loaded with people and provisions . . . then he told the Templar grand master: "Master, I know full well that I am not loved by everyone, and that if I set sail and it is known that I am at sea, there is no place I can land where I will not be killed or captured. So I ask you to lend me your brother knights and men at arms who will come sail with me. When we are far from here, they will lead me as if I were a Templar until I am back in my own country . . ." The grand master told him he would do so gladly, and he secretly summoned his knights and men at arms and had them board a ship. The king took leave of Count Henry, the Templars, and those native of that land and boarded the ship. During the evening he boarded the Templar ship and took his leave of his wife and her retinue. They sailed off in one direction, and the others continued off in another direction."[11]

These close ties between the Templars and Richard the Lionheart (who did not hesitate to don Templar dress), were such that certain authors, Rebold for example, were of the belief that the king was a grand master of the Templar Order.† There is not a shred of truth in this, but the respective power and prestige of the king and the Temple, closely allied, served to make both parties even stronger. When we

---

* de Tyr, *Histoire des Croisades,* vol. 4, 65–67, 183, 201. It should be noted that the same circumstances applied to Philip Augustus. Aymard, treasurer of the Temple in Paris, was his trustworthy ally when he was the administrator of the Royal Treasury (cf. Leonard, introduction to the *Cartulaire manuscrit du Temple,* 119).

† Rebold, *Histoire des trois Grandes Loges,* (Paris: Franck, 1864), 671, 681. This author, who is serious and capable all the same, indicates that the nomination of Richard the Lionheart to the chief mastery association of the Templars would have occurred in 1154 or 1155. Richard, however, was not born until 1157!

consider the importance of the London commandery, we can also imagine the size of the community of builders who worked there, first directly for the Temple, then for many years under its high authority.

The establishment of the Templars in Normandy also extends far back in time, having been encouraged by Richard, king of England, who also held the title of duke of Normandy. It was most likely Templar architects from Richard the Lionheart's entourage to whom we can attribute construction of the remarkable fortress that was built in the space of sixteen months (1196–1197) above the Andelys and on the right bank of the Seine and was gallantly baptized with the name Chateau Gaillard. It was so superior in construction to all its contemporaries that on its completion the king was compelled to cry out in admiration, "How beautiful she is, my one-year-old daughter!"

The Templars maintained numerous and important commanderies throughout Normandy. In the Seine Maritime region there was Saint Vaubourg; in the Eure there was Renneville, Chanu, and Bourgault; and in Calvados there was Beaugy, Bretteville, Voisinier, and Courval. It so happens that in Normandy, as in Flanders, the same coincidence holds true: the simultaneous creation of the guilds and the establishment of the Templars. Guilds did in fact exist in Rouen, where privileged sites were known as *franches aires*,[12] and in Caen, since the first half of the twelfth century.

Other characteristic examples of the formation of guilds can be singled out in France. One of the most important is the oldest known mastery association of lay builders, the Cloture Commune of Montpellier, which grouped masons *(maytres de payra* or *peuries)*, stone carvers, sculptors *(ymagiers)*, and carpenters. In 1196 this association had received a written guarantee of assistance and protection from William VIII, lord of Montpellier.[13] The Templars established themselves at the same time in this city, where they too enjoyed the protection of the lords. For example, William VIII left them properties in his will of September 29, 1172. Templars again appear in the Customs of Montpellier conceded by King Pierre of Aragon, lord of the city, on August 15, 1204.[14] As a rule, the Templars had been long established in these regions of the Midi, where they were of considerable importance. In 1146 they already had a seat in Nimes and in 1173 they had one in

Toulouse. It should also be noted that the lords of these provinces, just like those of Flanders and Hainaut, were particularly numerous in the earliest Crusades.[15]

In conclusion of our discussion of Templar influence on the existence of associations, guilds, and the Freemasons, we can cite the case of Metz, where the Templars had installed a commandery in 1133. As Templar establishments in Cattenom, Gelucourt, Pierrevilliers, and Richemont show, this initial commandery spread to surrounding areas. In the framework of the territorial organization of the Order, the commandery of Metz included in its jurisdiction the establishments of the Trois Eveches, Lorraine, and the BarDuchy. By 1147, when Saint Bernard himself came there to preach the second Crusade, the Temple had deep roots in the Metz diocese. Interestingly, toward the end of the thirteenth century a brotherhood of masons met in the oratory of the Metz commandery. From 1285 we have the name *Jennas Clowanges, li maires de la frairie des massons dou Temple* [Jennas Clowanges, mayor of the brotherhood of the masons of the Temple]. In addition, a tombstone discovered in 1861 in front of the chapel and now on display in the Metz Museum recalls the memory of *Freires Chapelens* [Brother Chapelens. He was master of the Temple of Lorene]. *Ki fut Maistres des Mazons dou Temple de Lorene,* who lived for some twenty-three years and died on *la vigile de la Chandelour lan* [Candlemas Eve] *M.CC.IIII.XX.VII* [1287].[16]

The Survival of the Templar Communities

The communities of free and exempted craftsmen (francs métiers) under the aegis of the Benedictines or the Templars did not vanish with the appearance of oath-bound associations or with the emancipatory movement of the communes from manorial bonds or, most important, with the dissolution of the Templar Order.

As we have seen, the status of many abbeys, with the exception of their manorial rights, was maintained for many centuries and royal authority did not have the power to impose its edicts in those areas under their jurisdiction. Interestingly, the crafts and trade exemptions recognized by the abbeys were often retained by the cities following their own emancipation. Thus as far as the Templar commanderies were concerned, their privileges and exemptions remained unchanged after the abolition of the Order. In fact, a bull issued by Clement V on May 2, 1312, decreed that all the properties, rights, and privileges of the Templars would pass into the hands of the Hospitallers of Saint John of Jerusalem (who went on to become the Knights of Rhodes and the still-existing Order of the Knights of Malta). This bull was applicable in all Christian countries and ratified by many kings, including Philip the Fair. The privileges the Hospitallers inherited from the Templars were subsequently and over the course of the centuries often confirmed by the popes,* and the Hospitallers continued to widely apply the right to asylum and the right of franchise so thoroughly that the francs métiers were assured of their survival after the dissolution of the Templar Order.

We have iconographic proof of this protection provided by the Knights Hospitallers to construction workers in a miniature from the end of the fifteenth century depicting the ritual reception of journeymen carpenters by the grand master of the Hospitaller Order of Rhodes on the worksite of fortifications of the city that the Turks besieged in 1480.† While workers are busy on the ramparts, the grand master, attended by his officers, is preparing to give the *collee* to a carpenter who stands with hands clasped at the knees and a large ax on his shoulder, followed by other journeymen carrying their respective tools: compass, square, hammer, and chisel. All are wearing ritual ribbons tied around their heads.

Moissac, connected to both the Benedictines and the Templars, provides a characteristic example of how things remained in the communal context of the presence of freemasons. Very ancient in origin, Moissac was erected by Charlemagne as a Benedictine abbey endowed with all the rights to administer justice, which were subsequently transferred to the "Consuls and Leaders of City Hall."[17] Today we can still admire the church of this important abbey, a masterpiece of early Romanesque art adorned handsomely with symbolic sculpture.

---

* H. de Curzon, in *La maison du Temple de Paris,* cites fifteen bulls of confirmation that were issued from the time the Hospitallers assumed the Templar's position until 1629.
† This miniature is reproduced in Pierre du Colombier's book *Les Chantiers des Cathedrales.*

There is no doubt that the Templars held a role of great importance in Moissac, for on the outskirts of the city discoveries have been made of towns with names like La Villedieu du Temple (the seat of a commandery founded in 1137) and la Bastide du Temple, as well as farms that are still called "the Temple." In Moissac itself there was until fairly recently a Temple Street (part of the current rue des Mazels) that got its name from an old building alleged to have once been the "seat of the Temple," which leads us to believe a Templar establishment once existed in close proximity. It just so happens that in this Benedictine and Templar city of Moissac—once a very important crossroads of different influences and one of the stations and pilgrimage cities on the road to Compostella—there is a rue des Francs-Maçons located in the old city. M. A. L. Bittard, the former master of conferences at the National Conservatory of Arts and Crafts and president of the Friends of Old Moissac, writes in regard to this subject:

> The rue des Francs-Maçons in Moissac is the same street that bore this name in the past—and no doubt quite earlier than the eighteenth century, the time when speculative Freemasonry first appeared in France. It therefore concerns corporative freemasons who, from the time of the Middle Ages in France, had inherited a name and professional traditions from the journeyman of Hiram . . . Moreover, it was also included in the quarter of those corporations that had probably been freed from the censive district of the abbey and whose old memory has been perpetuated by the names of other streets: rue des Mazels (butchers), rue de l'Escauderie (tripe butchers), and so forth.*

---

* The current nomenclature of the old streets of Moissac dates from 1824, but the names used then would have been even older ones that had been suppressed at the time of the Revolution. See also Lagreze-Fossat, *Etudes historiques sur Moissac* (Montauban: Forestié Printers, 1870). This author believes that the "seat of the Temple" that could still be seen in the eighteenth century "on the west side of the corner formed where rue Malaveille meets rue Saint Paul, was a vast building that displayed all the appearances of a former monastery inside. This monastery, according to tradition, had belonged to the Templars, which explains why rue Saint Paul was called rue des Templiers in 1824, in the alignment map of the city."

This old rue des Francs-Maçons bears proof that in Moissac there once existed builder craftsmen benefiting from exemptions; from this it is hardly an audacious jump to connect their origin to the Benedictines and Templars.

The Introduction of the Templars into Builders Associations

The last interaction the Templars had with the builders associations was their own introduction into these groups following the destruction of the Order.

Certain authors have taken this even further, maintaining that after the execution of grand master Jacques de Molay, the Order continued and that he was succeeded by other grand masters without interruption. Of course, the line of descent varies according to author. For Cadet-Gassicourt it was the grand master Molay himself who, foreseeing the tragic end of the Order and his own execution while in his cell at the Bastille, charged his nephew Beaujeu with the task of creating four great lodges in Paris, Edinborough, Stockholm, and Naples, whose purpose would be the destruction of spiritual power (the pope) and temporal power (the king).[18] In the *Acta Latomorum,* Thory explains it as follows:

> Jacques de Molay, foreseeing the misfortunes that threatened an order whose existence he wished to perpetuate, designated as his successor Brother Jean-Marc Larmenius of Jerusalem, who invested the grand masters destined to succeed him with patriarchal authority as well as magisterial power by virtue of the charter of transmission he was given in 1324. The original of this charter, consigned to the Treasury under the title *Tabula aurea* by order of the Temple, contains the acceptance, signed *propria manu,* of all the grand masters to have succeeded Larmenius.

Baron von Hund, the 1756 creator of the Rite of Strict Observance, provided this version of the story: After the Order's downfall, the provincial grand master of Auvergne, Pierre d'Aumont, fled with two commanders and five knights. In order to avoid recognition, the men disguised themselves as masons and took refuge on a Scottish island, where they found the high commander, George Harris and several other brothers, with whom they resolved to continue the Order. They formed a chapter on Saint John's Day of 1312 and Aumont was named grand master. To avoid persecution, they adopted secret signs and passwords similar to those of masons and called themselves free and accepted masons. In 1361 the residence of the grand master was transferred to Aberdeen, and this is how the Order was saved and spread.[19]

Despite all that can be said about this direct continuation of the Templar Order, the entire story is purely hypothetical. It is legend that sees in modern Freemasonry, or at least in some of its chapters, a direct survival of the Templars. But it is nonetheless true that the Templar influence on traditional freemasonry is undeniable as is obvious from our earlier observations here. History tells us that following the dissolution of the Order, the Templars entered the builders corporations. It is possible to deduce from this that they would have thereby continued to exert their influence.

> Following the abolition of the Order in Germany, England, and Italy, the Templars were obliged to give up their religious garb and start earning a living, either as warriors and squires for their noble friends, or as architects, foremen, craftsmen, and workers accepted by the guilds according to the duties they had fulfilled in the Temple.
>
> The constant relations between the Templars and labor associations make it possible to grasp the rapid incorporation of the fugitives into the construction crews that were primarily working on churches and castles."[20]

Many Templars fleeing persecution took refuge in Scotland; this was the case of those belonging to the Douai commandery. Since 1274 the king of Scotland had been Robert the Bruce, whose family was of Flemish origin and some of whose members had been Templar knights. This king gave aid and protection to the Templars for this reason. Furthermore, he had drawn to Scotland a large number of Flemish craftsmen organized into guilds, with his promise that their customs and traditions would be safeguarded. Documents remain from this time attesting to the favors and privileges granted to weavers, wool carders, masons, and carpenters. These Flemish guilds that emigrated to Scotland primarily consisted of natives of Bruges. It is significantly noteworthy that in Bruges itself, where the Templars had an important commandery, the guilds and others had welcomed fugitive Templars

The legend extends much further than does the historical data to support it. As recorded and handed down by several authors,[21] Robert the Bruce is said to have founded in favor of the Freemasons, the Royal Order of Heredom of Kilwinning. At this same time he is said to have raised the lodge founded in 1150 (concurrent with the founding of the Kilwinning Abbey) to the rank of Grand Royal Lodge of Heredom of Kilwinning. Ancient chronicles also say that the fugitive Templars in Scotland enlisted under the flag of Robert the Bruce, where they contributed mightily to the successful outcome of the Battle of Bannockburn, in which 30,000 Scots defeated 100,000 English. This can be taken as fact, but legend goes on to add that King Robert rewarded the Templars by creating, at their request, the Order of the Knights of St. Andrew of the Thistle, reserving for himself and his successors the title of grand master. Initiations into the Order were supposedly performed according to the style that had been practiced among the Templars. During the time of the Reformation, the Order was suppressed and all its goods confiscated. In 1685 the Stuart monarch James III restored it. In accordance with the king's intent, it was to be a sign of distinction and reward for Freemasons.

Just what value can be ascribed to these legends? Are they more likely to be true given the protection and favor showed the Templars by Robert the Bruce? Or should we think, to the contrary, that they were imagined after 1685 by partisan supporters of the Stuarts in order to give, for political purposes, titles of credence and nobility to the "Scottish" masons whom they governed? Historically speaking, it is impossible to answer these questions. Any explanations that can be made belong to the domain of hypotheses.

In the interest of sticking to verifiable facts and the probabilities they justify, we can summarize as follows the role attributable to the Templars in the formation of freemasonry:

1. The Templars formed monastic builders associations that possessed Greco-Roman traditions passed down by the Benedictines and Cistercians.

2. The Templars had close ties to Christian and Muslim architectonic associations in the East and were subject to their operative and initiatory influences.

3. In Europe the Templars were the source of the creation and development of builders associations that long enjoyed specific exemptions. The terms *francs métiers* and *freemasonry* are derived from these associations.

4. Following the dissolution of the Templar Order, a certain number of Templars were incorporated into the mastery associations of builders.

To give a wider illustration of the formation and survival of free builders associations over the centuries in the Templar domains, we will give close attention in the next chapter to the example of Paris, seat of the most important commandery in Europe and headquarters of the Templar Order following its abandonment of the Holy Land.

7

The Templars and the Parisian Builders

The Domain and Sovereignty of the Temple

From the very beginning of the formation of their Order, the Templars sought to establish themselves in Paris.

King Louis VI, who ruled from 1108 to 1137 and had the sobriquet Louis the Fat, received a visit at his palace in the city one day from Father Bernard (the future Saint Bernard), abbot of Clairvaux. The abbot had come in the name of Baldwin II, king of Jerusalem, to ask if two Templars, Andre and Gondomard, whom Baldwin had sent as envoys of Jerusalem, could hope to find aid and protection in France and whether Louis was disposed to give them a roof for shelter and a chapel where they could pray to God.

"I understand," the king answered, "that it is a church you are asking me for. I will think on the matter." The result of his thought was that he gave them a house next to the Saint Gervais Church, which was then outside the city walls. The two Templars settled in and soon invited other members of the Order until gradually the Order took root in Paris and the king gave them a large piece of land that was known as the Temple's field. It extended from the current entry into the Faubourg du Temple* to the rue de la Verrerie. The Templars saw to it that within their walls—the Enclos, as it was known—a church was

---

* [Now the Place de la Republique and the rue Faubourg du Temple. —*Trans.*]

built dedicated to the Holy Virgin and to Saint John the Baptist. They also erected a refectory, a colombier, a large tower—the famous tower of the Temple—and several houses.

This was the origin of the first two Templar establishments in Paris, the building near Saint Gervais and the Enclos of the Temple. In 1147 the Order had some fairly spacious buildings in Paris near Saint Gervais, where a domain called des Barres was located (Everard de Barris, or des Barres, was then grand master of the Order). This was used to hold a general chapter assembly, which both Pope Eugene III and King Louis VII attended.

The domain of the Templars expanded considerably in short order, either through acquisitions and donations or through construction. A harvest record from 1247[1] shows that their holdings covered one third of Paris at that time. Superimposed over a map of modern Paris, the Order's domain would include part of the first arrondissement (the areas approaching the Pont au Change and the Pont St. Michel, Châtelet, rue Saint Germain l'Auxerrois, rue Saint Denis, and the current area of Les Halles); part of the second arrondissement (rue Saint Denis and its immediate area); a large portion of the third arrondissement; a portion of the fourth arrondissement including the Saint Merri and Saint Gervais quarters as well as the central part of the cité* (between rue d'Arcole and the palace); a large part of the Sorbonne quarter (mainly Saint Julien le Pauvre, Saint Sevrerin, and Cluny) in the fifth arrondissement; and, finally, part of the eleventh arrondissement in the north, which served as the Templar's farmland at that time and thus had no construction.

Of course this domain did not form a territory with clearly demarcated borders. Only the Enclos† and its dependencies and the agricultural

---

* [*Cité* refers to the original borders of the city of Paris. —*Trans.*]

† Originally, the Enclos was designated as only the actual fortified enceinte (Seat of the Temple, church, and tower), but eventually this term was applied to the entire domain that can be approximately traced along the following streets: Place de la Republique, avenue de la Republique, rue de la Folie Mericourt, rue Oberkampf, boulevard and rue des Filles du Calvaire, rue de Turenne, rue de Throigny, place de Thorigny, rue Elzevir, rue des Francs Bourgeois, rue pavee, rue Malheur, rue du Roi de Sicile, rue de la Verrerie, rue du Renard, rue Saint Merri, rue Saint Martin, rue des Etuves, rue Beaubourg, rue Simon le France, rue du Temple, rue Reamur, rue Bailly, rue de Turbigo, and back to Place de la Republique. When the king undertook his struggle against the manorial justices, the original and more restrictive Enclos was restored. In its last incarnation, its perimeter was framed by what are now the rue Temple, rue Beranger, rue Charlot, and rue de Bretagne, and it was surrounded with thick, high walls with round defense towers. By 1820, however, the last traces of this enceinte had disappeared.

land had no break in continuity. The rest consisted of streets, land, and houses that were sometimes isolated enclaves in the jurisdiction of the provostship, the university, or another sovereign jurisdiction. The rights of the Temple were confirmed by the placement of the Order's coat of arms on the facades of their buildings.

Inside this vast commandery lived a large number of knights and an even larger number of brother servants, among whom were the brothers who concerned themselves with construction projects and who were placed under the command of an officer called the master carpenter, *magister carpentarius in domo templi parisiensis.* The rapid building of the quarters of the Templar censive district shows that numerous lay craftsmen, masons, carpenters, and other tradesmen had come to reside there.

Inside this huge domain, the Templars ruled as masters. As was the case for such orders throughout the Christian world, the Order was sovereign both spiritually and temporally. With regard to the spiritual, just like the Order of Saint John of Jerusalem, the Templars answered directly to the Holy See. The papal bull *Omne datum optimum,* issued on March 23, 1139, by Pope Innocent II and confirmed in 1162 by Alexander III, immediately transferred the affairs of the Order to the Holy See and removed them from the authority of the patriarch of Jerusalem—and the prelates of other countries. It also gave the Order complete authority to institute priests and chaplains to serve its churches.* Shortly afterward, another bull, this one issued by Gregory VIII in 1188, declared that the Templars did not have to acknowledge the supremacy of any bishop other than the pope. This enabled them to avoid the pastoral authority of the bishop in Paris. By virtue of these privileges, the Order not only was spared the necessity of Episcopal visits, but it also assumed visitation and jurisdictional rights over the dependent parishes of its commanderies, except for the ordinances of diocesen bishop's concerning the management of souls and the administration of sacraments. The Order had the power to consecrate its own oratories and churches without any intervention from the clergy and the right to possess its own cemeteries and inter people in its parish churches.

---

* This was the motive that prompted the bitterness of William, archbishop of Tyre.

In the temporal sphere, the Templar Order asserted its full manorial independence by exercising in its domain and censive district important rights concerning justice and authority over roadways.

Before we look at these rights in detail, a short digression is necessary to examine several points in the history of public law. In the Middle Ages, the justice handed down by the lords appeared in two distinct forms: manorial justice and feudal justice.[2]

Manorial justice was an infeudated dismemberment of public power. The lord served as the judge in civil, criminal, and administrative trials within his seigniorial borders and over all the inhabitants of his seigniorial domain. Not all lords had an equally extensive authority, however. Two degrees were recognized: high and low justice. High justice dealt with every criminal accusation that carried an afflictive penalty and all civil trials in which a legal battle could take place—in other words, all major criminal cases. All other cases were the purview of low justice. It could be quite possible that one lord administered high justice while another lord in the same location was responsible for meting out low justice.

During the fourteenth century an intermediary—middle justice—appeared. This feudal or land-based justice was the result not of public authority but of feudal contracts and tenures and the relationships they created between men. It had two applications. In the first, the vassal, through homage, was subject to the jurisdiction of the lord of the fief, and it was this lord alone that was recognized as a judge in civil or criminal proceedings. In the second, any lord ruling over a feudal tenure had the exclusive authority to resolve any litigation concerning this tenure. The lord of the fief was the natural judge of any actions against the vassal by virtue of his authority over that fief. Likewise the lord censier (who received a censine's taxes) knew the causes concerning the censive area. We should note that in towns and cities, feudal tenures applied to houses. We should also be aware that in terms of pure feudal law, manorial and feudal justices were all of sovereign jurisdiction; their verdict stood as final and there was no right to an appeal.

Now we can look at precisely how the Temple exercised these rights of feudal and manorial justice in its censive district. In the beginning, it appears that the Temple possessed the rights of both high and low justice over the Barres, the Enclos, and those lands located outside of the walls of Paris. The growth of the Templar's domain, however, called for a modification of this authority. The properties belonging to its censive district but located inside the Parisian enceinte (the wall built by Louis VI that determined the city limits of Paris until Philip Augustus's construction of another in 1190), were subject only to the feudal justice of the Temple or, at most, its low justice. After the construction of the new enceinte, Philip Augustus, along with all high justice lords, challenged the Temple regarding its rights of high justice over the part of its domain located inside the city's walls. This conflict lasted for close to a century until an agreement was finally reached between King Philip III and the Templars in August 1279. This accord was on the whole favorable to the king, though it did establish the rights of the Templars in a solemn and definitive manner. After that time, all the patent letters of the king as well as all the claims of the order were based on this document, summarized as follows:[3] In Paris the Templars will hold possession of, in peace and perpetuity, all their houses, gardens, streets, and squares, with the rights to all land taxes and rents incumbent to them as well as the domain and property justice attached to them . . . outside of which the king reserves to himself all other right of high or low justice. Outside the walls, they will retain over their lands, houses, and streets, over their subjects and goods, all their rights whatsoever with all high or low justice . . . The king promises for himself and his successors never to lay claim to any of these rights mentioned, and never to demand any tally, military service, watch, and so forth.

This legal agreement carefully established the limits of of high justice left to the Temple. It consisted of everything located outside the enceinte erected by Philip Augustus, between the Temple and the Barbette Gates, up to the line that would later demarcate the new wall of Charles V. The incorporation of this area into the city at that time did not effect any of the privileges that had been attached to it.

Here an important observation must be added: It is not out of the question that the rights of the Temple to administer justice—mainly high justice—remained much more extensive in the areas directly dependent on the Enclos, such as Saint Gervais and the Barres. Similarly, it is quite possible that they retained these rights of administration over the fiefs that entered into the Order's possession by means of donations or purchases. On the left bank this would have included the area of Garlande, donated to the Templars by Monsignor Guillaume de Garlande in 1216 and 1224, and the fief of the "Franc Rosier," consisting mainly of the rue Parcheminerie.[4] On Ile de la Cité the Templars owned the lands of Saint Eloi,* which they had acquired in 1175 as the result of an accord they concluded with the prior of the Benedictines of Saint Eloi. On the right bank they had properties in the Saint Merri, Saint Opportune, and Saint Honore *encloisteres*.

The Temple was not the sole sovereign jurisdiction in Paris to exist before the fall of the Ancien Régime; other abbeys and religious orders in the city enjoyed the same prerogatives,† but the Templars' jurisdiction was by far the largest. Because of this sovereignty, the Temple was independent of the king and he had no power over the inhabitants in this high justice area—which we could easily call a state. There the laws of the police were enforced and justice was exercised by a civil officer named by the Templar commander. This officer originally held the title of procurator, then mayor, then later, at the time of the Hospitallers, the title of bailiff.‡ His powers corresponded to those held by the king's provost in the rest of the city. For a long time this mayor or bailiff would pronounce his verdicts at the foot of the famous elm of Saint Gervais. This tree, located in front of the church, is known to have been there since the thirteenth century. It had long been the site of the rendering of justice as well as the fulfillment of certain civic duties, such as the payment of rents or tenant farm dues. The tree was cut down in 1811. The Paris municipality was well inspired when it elected to plant a new elm on the Place Saint Gervais to recall the tradition of this historic site.[5]

---

* It should be noted that the Saint Eloi Monastery first followed the rule of Saint Columban, then later that of the Benedictines of Saint Maur (cf. Abbe Lebeuf, *Histoire de la Ville et de tout le Diocese de Paris,* vol. 3 (Paris: Éditions Cocheries, 1887), 376.

† In 1674, when, in an effort to suppress them, Louis XIV gathered together at Châtelet the city's different legal authorities that were allowed to administer justice, Paris still counted sixteen feudal ecclesiastical justices: the archbishop of Paris in Fort l'Eveque; the officiality at the archbishopric; the chapter of Notre Dame, the chapter of the Temple; the abbeys of Sainte Genevieve, Saint Germain des Presm, Saint Victor, Saint Magloire, and Saint Antoine des Champs; the priories of Saint-Martin des Champs, Saint Denis de la Charte, Saint Eloi, and Saint Lazare; and the chapters of Saint Marcel, Saint Benoit, and Saint Merri.

‡ H. de Curzon, *Le maison du Temple de Paris* (Paris: Éditions Renouard, 1886), 51–52. In 1595 the famous jurisconsult Antoine Loysel was given this office as Temple bailiff.

In addition to the bailiff, the bailiwick of the Temple included, during the final days of the Order, a fiscal prosecuter, a court clerk, a court usher, and a sworn surgeon.

The Paris Temple and Craftsmen

Circumstances eventually prompted many craftsmen to seek protection in the sovereign censive district of the Temple. It was a fact that until the time of Saint Louis and the drafting of the *Livre des Métiers* in 1628 by the king's provost, Etienne Boileau, the working class suffered greatly from a lack of genuine laws whose texts could serve as reference when grievances were raised. The taxes and fees that weighed down working individuals were levied unequally with no standard rate. Eventually the situation became so intolerable for workers that many abandoned the quarters of the city belonging to the king to settle as best they could in quarters that fell under different jurisdiction.[6] The Templars' quarter, which was in full development at this time, must have been particularly appealing to them. "Because of the great hurt and great rapines they suffered in the provostship," writes Joinville, "the 'little people' dared no longer remain on the grounds of the king, but sought instead to dwell in other provostships and manorial holdings; and thus it was the lands of the king that became so sparse that when he held his plebiscite, no more than ten or twelve people would elect to attend."

Craftsmen were all the more inspired to dwell in the Temple's jurisdiction, for doing so, let us recall, gave to those who came seeking assistance and protection the benefit of two important privileges: asylum and trade exemptions. These privileges were expressly confirmed in Paris by the accord of 1279. Right to asylum was not unique to the Temple, however. The free lands of other abbeys and religious orders also offered this privilege. A manuscript from the beginning of the sixteenth century provides the following list of these other jurisdictions: the Notre Dame de Garlande land and all the land of the chapter of Notre Dame inside the city of Paris, the Evesque land, the land of the *franc-fie* of the Rosiers, the Saint Marcel land on Mount Saint Hilaire, the Saint Victor land outside the gates, the Sainte Genevieve land outside the gates, the Saint Germain des Près land outside the gates, the Saint Benoit Cloister, the Saint Eloi land on Ile de la Cité, the Saint Symphorien land, the Saint Denis de la Chastre land in the city, the Ostel Dieu land, the Dougnans land, the Saint Merri Cloister, the Sainte Opportune Cloister, the Saint Honnoure Cloister, the Saint Germain l'Auxcerrois Cloister, the Saint Martin land outside the gates, the Temple land outside the gates, the Saint Eloi land in the old Tisseranderie, the Saint Victor land at the crossroads of the Temple, and several easements in the city of Paris."[7] Saint Jean de Latran can also be added to this list.

It should be noted that the Temple's right of asylum applied only to its lands outside the city walls. These were the very terms laid out in the 1279 accord. But certain parts of the privileged enclaves listed above that were located within Paris entered into the Templars' possession. It is certain that the right of asylum necessarily followed the right of possession. Ultimately, of course, the right of asylum, which was so widespread in Paris during the Middle Ages, gradually disappeared. At the end of the Ancien Régime, there was no spot other than the Enclos of the Temple that existed *stricto sensu* as a sure place of asylum.

The right of craft and trade exemptions was much more exceptional. It existed in the censive districts of the Hospitallers of Saint John and the large Benedictine abbeys: Saint Germain des Pres, Saint Martin des Champs, Saint Eloi, the Enclos of the Quinze Vingts, and the rue Nicaise (Tuileries). But in these jurisdictions, where asylum was more or less limited in fact or in law, it was gradually beaten down completely by royal power as well as by city and community authorities. To avoid competition from free craftsmen "outside the walls," the Parisian bourgeois periodically pushed back the enceinte of the cité. This practice hindered the settling of the suburbs, especially the Faubourg Saint Germain.* Only the Temple granted and had the power to guarantee a very extensive franchise to craftsmen.

The right of franchise allowed the exercise of any craft or commerce

---

* Seine Prefecture, *Commission d'Extension de Paris Aperçu historique*, 1913, 12, 16, 17. A 1548 edict banned all new construction in the faubourgs [suburban areas], where "an infinite number of folk" were looking to settle "in order to enjoy the franchises and exemptions that were accorded to the inhabitants of these faubourgs."

outside the ordinary laws of the king, the city, and craft organizations. The exact territorial limits covered by the Temple's franchise are not known. It is quite certain that they went well beyond the Enclos itself. The 1279 accord stipulates in fact the rights and franchises for those artisans who lived and worked in the courts and the Enclos of the Temple. The franchise privilege obviously was exercised throughout the area where the Templars had the authority to administer high justice, a domain that was much more extensive than the Enclos and its direct dependencies. It is likely, however, that originally all the taxpayers of the Temple benefited from it.[8]

By virtue of this right of franchise, the entry into a craft would have been free in the Temple censive district, whereas in the royal provost-ship many crafts and trades had to be purchased from the king. Generally speaking, the subjects of the Temple, at least those in its high justice domain, were exempt from royal and municipal charges and most taxes: those attached to the tally, conscripted labor (the corvee), regulations concerning weights and measures, the giving of free gifts, and so forth. After 1279, they all escaped the servitude that the bourgeois and crafts masters found so unpleasant: the watch. In the provost-ship, on the other hand, it was quite rare that those crafts described as francs métiers in Etienne Boileau's book escaped this obligation. Among those that did were the mortar makers and stonecutters, but not masons and carpenters. In the Temple jurisdiction, all craftsmen were francs métiers and the masons who were established there were freemasons. The bourgeois there were known as *francs bourgeois,* such as a certain Simon le Franc, who lived around 1200 and left his name on a street in the censive district that neighbored the rue des Francs Bourgeois.

Thus privileges of asylum and franchise were not common. They long made the Temple highly popular among craftsmen. It was the influx of these artisans that helped populate and enrich the Parisian establishment of the Order—so much so that it was chosen to be the Order's headquarters when the Christians lost the Holy Land.

The Temple enclosed its population within its huge commandery, effectively a large city that manufactured everything needed to live there. The Parisian merchants, craftsmen, and bourgeois who lived under Templar jurisdiction were so numerous in comparison to those who were dependents of the royal provostship, and the tutelary action of the Order was so powerful, that the Templars can be credited with the transformation of the hansa, home to the Hanseatic League of Paris, into a municipality under Saint Louis, with freedoms and an administration that it helped to develop further.[9] In support of this theory, we can note that the seat of municipal government was originally located within the Templar censive district.

The religious seat of the Order, where the worship ceremonies of the Brotherhood were performed, was the Sainte Madeleine Church on the rue de la Juiverie, in the cité. This street, which was originally part of the censive and justice district of the Saint Eloi Priory and the order of Saint Eloi, had passed into Templar possession following the agreement reached by the two orders in 1175. As for the church, it was a former synagogue that had been converted in 1183, when Philip Augustus had driven out the Jews. It was in this church where the Brotherhood of Water Merchants would meet, followed by the Great Brotherhood of the Bourgeois of Paris around 1205. Abbe Lebeuf indicates that the church was not a dependency of any secular or regular body.[10] Such a franchise, irreconcilable with feudal law, could have been conferred only by the lord high justice of the Templars. The Great Brotherhood had its own censive district and an enclave in the Jacobin area near the rue Saint Jacques, the Clos des Bourgeois.

It seems that the office of the Brotherhood, what we could call its temporal seat, was originally in the Templar censive district, in the Maison de la Marchandise [Merchandise House] in the Valley of Misery, bordering the Seine to the west of the grand Châtelet. It was then transferred in 1246 to the Parloir aux Bourgeois, between the grand Châtelet and Saint Leufroy, still in the Templar censive district. It was in 1357 that the municipality was installed in the Maison aux Piliers [Column House], bought from the dauphin and located on the Place de Greve, neighboring the Templar domain.*

---

* It seems an error to place the Parloir aux Bourgeois of the thirteenth and fourteenth centuries on the left bank near the former Saint Jacques Gate. Cf. Rochegude, *Promenades dans toutes les rues de Paris,* rue Soufflot, no. 2 (Paris: Denoël, 1958); J. Hillairet, *Evocation du vieux Paris* (Paris: Éditions de Minuit, 1952), 128, 189, and 501.

The Temple and the Organization of Parisian Masons and Carpenters

Several facts demonstrate quite clearly that it was under the aegis of the Temple and under its sovereign jurisdiction that the organization of Parisian masons and carpenters formed.

At the time the *Livre des Métiers* was written in 1268, a Templar known as Master Fouques held the office of the king's master carpenter and, by virtue of this title, had jurisdiction over the carpenters of the royal provostship.

At the same time Master Fouques was the master carpenter of the Temple. In fact, the preamble to the rules for carpenters (tit. XLVII from the *Livre des Métiers*) states: "These are the ordinances of the crafts that belong to carpentry in the suburbs of Paris, in accordance with how Master Fouques of the Temple and his predecessors have used and maintained them from times past." The jurisdiction of Master Fouques, then, as for his "predecessors," was outside the provostship of Paris. In this regard, the rule was not exercised by virtue of the king's master carpenter, but by virtue of similar but earlier powers conferred within a sovereign censive district that could only be that of the Temple. The mention of predecessors shows that their origin—and consequently that of a Templar carpenter association—was already old history.

Master Fouques's dual role is again confirmed by the first article of the rule: "Firstly, Master Fouques of the Temple says, when the craftsmen and the masters of the said carpenter trade of the king was given him, he was sworn to all the masters of said crafts . . ." There is quite a distinction between the "trades (of the carpenter of the Temple)" on the one hand, and the trades of the "king's carpenters" on the other. It also appears that the custom of Temple carpenters, which became the rule of the organization of carpenters of the provostship when Master Fouques was placed at its head, went back to an already remote past. This underscores the importance of the Temple in the construction craft—and it is not foolhardy to venture that the carpenter's association of Paris originated with the Templars.

The Templars remained at the head of this carpenters association known as the king's carpenters until the dissolution of their order. At that time, in fact, the position of the royal carpenter was abolished under Philip the Fair by an act of Parliament in 1314 on the Tuesday before Palm Sunday.[11]

What proves that this suppression was only circumstantial in nature and targeted only the officeholder is that the position was later restored. In fact, in the epitaph record of Saint Paul Church we can read: "Jean, son of Jacques Barbel, known as de Chastrel, sergeant of arms, *carpenter of the king* for his kingdom, who died on November 24, 1882" (emphasis mine).

We know what kind of authority over the building crafts was held by the magister carpentarius, the master carpenter, in the Templar domain. As a result, Master Fouques had oversight of both carpenters and masons in the Parisian domain of the Temple. By way of contrast, in the royal provostship his authority extended only to the carpenters. This provostship in fact had a king's master mason, at this time Guillaume de Saint Palu, who held authority over all the masons in the provostship. The two trades of carpenter and mason were nonetheless connected throughout the entire city and the influence of the Templars is equally evident where masons are concerned.

This Templar influence is noticeable in the rule of the masons in the *Livre des Métiers*. It was because of the Templars that the masons enjoyed free status, which, as we have seen, was the rule for all trades exercised in the jurisdiction of the Temple, whereas in the royal provostship, the majority of trades had to be purchased. "He who so wishes can be a mason in Paris, provided that he knows the craft and that he employ it according to the usages and customs of the trade" (tit. XLVIII, art. 1). An even rarer privilege characterized the franc métier in Etienne Boileau's book: The trades of mortar maker and stonecutter were exempted from watch duties.

The drafting of the *Livre des Métiers* in 1268 by the king's provost, Etienne Boileau, did not result in unification of all organizations for a particular craft existing in different jurisdictions. The autonomy of these areas stood in opposition to any such unification. The *Livre des Métiers* and the system of sworn confraternities it instituted were applicable only within the jurisdiction of the city's provostship. Even when the statutes and standards for craft mastership were identical, as was the case for carpenter mastership, no merger was possible. Master

Fouques held his dual jurisdiction from two different sovereign powers: the king and the Temple. The identical nature of their statutes and craft mastery were circumstantial in nature; they could cease to be so, which did not fail to happen on an individual basis to start. The kings could have the tendency to regulate the trades—including those of carpenters and masons—with greater strictness by creating sworn carpenters and masons who had purchased their craft, but in the jurisdiction of the Temple all crafts would retain their freedom. Furthermore, the franchises given Temple craftsmen went beyond the professional framework, touching on personal status, fiscal authority, and exemption from the watch.

Under these conditions, the influence of the Temple continued to make itself felt, as we can see from the creation of craft associations, the maintenance of free associations, and the francs métiers, all contrasted to sworn trades of the royal domain. This influence and the distinguishing features of trades exercised inside its censive territory did not disappear with the Order's dissolution; instead, they survived up to the time of the French Revolution and tradition has maintained remnants of them even into the present.

The Survival of Templar Communities and Their Franchises after the Dissolution of the Order

The Templar Order was abolished by Pope Clement V on March 22, 1312. In a bull issued on May 2 of that same year, he decreed that all Templar properties, with the rights and privileges granted their owners, would be transferred to the possession of the Hospitallers of Saint John of Jerusalem. Philip the Fair ratified this transfer in France on August 24, 1312.*

The Hospitallers, who were known as the Knights of Rhodes since 1309 and later the Knights of Malta (1530), were thus made surrogate holders of the manorial rights of the Templars and over the centuries preserved them with all the privileges of their predecessors. There was

---

* This was by no means a gift freely given to the Hospitallers. On several occasions, payment of considerable sums was demanded of the Order by Philip the Fair and his successors.

never any legal confusion between the Hospitaller's own domain and what they owned in the name of the ex-commandery of the Temple. Distinguishable was the "censive district of high, middle, and low justice of Milord and the high prior of the town, city, and university of Paris, because of the commandery of the Temple." This was the phraseology used during the fifteenth, sixteenth, and seventeenth centuries in the accounts and inventories raised by the high prior of the Hospitallers.* For a long time the high prior of France pronounced his title to be: "Humble prior of the Hospital in France and commander of the bailiwick that formerly belonged to the Temple."

The Hospitallers were not only surrogates for the manorial rights of the Temple, but also for its purely ecclesiastical and spiritual privileges. On certain holidays until the eve of the Revolution, the clergy of the parishes of Saint Nicholas des Champs, Saint Jean en Greve, and Notre Dame de Bonne Nouvelle, all dependencies of the Templar censive, continued to march in procession to the church of the Temple, as they had at the height of the Templars' influence. The homage that was once rendered to the Templars was thus transferred to the Knights of Malta.

The Temple church always maintained its independence from the archbishop of Paris, which was why, in 1787, free masons went to the Temple after encountering difficulties from the Paris archbishop Monsignor de Juigné for their wish to have a High Mass sung "with a large choir." In the Temple, the Mass was sung and on the next day a service was celebrated for brothers who had died over the course of the previous year.[12]

This independence even extended so far as to allow those who had been excommunicated by the Church to be buried with the sacraments in the cemeteries of the Temple.

The kings tried their best to restrict rights and privileges inherited by the Hospitallers from the commandery of the Temple, either by limiting exercise of these rights within the confines of the Enclos itself or, in a more general way, by fighting against the sovereignty of manorial

---

* Lebeuf, *Histoire de la Ville et de tout le diocese de Paris,*vol. 2, 465 ff. The Hospitaller Order, governed by a grand master, was divided into eight provinces, or *tongues,* each with a high prior at their head who was assisted by a chapter of commanders.

justices through appeal of royal cases and, in 1674, through the pre-
vention and suppression of high justice rights (criminal cases). They
never, however, contested the legitimacy of these rights. It is important
to note that the 1279 accord, which included a transferring of rights to
the Hospitallers, was confirmed by all subsequent kings of France from
1287 to 1718—thirty-four confirmations in all. The last were made by
Louis XV in 1716 and 1718.

One of the rights of the Temple that had been transferred to the
Hospitallers stemmed from privileges and franchises that benefited the
craftsmen in the Templar domain. This meant that Templar communities of craftsmen, who were otherwise laypersons and outside the
Order, did not disappear with the Order.

The right of asylum in the Templar domain was confirmed for the
Hospitallers by numerous papal bulls, notably in 1523 and 1539. We
have some interesting texts from the eighteenth century showing how
far this right extended. A November 3, 1701, memorandum of the high
prior Philippe de Vendôme[13] attests that not all were suffered to seek
sanctuary in the Temple Enclos and that the officers there were charged
with quelling any misuse of this privilege. A police regulation from the
high prior of Crussol on February 5, 1780, stipulates that asylum was
not granted to exiles, fugitives from justice, bad-faith debtors, fraudu-
lent bankrupts, and those who led criminal lifestyles. These kinds of
individuals would be given twenty-four hours to leave the Enclos.

Sometimes, for opportunistic reasons, the Temple refused to grant
to craftsmen the right to asylum in the Enclos. Thus in 1645 the
Compagnons Cordonniers du Devoir [Companion Cobblers of Duty]
were denounced among the Sorbonne's faculty of theology because of
initiation practices they employed to make an apprentice into a journeyman. This exposure led to the targeting of other such practices
among the hatters, tailors, and saddlers, and condemnation of these
rites by verdict of the Officiality of Paris on May 30, 1648. Confessors
were ordered to see to it that their penitents atoned for all the rites in
compagnnonage [journeyman rituals], to make public confession of
their mysteries, and, most important, to renounce these mysteries. In
order to escape prosecution by the archbishop of Paris, the compagnnonages reunited within the enceinte of the Temple, but the right of asy-

lum was not granted them and they were driven out by an order of the Temple bailiff on September 11, 1651.[14] These instances remain the exception to the rule, however; the compagnnonages, especially those of the masons, always had their headquarters, their *cayennes,* in the jurisdiction of the Temple.

The privilege of franchise for craftsmen was maintained all the more easily by the Hospitaliers of Saint John, for they had already recognized such a privilege in their own censive district on the left bank of the Seine. Workers, though in small numbers, remained in the commandery of Saint John of Latran, where they could plie their craft without purchasing a trade.[15]

The right of franchise within the Templar censive district survived intact until the end of the seventeenth century, the time when the king's council began to batter it. A council decision on January 28, 1678, declared the rights of high justice belonging to the Enclos would be respected and added that it would not allow "the craftsmen and workers plying their trade or crafts to settle in the Enclos without being subject to inspection by masters, guards, and the sworn servants of the city."

Overall, however, the right of franchise appears to have remained fairly intact through the years, as can be seen by another passage from a 1701 memorandum of the high prior Philippe de Vendome:

It is not without good reason that it pleased the king to confirm said privileges . . . because it is obvious to each and all what the famous merchants and traders of Paris are in a position to confirm—that is, if said Enclos was not an asylum and a free retreat for different merchants and other folk for whom a fall from grace was precipitated by an unexpected misfortune in business that not all the prudence in the world could have avoided, there would be an infinite number of merchants and traders in Paris, and likewise outside, who would find themselves forced to move into foreign lands and carry with them their effects because there is naught but this place in Paris that is regarded as an established haven. This would be a consequence more dangerous than it is possible to say.

Only the crafts masters' visits to the Enclos were authorized. Thus we can read that on June 28, 1705, a declaration from the king to the carpenters association granted:

> [p]ermission to the sworn syndics of said community to make their visits to all the studios and worksites, whether in the Faubourg Saint Antoine, the Enclos of the Temple, of Saint John of Latran . . . and other privileged places. And in the case they find there shoddy products, defective wood, or works that violate police regulation and the art of carpentry, said sworn syndics will make their report and appear before the lieutenant general of the police, in the places where said visits were made . . . [16]

Up until the end of the Ancien Régime, then, we find existing inside the Temple domain craftsmen benefiting from privileges and franchises that go back to the medieval Templars. These craftsmen formed more or less marginal communities in relation to the sworn confraternities and corporations of the city of Paris.

It is certainly much harder to find traces of these Templar associations than of the sworn associations. The latter were regarded as legal entities: They had statutes, they possessed properties, and they contracted and operated under terms provided by the justice system. It is therefore possible to rediscover documents concerning them. The Templar communities, however, were not legally formed groups. There could be no question of this in the area of the Temple; such a legal entity would have been irreconcilable with the exercise of francs métiers, which was the rule of the Temple—they were de facto communities. Yet these groups were more than simple assemblies of workers, craftsmen, and merchants of the same status within the same quarter. That a trade was franchised did not mean it could not be regulated. The rule that existed for carpenters, for instance, was modeled on the sworn association that preceded it. *Franchise* merely meant that a master did not have to purchase the trade, that he was exempt from royal and municipal fees and charges, and that every journeyman could freely establish himself as a master, but it did not mean that a trade was no longer subject to traditional rules concerning length of apprentice and journeyman status, operative oaths, and celebration of patron saints' holidays—all specifics that clearly imply an organization.

To compensate for the absence of a judicial body charged with protecting common interests and ensuring that the rules of the profession were respected, craftsmen of francs métiers were likely more inspired to follow traditional and symbolic rites and practices. Such customs are much more strictly respected when they take on the force of law.

The free craftsmen living in the Temple commandery did not, then, scorn the prospect of becoming part of a sworn confraternity. With it they were able to exercise their talents in two arenas. As Templar subjects, they benefited from certain privileges and franchises. As associates of the community, they were assured of being able to work and of being protected throughout the territory of the city. "It was in the best interest of the worker who, placed under the jurisdiction of an abbey, shared the legal status of the area in which he lived, to submit at the same time to royal jurisdiction so that his affairs would prosper."[17] Joint allegiance—to the Templars and to the royalty—ensured commissions from both.

This state of affairs does not make the historian's task an easy one. Templar documents are fairly scarce.* We do have useful testimonies that help us pick up the trail of craftsmen in the former Templar censive district: the old epitaph records in Paris churches; street names; records of pious and charitable foundations, chapels, and trade groups. All of these are sources of evidence that help us follow through the centuries until the French Revolution the existence of what we call Templar communities. The example of the builders—masons, carpenters, mortar makers,

---

* The most valuable source for documents is glaring by its absence. It is known that, much to the chagrin of Philip the Fair, the general archives of the Templars, as well as those concerning individual houses—just as the considerable treasure of the Order—mysteriously disappeared before the arrest of Jacques de Molay. Were they destroyed? Housed in a safe place? Their disappearance is one of the great enigmas of history. Henri de Curzon surmises that the disappearance was to someone's personal advantage. The most likely hypothesis is to view the Templars themselves as the architects of this disappearance some time prior to the fall of the Order. See also Gérard de Sède, *Les Templiers sont parmi nous, ou l'Enigme de Gisors* (Paris: J'ai Lu, 1962), a work that judiciously and methodically examines a number of important clues that were corroborated by the 1970 discovery in Gisors of a bronze vessel containing 11,359 coins, most of which were minted during the twelfth century. They are currently housed in the Cabinet des Médailles in the Bibliothèque Nationale.

stonecutters, and so forth—is particularly significant. To this extent we can safely claim that the Temple survived, even under its own name, the destruction of the Order. This fact has escaped most of those studying the history of Freemasonry, for they have often been overly prone to focusing on only the religious and spiritual aspects of the Templars and to seek—or refute—the survival of the Order within what can be characterized as chivalrous or philosophical organizations.

Templar Traditions and Parisian Builders

The bond between the Templars and the masons and carpenters was so strong that traces of it remained for centuries. The Templar's domain in Paris was, throughout its entire existence, the preferred dwelling place for these builders. Convincing evidence of this can be found simply by taking a stroll through time and space within this former Templar area. We will begin our walk at the Temple itself. From there we will go to Saint Nicolas des Champs and Notre Dame de Bonne Nouvelle, then down toward the Seine by way of Saint Gilles, Saint Leu, and Saint Merri. We will linger momentarily at Saint Paul, Saint Gervais, and Saint Jean en Grève before crossing the Seine to Ile de la Cité. We will then end our visit to the Templar commandery on the left bank of the Seine, at Saint Julien le Pauvre and Saint Séverin.

The House of the Temple inside the Enclos, the church, and the famous Templar tower were built on the territory of Saint Nicolas de Champs parish. The Templars' original church, the rotunda, was built some time around 1140 and was modeled on the Holy Sepulchre. The nave and choir were built at a later date and the church was definitively consecrated on January 11, 1217.

This rotunda is comparable in every respect to the one built later in London and dedicated in 1185. It seems that the same architect designed both churches.[18] We know that a Christian architectonic association brought over from the Holy Land by the Templars built the Temple on Fleet Street in London. Could this same association be credited with construction of the Temple in Paris? It is almost a certainty that no mason and carpenters association existed at that time in Paris. The oldest merchant brotherhood of the capital, the *mercatores aquoe,* is not mentioned before 1130.[19] Yet, the rapid erection of large and important buildings of the Temple and of the city adjoining it presumes the existence of an extensive organization. It could be that it was only the Templar community led by the magister carpentarius and that this organization was the source of the Parisian *matrises* of masons and carpenters. It is also within reason to suggest that the Parisian métier was organized before that of London and that the craftsmen in the English capital were influenced by it.

One bit of proof within the Templar rotunda suggesting a link between the Parisian builders and the Templars is the Saint Anne Chapel or Altar that lies to the left of the nave and choir and is maintained by the *toicturiers* (roofers) of Paris.[20] There was also a small Saint Nicolas Chapel in the Templar Church at one time that may have been the seat of a confederation of carpenters. Masonry, carpentery, mortar making, stonecutting, plastering, and other trades involved in the construction of buildings would have required a number of patron saints among which are Jesus Christ, Saint Blaise, Saint Nicolas, Saint Anne, Saint Thomas, Saint John the Baptist, and Saint John the Evangelist.

Right next to the site of the former church of the Temple on the rue Saint Martin, we find the church of Saint Nicolas des Champs, which is also dedicated to Saint John the Baptist. A church dedicated to Saint Nicholas had already been built on this spot at the beginning of the twelfth century, before the arrival of the Templars.

The parish district was always under the jurisdiction of Saint Martin des Champs, a priory of the Cluny Order. A bull from around 1119 issued by Calixtus II mentions a parish Saint Nicolas Chapel that was separate from the convent church.[21] With respect to the administration of justice, the parish territory was divided between the priory of Saint Martin and the Temple—another example of the closeness of Templar and Benedictine neighbors in the city itself. An agreement concluded in 1292 confirmed the rights of the Temple over the moat of the Saint Martin Convent (on rue Frépillon, or today's rue Volta).[22] We are quite certain that until the Templars settled there, the town was only a collection of peasant huts around the priory of Saint Martin. The monks, who mainly devoted themselves to intellectual tasks customary of Benedictines, hardly inspired any craftsmen to settle in their censive district. This situation changed when the Templars moved onto parish territory. The increased peopling of the area seems to have been a direct result of the arrival of brothers of the Militia of the Temple. In fact, population growth in this area was so great that in 1220 it proved necessary to create a new parish cemetery.

In 1399 the church was expanded:

> The church wardens of Saint Nicolas des Champs . . . decided, after obtaining the consent of the priest and the bishop of Paris and the counsel of the king's sworn representatives of masonry and carpentry—masons *Remon du Temple* [emphasis mine], Jehan Filleul, Regnault Lorier, and Adam Ravier (known as de Moret), and carpenters Robert Focuchier and Philippe Milon—to see to the construction of the masonry of the three chapels in the alley between said church and the hostel of said priest . . .[23]

The mention of Remon du Temple, sworn master mason, must be singled out. This master, better described as an architect and sculptor, practiced between 1363 and 1404. He was the master builder of Notre Dame in Paris and built the famous Beauvais College on rue des Carmes. His seal depicted a shield bearing a hammer flanked by a square and trowel, with both crowned and flanked by fleurs de lys.[24] While working on the Louvre and performing construction miracles there, he drew the recognition of Charles V, who called him his "beloved sergeant of arms and mason."*

At this time there could be no question of any kind of alliance with an order that had been suppressed since 1312. Master Remon must have belonged to an operative organization of the Temple, such as the one that survived in Saint Gervais Parish in the seventeenth century.

Builders continued to show an affection for the church and parish of Saint Nicolas des Champs for years to come. The entire quadrilateral

---

* With regard to Notre Dame, it should be noted that two of its most famous architects, Jean de Chelles and Pierre de Chelles, were natives of Chelles, where the Templars had one of their centers. During the thirteenth century, Chelles was considered a *franche* commune, a franchise similar to that of the Templars that went back to Louis VI. After the dissolution of the Order, this franchise was lost in 1320 by an act of the Parliament in Paris, at which time it fell under the subordination of the women's abbey that also existed in Chelles. (Cf. Georges Poisson, *Evocation du Grand Paris. La Banlieue Nord-Est* (Paris: Éditions de Minuit, 1961), 398.

formed by the streets rue des Archives (the former rue du Grand Chantier), rue des Quatre Fils (formerly the Quatre Fils Aymon), rue Vielle du Temple, and rue des Francs Bourgeois (the current site of the national Archives) was long occupied by the workshops of entrepreneurs and retained the name of Worksite of the Temple.[25]

The church of Saint Nicolas des Champs was also the seat of a confederation of carpenters dedicated to Saint Joseph.[26] In 1588 one of this church's chapels was granted to Jean Jacquelin, treasurer of the king's buildings. In it we can read the epitaphs of Robert Marquelet, concierge and guard of the king's furnishing in his palace of the Tuileries, sworn servant of the king in the office of masonry, and bourgeois of Paris (April 20, 1625); Charles de la Champagne, sworn representative of the king for works of carpentry (May 25, 1608); Barthélémi Camuset, merchant in the roofing of houses and bourgeois of Paris (May 5, 1601); Marguerite du Saussay, his wife (February 13, 1587); Jean Camuset, their son, roofer (16??); Marie Aubert, his first wife (Kuly 16, 1594); Blaise de la Champagne, his second wife (16??); Barthélémy Beaulieu, master mason and bourgeois of Paris (October 10, 1572); Thomasse Léger, his wife (October 11, 1571); Jean de la Vallée, master mason and bourgeois of Paris (April 22, 1600); Anne Le Roy, his first wife (September 30, 1597); Jean Fessart, master mason and bourgeois of Paris (16??); Elisabeth Davy, his wife (March 26, 1639); Louis Le Rambert, keeper of the king's marble and bourgeois of Paris (August 12, 1614); Madeleine Maillard, his wife (September 21, 1610); François Angoulvant, Lord of Launay and Gasserant and master builder of locks for the king's buildings (December 18, 1603); Charles Prevost, master mason and bourgeois of Paris (16??); Fleurie Le Gendre, his wife (April 3, 1606); Guillaume Chéron, master mason and bourgeois of Paris (n.d.); Antoinette du Chaume, his wife (April 9, 1608).* Paul Lacroix added another name to this list: Nicolas the Younger, mason (December 13, 1608).[27]

---

* For more on the epitaph records of Paris, see the Bibliothèque Historique de la ville de Paris, ms CP 5484, an interesting copy of almost all the city's important epitaphs. There are also several manuscripts in the Bibliothèque Nationale and the Bibliothèque d'Arsenal. See also E. Raunié, *Epitaphier du Vieux Paris, 1890–1918*, 4 volumes, and A. Lesort and H. Verlet, *Epitaphier du Vieux Paris, 1890–1918*, vol. 5. Earlier we have Cocheris's additions to Abbe Lebeuf's *Histoire de la Ville et du Diocèse de Paris* (Paris: Éditions Cocheris, 1883). All of these works, however, remain incomplete. It should be noted that these epitaph records make no mention of individuals buried before the sixteenth century.

If we consider that on the whole this epitaph record contains only a few names and that the vocations of many are not indicated, the proportion of builders appears sufficiently strong to show that Saint Nicolas Parish was clearly a builders' neighborhood at one time. This same holds true for the neighborhoods near Saint Sauveur, Saint Gervais, and Saint Paul, as we can see from epitaph records from these parishes.

Near Saint Nicolas des Champs was the small parish of Saint Sauveur, throughout whose territory the Temple had its domains. Here again, Saint John the Evangelist served as the second patron saint. The church here was demolished in 1787 and its site is now occupied by a house on the rue Saint Denis.

As the short epitaph record suggests, the parish of Saint Sauveur was home to numerous masons: Pierre Morin, mason and bourgeois of Paris (December 15, 1623); Gilles de Harlay, master mason and sworn mason to the king (February 24, 1579); Jeanne Legrand, his wife (July 13, 1580); Pierre Bréau, employed on royal construction projects and excelling in masonry (January 8, 1606); Anne Bréau, his wife (October 18, 1617).

An intriguing indication of the connection of Saint Sauveur to the Templars is its proximity to Trinity Hospital, located on the corner of rue Saint Denis and the rue Darnétal or Greneta in the censive district of the Temple.* This hospital, one of the oldest in Paris, was founded in 1202 by two private citizens, Jean Palée and Guillaume Estuacol, to take care of "poor pilgrims." Sometime around 1210 a chapel was erected at the hospital, which was long administered by the members of a religious community, the Premontrés d'Hermières. "This order," writes Pierre Bonfons, "was continued charitably for a good length of time until the abbot of Hermières placed there other monks who were more inclined to seek their own personal profit than to give charity of

---

* This is indicated from the status of the Templar domain according to the harvest record of 1247: "It is in a splendid site before the Trinity." Also: "In the year 1217, there was mention of the church of the Trinity, in front of which church there were houses of the Episcopal censive district belonging to the Templars" (Lebeuf, vol. 1, 115). It should be specified that the rue Greneta was also partially in the censive district of the Benedictine abbey Saint Magloire.

either a spiritual or temporal nature." In 1547 the court of Parliament reorganized Trinity and delegated five "good bourgeois of the city of Paris to administer it."[28]

Cocheris points out the existence in Trinity Chapel of a Confederation of the Ascension, which he connects to tailors of religious habits. It may be more likely, however, that this was the seat of a confederation of stonecutters, for the Ascension of Our Lord was depicted on the coat of arms of the association of masons and stonecutters.[29] According to a trade legend, it was a stonecutter who unsealed the stone that covered the tomb of Jesus and a mason who demolished the rest of it to enable Jesus to ascend to Heaven.[30] Trinity Chapel was also the seat of the Confederation of the Passion and Resurrection of Our Lord, which received patent letters from Charles V awarding them the privilege of staging the Mystery of the Passion and other Catholic mystery plays. Such performances, which were very popular during the Middle Ages, offered religious and initiatory amphibological sense relevant to the rituals of craftsmen. Over time, however, their meaning was lost and they eventually became spectacles deemed impious by the clergy and justice authorities. Nonetheless, the attraction of these plays survived for an audience of diverse quality made up mostly of the "mechanically minded," meaning artisans, according to Pierre Bonfons, who was a contemporary of this era. (The first edition of his book, itself a revision of the 1532 book by Gilles Corrozet, was published in 1586.) Eventually, similar Passion confederations were formed in Paris and its suburbs, causing the confederation of Trinity Church to assert its privilege and request the authorities to ban these rival associations. With an act of November 17, 1548, the Parliament of Paris satisfied this request by forbidding the staging of all sacred mysteries, including those of the Passion of Our Savior, and permitting the staging of only "profane, honest, and licit mysteries."

Trinity Hospital, originally intended to give succor to "poor pilgrims," was eventually also used to house *transients*,[31] a term that is worth some additional attention. As we will see when we discuss Saint Gervais Hospital, it refers not only to pilgrims, but also to workers in transit, who traveled a kind of "Tour de France" of journeymen. We might assume, therefore, that many of those who attended the Mystery of the Passion and other Catholic mystery plays belonged to this group. At the time of the hospital's reorganization, supported by an act of Parliament on July 1, 1547, it was decided that children of the poor would also be raised there and educated in craft techniques by male and female workers in return for the privilege of obtaining, in six years' time, recognition as masters in their crafts without the requirement of any fee or masterpiece. Justification for their status would be provided by the professional skills of their eventual students, who would themselves enjoy the status of the sons of masters.* By a declaration of Henri II given in Paris on February 2, 1553, craft masters in the city of Paris could take on a second apprentice only from among the children raised at Trinity Hospital. Two acts of Parliament, one of December 3, 1672, and one of August 22, 1798, specifically confirmed "the rule over the rights and privileges of those who taught the art of craft and masonry in the hospital of the Trinity and those who have learned it in said hospital."[32]

These institutions prove the long existence of social work among craftsmen, notably masons. Other examples can be found in connection to Saint Gervais Hospital and a second Trinity Hospital located on the left bank.

Bordering the Saint Nicolas des Champs and Saint Sauver Parish were Notre Dame de Bonne Nouvelle on the north and, to the south, the parishes of Saint Gilles and Saint Loup and Saint Merri, located in the Templar's domain. The church of Notre Dame de Bonne Nouvelle is the most recent church, having first been erected from 1624 to 1628. The masons who lived in neighboring parishes likely came to settle in this quarter under construction in fairly large numbers. In fact, in 1663 the church became the seat of the Confederation of Stonecutters, instituted under the name of the Ascension of Our Lord.†

In the proximity of Saint Nicolas des Champs, between the current rue Saint Denis and boulevard de Sépastopol, is located the very old

---

* Abbe Lebeuf's citation of this date as 1545 is an error.
† R. de Lespinasse and Bonnardot, *Le Livre des Métiers d'Etienne Boileau* (Paris: Imprimerie Nationale, 1879), 600. A small chapel dedicated to Saint Louis and Saint Barbe that existed on this site was demolished by the Religious League in 1591. With the exception of the belltower, which dates to the seventeenth century, the current church was constructed from 1823 to 1830.

church of Saint Gilles and Saint Leu, or simply Saint Loup. This church was originally a dependency of the Benedictine Saint Magloire Abbey, which still exercised the right to administer high justice in its domain. The Templars owned important properties in the territory of the Saint Leu Parish, providing another piece of evidence that testifies to the relationship shared by the Benedictines and Templars.*

Saint Leu was formerly the seat of a confederation of Saint Anne—who, we know, was venerated by roofers—and also housed chapels dedicated to Saint John the Baptist and Saint John the Evangelist. In addition, it served, for several different periods of time, as the sanctuary of the Order of the Knights of the Holy Sepulcher of Jerusalem, who were instituted in the fifteenth century by Pope Alexander VI. This church's neighborhood had always been a frequent haunt of the Compagnons Étrangers du Devoir de Liberté [Foreign Companions of Duty to Freedom]—the Loups [wolves]—perhaps because of the patron saint of the parish, Saint Loup. Even into the nineteenth century the compagnons still met in cabarets located on two colorful streets: the rue du Grand Hurleur (formerly the rue Grand Hue Leu, or Hue Loup) and the rue du Petit Hurleur.[33] The term *hurler,* meaning "to howl," is still a compangonnage term, which is significant given that these streets were already in existence in the thirteenth century. From 1242 to 1540, the rue du Petit Hurleur was known as rue Jean Palée, referring to the name of the founder of Trinity Hospital. This quarter also had a rue du Renard [fox] (which should not be confused with the current street that holds that name)—which is interesting given that journeymen designated as "foxes" those aspirants to their ranks.

Saint Merri Church is also of ancient origin. In the seventh century there was already a chapel by this name built on a site that was then part of the territory of Saint Gervais. Saint Merri was raised to parish status sometime during the seventeenth century.[34] According to Rochegude, the current building was constructed between 1520 and 1612. Above the main portal, set between two figures on the keystone

---

* Dr. Vimont, *Histoire de l'eglise et de la paroisse Saint Leu Saint Gilles,* 4 volumes (Paris: 1932). The original church, built in 1235, was rebuilt in 1320 and was renovated and transformed in 1611, 1727, and finally in 1858 with the excavation and construction of the Boulevard de Sebastopol.

of the arch, there is an enigmatic figure that some believe represents the Baphomet of the Templars.[35]

The presence of masons in this parish was confirmed as early as 1229 by a charter of that year that makes mention of the house of a certain Guillaume, *cementarius*. In older eras, chapels could be found in Saint Merri dedicated to Saint Blaise, the patron saint of masons and carpenters; Saint Nicholas, patron saint for carpenters alone; Saint Anne, protector of home roofers; Saint John the Baptist; and Saint John the Evangelist.[36] Saint Merri was dependent on the priory of the same name, but was contiguous to the Temple's censive district. The rue de la Verrerie, which was shared by the priory and the Temple, was inhabited by a specific category of artists working on the construction of churches and fine homes: the glassworkers and painters on glass, whose confraternity, according to Rochegude, was established there in 1187.

Within the territory of Saint Merri was the chapel of the Holy Sepulcher, erected in 1326, where sculptors and stone and plaster engravers had a confraternity that celebrated Saint Jean Porte Latine on his feast day of May 6. This church also housed an altar dedicated to Saint Nicholas and Saint Giles and a chapel of Saint Nicholas. The chapel of the Holy Sepulcher belonged to a confraternity who shared its name. It was originally administered by pilgrims who had been to the Holy Land, then later by four directors elected by the confraternity of Saint John and assisted by a council. In 1454 an individual named Yves Petit, a sworn mason of the king, was a member of this counsel.[37]

In very close proximity to Saint Merri are Saint Paul, Saint Gervais, and Saint Jean en Gréve. These churches, among the oldest in Paris, were connected to the Benedictine Orde, another suggestion of an association between these monks and the Templars.

The former church of Saint Paul, which should not be confused for the current church of the Jesuits (Saint Paul and Saint Louis Church), was located at the site of what are now numbers 30–34 on the rue Saint Paul. An earlier oratory of this name is supposed to have been erected by Saint Eloi. In 1107 it was reunited to the Benedictine priory Saint Eloi, then later with the abbey of Saint Maur des Fossés. The church was expanded and repaired under Charles V and was demolished in 1798.

The first church dedicated to Saint Gervais was built in the seventh or eighth century. In the tenth century the counts of Meulan took possession of this church and its properties and remained its masters for a time until the difficulties connected to the administration of an ecclesiastical property induced them to make a present of it to the monks of Saint Nicaise Priory, who were Benedictines of the Saint Maur congregation, which they had founded in Meulan. In a charter of 1141, Waleran, count of Meulan, numbers this monastery among his properties: *Ecclesias Sancti Gervasii et Sancti Joannis quoe Sunt Parisius in vico qui dicitur Greva*. Le Pouillé, a Parisian of the thirteenth century, mentions that the parish district of Saint Gervais was named as such by the prior of Saint Nicaise de Meulan.[38]

Saint Jean Church was originally only a baptistery of Saint Gervais, but later it became a separate chapel, which was expanded in the eleventh century, then raised to the status of a cure in 1212, when Saint Gervais underwent redistricting due to its "multitude of parishioners"—a sign of urban development in this area. Saint Jean Church, rebuilt in 1326, was demolished in 1800, with the exception of its communion chapel, which was annexed to the Hôtel de Ville,* where, as the Saint Jean Room, it long served as a meeting place for various groups until it was torn down in 1837.

We know that it was in the proximity of Saint Paul and Saint Gervais that the Templars had their first establishments in Paris before 1137. In 1152 the count of Beaumont donated "to God and the brothers of Solomon an oven and a house, which had belonged to Frogier l'Asnier." This house gave its name to the street that today bears the erroneous name Geffroy l'Asnier. An act of 1175 indicates that the Templars then owned fairly large properties in the censive district of Saint Eloi, which has since become Saint Paul Parish. For a long time this quarter served as the Templars' principal establishment until the definitive Templar church was consecrated in 1217.

Until 1217, then, the commandery's seat was in the Barres area, the site mentioned in the 1152 donation charter for the house of Frogier l'Asnier *(domum Frogerii Asinarii ante barras sitam)*,[39] which, to be more specific, sat by the south chevet of Saint Gervais. On a 1618 map,

---

* [Hôtel de Ville refers to City Hall. —*Trans.*]

we can still see at this location the House of the Temple designated as such by name, on the rue des Barres. The maps of Truschet (1551) and Nicolay (1609) depict at this spot abutting Saint Gervais a large building with two facades, one facing the rue de Longport (the rue de Brosse today) and the other overlooking the rue des Barres.* In reference this property is often referred to as Old Temple, Small Temple, or Hotel of the Garrison. Its division into parcels prompted a legal action between the church wardens of Saint Gervais and the grand prior of Malta, acting in the name of the "Noble Lords of the Temple." The subsequent trial ended in an agreement following two acts of Parliament on February 6 and 24, 1618.† The house, rebuilt in 1623, was demolished in 1945.

Following the transfer of its seat, the Temple retained its port, mills, and barns in the Barres area. In 1250 the road was called the ruelle aux Moulins des Barres; in 1293, the ruelle des Moulins du Temple; then the rue Barres or Barris. Historical dictionaries of Paris remain mute on the origin of this name, though it is possible that it derives from Evrard des Barres or Barris, who was grand master of the Temple from 1146 to 1149, the exact time a general chapter of the Order existed in this area.

In the middle of the thirteenth century, a large building, the Hôtel des Barres, was erected on the rue des Barres, occupying a large site on what is now the corner of rue des Barres and rue de l'Hôtel de Ville. Remnants of this Hôtel des Barres are still in existence: At number 56 of rue de l'Hôtel de Ville (the former rue de la Mortellerie), we can see a strange ogive-shaped cavern in two bays. One of the arch keystones adorning the first bay is adorned with a crest that includes a cross; the keystone of the second bay is decorated with a rose window with a leafy border.[40]

In three parishes with confused borders—Saint Paul, Saint Gervais, and Saint Jean en Grève—the number of properties owned by the

---

* J. Hillairet is mistaken in his assumption that the first Templar establishment was slightly more to the north, at the site of the Napoleon Barracks (J. Hillairet, *Evocation du vieux Paris,* 134), an opinion he borrowed from Rochegude and Dumolin, 71 and 150. For more on this topic, see also C. Piton, *La Cité* (1911), 105–76.

† Probst-Biraben (*Les Mysteres des Templiers,* 165–67) sees in "these Noble Lords of the Temple" a survival of the Templars in the form of a third order, whereas they were simply the Knights Hospitallers.

Templars increased rapidly. The 1632 list made by the grand prior of Malta showing the definitive status of the censive district of the former Templar commandery notably indicates these holdings: "rue Frognier l'Asnier; rue Garnier sur l'Eau (Grenier sur l'Eau); rue des Barres or Barrys; Saint Gervais Church, cememtery, chevet; Beaudoyer Gate; rue du Gantelet; rue Jean en Grève; Martlet; chevet of the church (Saint Jean); Hôtel de Ville of Paris; Grève; old Saint Jean Cemetery, rue de la Mortellerie: the Seine River: the Vannerie and Jean de l'Espine: rue Vielle Tissanderie (today Francois Miron)."[41]

The presence of organized builders in this quarter is visible from the time the Templars installed themselves, long before the existence of a sworn association of masons in Paris. Toward 1170, according to Lebeuf, a mason named Garin and his son Harcher, priest of the parish district of Saint Jacques de la Boucherie, founded a hospital on rue de la Tissanderie (Francois Miron).[42] This hospital was created "to shelter poor travelers, to whom bed and board were given for only three nights." Originally, the institution had a master and brothers to provide hospitality. It is possible to believe that the monks who managed this hospital, called Saint Gervais, were affiliated with the Temple, for in the fourteenth century, following the dissolution of the Order, the bishop of Paris entrusted its administration to the clergy. The chapel of Saint Gervais Hospital was rebuilt in 1411 and consecrated in the name of Saint Anastasius. In 1657, the hospital was transferred into the Hôtel d'O at 60 rue Vielle du Temple. Abbe Lebeuf states that in his day (1754) nothing remained of the old hotel except its chapel, which people called the Saint Nicholas Chapel. The number of guests it sheltered, which varied every year from 15,000 to 16,000, reached the astounding figure of 32,238 people in 1789. These "poor travelers" just like the "transients" we saw earlier in relation to Trinity Hospital, were originally pilgrims, most often those beginning the journey to Saint James of Compostella. Later, it was more than likely that these transients and travelers were not only the faithful on pilgrimage, but mendicants and vagabonds as well. A vagabond was one who had no profession, trade, or sure abode, while valid mendicants were "the homeless who wandered the land."[43]

The police always acted ruthlessly against these mendicants and vagabonds: In 1270 the ordinance of Saint Louis pronounced the penalty of banishment against them; Henri II's ordinance of April 18, 1558 declared the crime of being a vagabond to be punishable by hanging; and a declaration of August 27, 1702, banned these homeless from the jurisdiction of the provostship and viscounty of Paris and, in the case of repeat offenders, sentenced them to three years in the galleys.[44] Through the declaration made by the grand prior of Vendôme, we also know that such individuals could not benefit from the right of asylum in the Temple's jurisdiction. Finally, a police ordinance issued on February 19, 1768, made it "a crime for mendicants and vagabonds, and persons without the proper credentials, and so forth, to seek lodging at Saint Gervais Hospital, and for pilgrims and travelers to present themselves there without certificates and passports in the proper order."[45]

We can easily deduce from these texts that the "poor transients" and "travelers" housed in such large number at Trinity Hospital and especially at Saint Gervais Hospital were in possession of a trade. Quite often they were nothing more or less than transient journeymen in search of a master to employ them. We could maintain they were simply a "Tour de France" of guildsmen. Their wandering of the countryside echoed the route taken by those on pilgrimage, which was how they would obligatorily visit Saint Baume to pay homage to Saint James, in whom they saw their patron saint (Maitre Jacques), who would have lived near Saint Magdalene and been buried in her famous cave.

At this point, how could we not bring up the famous Compagnons du Devoir? The journeymen stonecutters and carpenters of the Duty called themselves the Compagnons Passant. It was they who were nicknamed the Loups Garoux [werewolves] and the Drilles [good fellows]. They presented as their remote founders this same Master Jacques [James], who would have been the overseer of the works of the Temple, and Father Soubise, Solomon's head carpenter. They stated that their modern organization dated from the Templars and some identified Master Jacques as Jacques de Molay, the last grand master of the Templars.[46] C. H. Simon, in his *Etude historique et morale sur le Compagnonnage*,[47] considers it likely that "the Children of Solomon" received a new "duty" from Jacques de Molay. He sees a great connection between the legend of Master Jacques of the Companions of Duty and the history of the grand master of the Templars. The long ironshod cane of the "children of Master Jacques," so dreadful to the "Gavots," * would be considered as a souvenir of the Templars' terrible lance. Others have compared it to the Templar cross.[†]

The Companions of Duty obligatorily professed the Catholic faith. A confession of belief in the divinity of Jesus Christ was required to be accepted into the rites of Master Jacques or Father Soubise. It was the Companions who gave particular honor to the Ascension and the Holy Savior.

The Compagnons Étrangers du Devoir de Liberté (the Loups),[‡] however, accepted into their ranks men of all nations and creeds. According to Agricole Perdiguier, in his book on compagnonnage, the *Compagnons Passant* [Traveling Journeyman] lived on the right bank of the Seine and the *Compagnons de Liberte* lived on the left bank. What we find here is actually an entire quarter inhabited by masons. Both were obliged by their conventions to work on the side of the river where their homes were located.

The "traveling journeymen" housed at Saint Gervais Hospital

---

* The Gavots, or "compagnons of liberty," were accused of supporting the Reformation in the seventeenth century, while the "children of Master Jacques" supported the Catholic Church. —*Trans.*]

† From an historical point of view, another more recent comparison could be made. In 1667, the grand prior of Malta and the Temple was Jacques de Souvré. He saw to it that the former walls of the Enclos were demolished and that large mansions (Hôtels des Bains, de Guise, de Boufflers, and so on) were transformed into houses that were rented to private individuals. He also entrusted to Mansart the task of rebuilding his palace (cf. J. Hillairet, *Evocation du vieux Paris,* 352). Could this Grand Prior Jacques de Souvré have been the journeymen's "Master Jacque?" It should be added that the Hôtel de Clisson, built on the grand worksite of the Temple (the current rue des Archives) was acquired by the Soubise family in 1697. The Hôtel de Soubise or Rohan Soubise (today the National Archives) was built from 1705 to 1709 on the site of the former gardens at the same time that the Hôtel de Rohan was built alongside on the rue Vielle du Temple. Gould *(A Concise History of Freemasonry),* does not hesitate to connect the origin of the "children of Father Soubise" to the illustrious Rohan-Soubise family. Whether true or not, it is certain that these magnificent dwellings were built by masons who lived in the censive district of the Temple.

‡ According to Macrobe, the wolf represents the initiate, he who has received the light, because of the kinship the ancients felt existed between the wolf and the sun. "In fact," they said, "the flocks flee and disappear when the wolf approaches just like the constellations, flocks of stars, disappear before the light of the sun." (Clavel, *Histoire pittoresque de la Franc Maçonneire,* 361.)

could easily find work with the numerous master masons residing in that quarter, notably on rue de la Mortellerie (later the rue de l'Hôtel de Ville), which earned its name from the many mortar-maker workshops located along its length.

Rue de la Mortellerie was cited under this name as early as 1212 in the act establishing the parish district of Saint Jean en Greve,[48] which serves as proof that during the time of the Templars it was already inhabited by numerous masons. In 1348 of the following century, a certain Richard "the *mortellier*" [mortar maker], who lived on this street, established the seat for a society of masons in his house. The Office of the Master Masons remained fixed there for centuries, until the French Revolution. In 1787 the building also housed the offices of the carpenters, joiners, cabinetmakers, miniature furniture makers, and turners. This house stood there until the nineteenth century, when it was removed to accommodate the expansion of the Hôtel de Ville. Close by it, also on the rue de la Mortellerie at the current location of the garden of the Maire de Paris, stood the so-called chapel of the Haudriettes, which the society of masons and carpenters bought from the Sisters of the Assumption on December 22, 1764, in order to install the confederation of Saint Louis and Saint Blaise there after it was transferred from the rue Saint Jacques.[49]

Other streets in this quarter that formed part of the Templars' censive district also evoke the presence of builders: the rue du Platre or Plastriere, or the rue du Jean de Saint Paul, still in existence today. A plaster works once existed there and numerous plasterers had established homes along its length.[50] Another rue Plastriere or Lingariere, which should not be confused with the first one mentioned, ran from the rue Beaubourg to the rue Saint Martin.

There are many other pieces of evidence of the affection that masons have always felt for the old Templar quarter of Saint Gervais and the Greve. There are stalls dating from the sixteenth century in the choir of Saint Gervais Church that depict images of the quarter's corporations sculpted on the misericordes: bargemen, wine merchants, cobblers, meat roasters, masons, and stonecutters.*

---

* For more on the stalls of Saint Gervais, see the reports of L. Lambeau and Abbe Gauthier (with photographs): *Proces-verbaux de la Commission du Vieux Paris* (1901), 104–5 and 159–60.

In the epitaph record of the persons buried at Saint Gervais, we can read these names: Marguerite Rousset, wife of Claude Monnart, sworn mason to the king and bourgeois of Paris (September 18, 1632); Guillaume Chappeau, architect mason; Claude de Villiers, his first wife (September 25, 1546); Balthazar Monard, master mason and bourgeois of Paris (June 11, 1637); Pierre Chambiges, master of works for masonry and paving in the city of Paris (June 19, 1544); Jacqueline Laurens, his wife (June 3, 15??); Guillaume Guillain, master of works for masonry and paving in the city of Paris; Gillette de la Fontaine, his wife (February 15, 1558); Percevel Noblet, bourgeois of Paris and sworn mason to the king (May 23, 1632); Catherine Denison, his wife; Guillaume Marchand, architect of the king (October 12, 1555); Claude du Puys or Dupuis, master glazier and glazier for the king's buildings (April 23, 1599); Jean Jacquet, master mason, bourgeois of Paris, and mason of Saint Gervais (July 12, 1603); and Renee Fezari, his wife.

In the epitaph record of old Saint Paul Church, we find the following names: Augustin Guillain, master of works, keeper in charge of the fountains of Paris, sworn servant of the king for works of masonry (June 6, 1636); Jeanne de la Robye, wife of Mederic de Donon, equerry, lord of Chastres, counselor of the king, and general overseer of his buildings (date?); Pierre Biard, master sculptor, painter, and architect (September 17, 1609); Michel Richier, master of paving works in the king's buildings (January 26, 1610); Louis Coulon, king's sworn master carpenter and bourgeois of Paris; Louise Thévenard, his wife (December 4, 1639); François Pinart, master mason (November 21, 1622); Jaquette Chardon, his wife (1623); Pierre Pinart, their son, master mason (163?); Marie Autin, his wife; Jean, son of Jacques Barbel called of Chastres, sergeant of arms, carpenter of the king for his kingdom (November 24, 1382). We can also add the names of François Mansart, who was notably the architect of Jacques de Souvré, Grand Prior of Malta (1666); and of Jules Hardouin Mansart (May 11, 1708).

Finally, how could we note the name of Rabelais? The epitaph record of Saint Paul parish gives us the date of his death: François Rabelais, deceased at the age of 70 years, rue des Jardins, on April 9, 1552, was buried in Saint Paul Cemetery."[51] Rabelais, who was then the priest beneficiary of Meudon, seems to have lived the last two years of his life on the rue des Jardins Saint Paul, which was in the jurisdiction of the censive district of the Benedictines of Saint Maur, for whom he was a canon. This mention of Rabelais and his home in the masons' quarter, the quarter of the mortar makers, is really not tangential to the topic at hand. Everything leads us to believe that he enjoyed the company of craftsmen quite often and that he was at the very least the chaplain for a confraternity of masons. Doesn't he admit as much in the prologue to Book Three of *Pantagruel,* and again in the prologue to Book Five, when he reveals his status of "accepted mason?": "I am resolved to do as did Regnault de Montauban; to serve the masons and put the pot on for the masons; then, since their journeyman I am not, they will have me for their indefatigable audience for their heavenly writings."[52] This confession takes on its full meaning when placed in context with the one that appears earlier in the prologue to "Gargantua": "To me it is all honor and glory to be dubbed and esteemed as a good *gaultier** and a fellow companion." The word *gaultier* can be related to the *gault,* meaning "cock," that medieval- and Renaissance-era masons took as a sobriquet.

The Sainte Catherine du Val des Ecoliers was located not far from Saint Paul Church, on the current site of the rue d'Ormesson where the masons confraternity celebrated Saint Louis on August 25.[†]

No masons' names were left in the epitaph records of Saint Jean en Grève Church. The building nonetheless includes a chapel dedicated to Saint Joseph, the patron saint of carpenters, and one dedicated to Saint Nicholas, who was also honored by carpenters. Both of these existed before 1325. In these, masons celebrated the feast day of Saint Blaise on February 3.[53]

To bring our stroll to an end, we cross the place de Grève and the Notre Dame Bridge over the Seine. Now we are in the Cité. Here the Templars long held ownership of a large domain between Notre Dame and the palace. As we can recall, the rights of the Temple over this domain were the result of the accord concluded in 1175 by the Order and the prior of the Benedictines of Saint Eloi. Their territory mainly

---

* [*Gaultier* refers to "one who enjoys his drink" or, less delicately, "boozer." —*Trans.*]
† J. B. Le Masson, *Calendriers des Confréries de Paris,* 47. This church was not in the Templars' censive district but in that of the Couture Sainte Catherine, an Augustine priory.

consisted of the rue Saint Landry and rue de la Regraterie, the new Notre Dame, the rue Saint Christopher and rue Saint Genevieve, the crossroads, and the Palu Market.

Crossing the Seine again, we arrive at the Ile de la Cité, by the Petit Pont. This brings us to the Left Bank, the old university quarter. We are still in the Templar's censive district, although at its southernmost point. This domain belonged in large part to the free and franchised fiefs of Garlande and the Franc Rosier. It encompassed: the rue de Garlande (now the rue Galande, which should not be confused with the rue de la Calandre on Ile de la Cité), the rue de la Huchette, the lower part of the rue Saint Jacques, the rue de la Parcheminerie,* the rue Erembourg de Brie or Boutebrie, the rue du Foin (which started at the rue Saint Jacques and ended at the rue de la Harpe), the rue des Mathurins (now rue Sommerand), the rue des Massons (rue Champollion), the rue de la Harpe, the rue Platriere or des Plastriers (rue Domat), and the Palais des Thermes.†

Here, too, we find the presence of masons and builders. First there is the rue des Massons (or des Maçons; called the rue Champollion after 1868), which has been in existence since 1254 *(vicus cementariorum)*‡ in close proximity to two other streets that should not be confused with each other or their namesakes on the Right Bank: the rue des Plastriers or Plastriere (rue Domat), and the rue Plastriere (rue Serpente today). The rue des Plastriers was at least partially within the Templars' censive district. It has been in existence since the thirteenth century. In 1247, 1250, and 1254 it was referred to as both *vicus Plastrariorum* and *vicus Plasteriorum* and is mentioned in fourteenth-century titles as Plastriers or Platriers. In the sixteenth century it became the rue du Platre and in 1864 it became the rue Domat. Interestingly, in the thirteenth century a house called the domus Radulphi plastrarii is mentioned as having stood there and, in the fifteenth century, mention is made of a Maison

---

* A mansion called the Franc Rosier (the Maillets) was located on this street in the sixteenth century and was under the jurisdiction of the grand prior of Malta's censive district. Refer to Berty, Tisserand, and Platon, *Topographie historique du vieux Paris (region centrale de l'Universite)* (Paris: Imprimerie Nationale, 1897), 305.

† [This refers to the construction built over the ancient Roman baths. —*Trans.*]

‡ There is a reference in 1263 to the name *vicus lathomorum*. The street was shared by the censive districts of the Temple and Saint Germain.

des Maillets (House of Mallets) that was to have faced the rue Saint Jacques and a Hostel de la Palastriere.[54]

As for the rue Platriere that now forms part of rue Serpente and is known to have existed as early as the thirteenth century,[55] it connected the rue Hautefeuille (whose upper half was called rue des Veieils Plastrieres or Ville Plastriere from the twelfth to sixteenth centuries) and rue Cauvain (rue de l'Eperon).

The rue des Maçons was part of Saint Benoit or Holy Trinity parish, whose church was located on the rue Saint Jacques, near the Palais des Thermes. Saint Benoit Church housed a chapel dedicated to Saint Blaisel, the patron saint of masons and carpenters, and two chapels to Saint Nicholas, two to Saint John the Evangelist, and one to Saint John the Baptist.[56] This veneration of the two Saint Johns was primarily related to printers and booksellers, who also resided in this quarter. We know that patronage of Saint John was also invoked by sculptors and engravers, the ancient "ymagiers" who worked with stone and plaster.

The rue de la Bucherie dates from the twelfth century and owes its name to the numerous merchants who lived there during the Middle Ages and sold wood for both heating and building purposes. The wood was floated on the Seine to Paris, where it was received and collected on the Left Bank at the spot called the *port aux buches*. The thirteenth century Livre de la Taille provides the names of numerous buchiers, carpenters, masons, and joiners who lived in this area.[57]

The greater portion of this Templar quarter on the Left Bank was a dependency of Saint Julien le Pauvre Parish, which later became Saint Severin Parish. It was also placed under the protection of Saint John in memory of an old baptistery that once existed near the original church built in the eighth century by Saint Julien the Hospitaller (or Saint Julien the Poor), bishop of Brioude. The current church called Saint Julien le Pauvre is the the chapel of the small priory that was erected on this site in the twelfth century by the Benedictines of Notre Dame de Longpont (near Montlhéry).[58]

Formerly on rue Garlande (Galande) near Saint Julien Church was Saint Blaise of the Masons and Carpenters Chapel, situated on the site of the old refectory of the Benedictine Priory. According to Breul, the old confederacy of masons and carpenters, which existed prior to 1268, was established in 1476 in Saint Blaise Chapel, which was also placed under the patronage of Saint Louis and Saint Roch.[59] During the seventeenth century, the brotherhood gathered in this chapel once a year on February 3.[60]

The ownership of this chapel was the object of a lawsuit between the masons and carpenters association and the General Hospital that lasted from 1473 to 1713! As the result of some highly complex legal maneuvering, the General Hospital's claim was dismissed, but because it strongly desired ownership of Saint Blaise Chapel as well as the two houses adjacent to it, it purchased this property from the master masons and carpenters in 1764. At that time the chapel was threatening to collapse and it was totally demolished around 1770.[61] The service of the Brotherhood of Masons and Carpenters was then temporarily transferred to Saint Yves Chapel on the rue Saint Jacques before being installed once and for all at the old Haudriettes Chapel on rue de la Mortellerie.

It also seems that around 1760, a brotherhood of masons and carpenters met in the Chapel of the Nation of Picardy on the rue de Fouarre (rue Lagrange) and that their corporation kept an office on rue de la Harpe at this time.[62]

The Temple's domain ended south of the rue des Mathurins, which formed part of their district. The area beyond this point fell under the jurisdiction of Saint Jean de Latran—that is, the Knights Hospitallers. This street owed its name to the Hospital of the Mathurins or the Trinity, which had been created around 1206. This facility was administered by the Mathurin Order, the donkey driver brothers founded by Saint Jean de Matha with an eye to ransoming prisoners held captive by the Muslims. This indicates that it had a relationship with the Templars, although it was a direct dependency of the chapter of the Paris Cathedral. The Templars, who were not priests, were affiliated furthermore with several religious orders, such as the Mathurins or the Carmelites, from whom they recruited their chaplains. Following the abandonment of the Holy Land and the end of the Crusades, it is quite probable that the Mathurins' Trinity Hospital, just like its namesake on the rue Saint Denis, would have given shelter to the poor "walkers," meaning both pilgrims and journeymen.

Masons and builders must have been numerous in the Templar Quarter on the Left Bank, although the epitaph records have only passed down a handful of their names. At Saint Yves Chapel we find only Jacques Dyche, house roofer and bourgeois of Paris (1400) and Jeannette, his wife. At Saint Severin there are only a master mason, Austicier (May 28, 1615), and his wife Marie Foliot (February 17, 1601). Saint Benoit lists the famous Claude Perrault, architect (October 9, 1678), and Mathurins Chapel has Claude Roman, architect and entrepreneur of buildings (1675).

This brings us to the end of our excursion through the old Paris of the Templars. It seems, from the evidence we have encountered, that during the entire time of the Ancien Regime it was also the Paris quarter of masons and carpenters. Here they had their homes and their religious and charitable foundations; here they enjoyed exceptional rights and privileges. Royal authority definitely sought to restrict them and limit them *ratione loci* to the area of the Enclos and its immediate dependencies, such as the Old Temple, near Saint Gervais. Elsewhere, in fact, the necessity of police and the maintenance of public order strictly prohibited the overlapping of authority. Nonetheless, the singular legal system instituted by the Templars during the twelfth and thirteenth centuries survived inside the Enclos until the Revolution; throughout the rest of the former commandery, it survived in the form of traditions.

To be absolutely thorough and give this demonstration all its conclusive value, it is important not only to establish, as we have done here, the bonds that existed between the Templars and craftsmen builders, it is also necessary to demonstrate that there are no profound traces of masons and carpenters having settled outside the boundaries of the Temple's former jurisdiction. In other words, it is just as important that we look closely at the other neighborhoods of ancient Paris for signs of populations of builders. Having researched fifty-eight of the main churches of Paris during this same time, here is what we can conclude: To be precise, there were neither evocative street names nor chapels or brotherhoods of masons and carpenters in any other areas of the city. The epitaph records rarely reveal any names of builders. Notre Dame and its dependencies and Saint Louis en l'Isle, the Blancs Manteaux, Sainte Croix de la Bretonnerie, Sainte Opportune, Saint

Merri, Saint Jean de Latran, Saint Jacques du Haut Pas, Saint Victor, Saint Laurent, and Saint Lazare reveal not a single mason or carpenter in their records. Only one was found at Saint Jacques de la Boucherie (Jean Douillier, 1562) and at Saint Germain des Pres (the famous Pierre de Montreuil, deceased March 17, 1266), and only two each were found at Saint Eustache and Saint Martin des Champs. The epitaph record of the charnel house of the Holy Innocents, which is quite considerable and the largest in Paris, gives only three builders' names.

Likewise, it seems that very few masons appear to have settled in the juridictions of the large abbeys where other trades enjoyed franchises. We learned earlier that Saint Nicolas des Champs Parish, a dependency of the Saint Martin Priory, was only a peasant village before the Templars installed themselves there. The settlement of the abbey of Saint Germain des Pres was also quite slow. A 1523 cartulaire confirms that the abbey exercised the right of all justice in its censive district and specifically stated that "said religious lords can make sworn masters of every trade in the forsbourgs of said Saint Germain, just solely as bakers, wine sellers, butchers, fishmongers, drapers, couturiers, stocking makers, cobblers, locksmiths, chandeliers, grossiers, apothecaries, barbers, surgeons, and generally of all other trades as it pleases said lords, with neither the king nor any others having the right to prevent it."[63] Not a single building trade figures in this list, which implies that none were practiced within the abbey's jurisdiction.

The Temple and Contemporary Masons

Neither the disappearance of secular privileges and franchises with the Revolution nor the suppression of the Order of Malta by Bonaparte in 1798 caused any change in the localization and traditions of crafts and commerce in the former Templar censive district. Up into the present day, this localization has given a very distinctive physiognomy to the third and fourth arrondissements. The construction of the Marais and its splendid mansions in the seventeenth century did not manage to change this character. Crafts and small businesses prevailed. This is something everyone knows, though it is a social and historical reality that those responsible for the renovation project of the Marais have overlooked to some extent. Few, however, are aware of one other quarter to which mason artisans have long held a traditional attachment: the Hôtel de Ville neighborhood.

In the middle of the nineteenth century, this is where masons lived in order to find employment. In a work that was published in 1840[64] we can read the following text, illustrated by an engraving made from a daguerreotype:

> During ordinary times, when it is not troubled by moments of public unrest, the Place de Greve is fairly calm but still not in a state of perfect tranquility. This is the place where workers, primarily masons in search of employment, have chosen to rendezvous . . . Around six in the morning one can see a crowd of individuals emerging from all the tiny streets in the neighborhood of the square. They are all clad in a garb that, because of its many patches, would rival the clothes of a harlequin if it were not for the whitish layer that is uniformly spread atop the garments' surface. They all carry on their backs what could be well called their insignia: a small basket inside of which sits a wooden spade whose handle emerges from a small hole contrived in the back of the basket. This is how the entrepreneurs who come there in search of workers recognize the men they need."

In 1835 the name of rue de la Mortellerie was changed to rue de l'Hôtel de Ville. But it's character still remained that of rue de la Mortellerie. Before the concerns of hygiene and urbanization that followed the Second World War led to the razing of this old quarter, at that time referred to by the bureaucratic title of insalubrious block number 16, numerous suppliers of mason's tools—trowels, brollys, squares, plumblines—could be found there, as was the case during the time of the mortar makers.[65] There were also numerous rooming houses where many of these workers in stone, plaster, and cement lived. Being for the most part natives of the provinces of central France who had come to Paris to ply their trades, these men were popularly known as *ligorgneaux* or *limousins*. The names of several of hotels in the area are quite significant in this regard: no. 7, Restaurant du Batiment; no. 33, Au rendezvous de la Haute

Vienne; no. 51, Au rendezvous des Creusois; no. 73, Au rendezvous des enfants de Limoges; no. 12, Au chantier de l'Hôtel de Ville; no. 36, Au rendezvous des Cimentiers; no. 50, Au rendezvous des Compagnons; no. 52, Hôtel de la Creuse; no. 74, Au rendezvous des Maçons.

Several of these establishments must have served as meeting places (cayennes), for the Journeymen of Duty. Until the expropriations motivated by the renovation of "block 16"—a small hotel and restaurant— the Rendezvous des Maçons on the rue de Brosse at the very chevet of Saint Gervais served such a purpose. It sat partially on the former site of the Old Temple or Small Temple, or the Garrison Hotel. The facade of this building, whose enseigne remained until 1955, fortunately escaped the pickaxes of the demolition team, though not, incidentally, for the memories it evoked but to "shore up" the southern side of Saint Gervais Church. Expanded and embellished, it has since been incorporated into a pastiche composition.

Today the Compagnons du Tour de France have a building in close proximity at 84 rue de l'Hôtel de Ville, which they have carefully restored. The Compagnons du Tour du Devoir thus continue a tradition and help us to grasp how they are right to claim to be the successors to the Templars. Freemasons could make this same claim if their history was not so poorly known. Their story does, however, reveal a different reality, if not too far off—one of certain people religiously repeating legends that induce a smile among those who don't believe in articles of faith.

PART 2

From the Art of Building to the Art of Thinking

8

Mason Corporations in France

In the first half of this book we examined the remote ancestry of Freemasonry and its birth as a craft brotherhood in the Middle Ages, notably under the aegis of the Templars. In this second half we are going to undertake the examination of the professional building trade organizations in the major countries of Europe and then look at select circumstances of how the art of building, which primarily implies and illustrates an art of thinking and living, gave way to an art of thinking alone. We will also look at how modern speculative Freemasonry succeeded the operative freemasonry of the past.

First, though, an observation concerning terminology: It is customary when characterizing the trades of the past to use the generic word *corporation*. It is important to emphasize that this term, which is etymologically English, is of modern origin. When this kind of group appeared at the beginning of the twelfth century, the name it assumed, depending on the region, was either guild or brotherhood, the terms for the associations from which it emerged at a time when, in addition to their origional religious and social purposes, they took on a secular and professional nature.

In the thirteenth century, notably in Paris, a division occurred between the religious and charitable organization—the brotherhood—and the professional organization that the *Livre des Métiers* calls the trade, the trade body, or the regular tradesmen. Later, in the seventeenth century, trade was denoted in France as the trade community, then in the eighteenth century, as the corporation. "This word is not used in official acts before the memorandum of January 1776 in which Turgot presented to the king the edict that would abolish, over the following months, mastery associations and oathbound groups."[1] So this term can be employed only in the broad sense, which is how we will use it: to designate the former professional organization.

We will examine in succession these organizations in France, Germany, Italy, Switzerland, and in Great Britain, concentrating particularly on those of masons and builders.

The Origins of Mason Corporations in France

As we have seen, guilds and secular brotherhoods of craftsmen appeared during the twelfth century. Though the statutes of these sometimes make reference to earlier guilds, their existence is not certain.

These guilds and brotherhoods gradually organized into trade communities under a sovereign authority, generally the king. We know that Flanders, Picardy, and the Artois region witnessed the organization of craftsmen into corporations very early on and we have determined the synchronism between this organization and the establishment of the Templars. In Rouen the cobblers guild was confirmed by a charter granted by Henry I of England (1100–1135) while those of the tanners and furriers were confirmed by Henry II (1154–1189). The origins of crafts in Caen and Coutances go back to a date in the remote past.

The oldest statutes for a community of builders are those we have already cited, coming from the common cloister of Montpellier, which date back to 1196 and which were sanctioned by Guillaume VIII, lord of Montpellier.* The names of several particularly skilled architects of this "mastery association," such as Bertrand, *maistre de piéra*, and Guillaume Alesta, *magister lapidum* in 1273,[2] have been preserved

It seems that the masters of stone *(magistris lapidum)* of Nîmes

---

* These statutes were reformed in 1284.

formed a community at a very early date. In 1187 Raymond V, count of Toulouse, granted them jurisdictional privileges in return for certain fees and for personnel to give military service aiding in the demolition of enemy castles.[3]

In Paris the oldest brotherhood, that of the *mercatores aquoe* [water merchants], is first mentioned in 1121. It maintained its seat at the church of Saint Mary Magdalene. Royal certificates from 1162 mention the privileges enjoyed by butchers of the La Grande Boucherie Parisienne. These privileges were confirmed by patent letters issued from 1182 to 1183 by Philip Augustus. The drapers had established themselves in the community in 1183 and in 1188 they founded the Brotherhood of Saint Peter in the chapel of Saint Mary the Egyptian. In all the relevant documents of this era the members of this Parisian brotherhood are called *fraters,* which is exactly the case in a 1219 charter, conserved in the city archives of Paris, concerning the acquisition of a house sitting behind the butcher shop of the Petit Pont next to the brotherhood of drapers.

Everywhere, just as single individuals were, these groups of merchants and craftsmen remained subject to the public authority of the land—that is, to the lord chief justice. Thus in a city such as Paris that was under the jurisdiction of several chief justices, we can see the development of several different communities according to the rights they were able to enjoy in their respective jurisdictions. This subordination is often displayed by a very clear feature: in Paris, for example, the king quite frequently "sold the trade," meaning he levied a tax on the merchant or craftsmen who was setting up in his trade. But all the dismemberments of public law that were so skillfully enacted during the Middle Ages had an effect on the rules and policing of trades. As was quite often the case, in order to better establish legal autonomy of a trade, a lord would entrust jurisdiction of it to a master of that trade. In Chartres, the post of master of taverners designated by the count had been in existence since 1147. In that same year, Louis VII gave the bakers of Pontoise a monopoly on the making of bread and in so doing put them under the authority of a master he had chosen. The master was often a king's officer whose domestic duties had some connection to the corporation in question. He might be the head of the corresponding service in the royal domicile. Thus the masons were under the master builder of masonry and the carpenters under the king's master carpenter.[4]

The Corporative Organization in Paris
According to the *Livre des Métiers*

The drafting of the *Establissements des mestiers de Paris,* known as the *Livre des Métiers,* in 1268 under the direction of Etienne Boileau, provost of the king, sheds full light on the corporative organization.[5]

With the creation of this book in mind, Etienne Boileau asked the representatives of the brotherhoods to give him the rules of their trades. This book is therefore a codification of earlier existing statutes. The system of the *Livre des Métiers* placed labor under the control of Church and state. But it is important to remember that this regulation was valid only within the royal provostship. It did not apply in the jurisdictions of other sovereign authorities that essentially derived from the Church and the Ecclesiastical Orders, among which the Templar quarter figures prominently, especially with regard to jurisdictions where trades were exercised in franchise. These francs métiers, escaping royal or sovereign tutelage, did have their own rules and rites however, and we know they even served as models for the sworn trades. The internal organization is thus equally valid for both kinds of trade associations.

According to Boileau's book, trade taken in its entirety is based on a fundamental division made up of three classes: apprentices, valets (the term journeymen later replaced this), and masters. The length of apprenticeship varies from two to twelve years, depending on the trade. Once his time of apprenticeship had ended, a young artisan could immediately become a master. It was only in the fifteenth century, or at the end of the fourteenth at the very earliest, that the disposition was introduced into the rules that made journeyman a separate stage of apprenticeship that the artisan was expected to undertake before obtaining the brevet of mastery.

According to the *Livre des Métiers,* the master could and should require the worker (valet) he hired to produce certain justifications of his skills, first giving notice that he had completely finished his apprenticeship, and then establishing that he was free of any earlier commitment.

The contract was concluded orally, but before this the valet swore on the saints that he would perform the trade "faithfully and well." Depending on the profession, this swearing might involve the relics or images of the patron saints of the trade or the Holy Gospels.[6] A. Lantoine is therefore mistaken when he claims that the oath could not have been made on the Bible in the lodges of operative Catholic masons. We find this oath on the Bible in corporative English masonry, which was also Catholic. The "Bible upon the altar" is therefore not an example of "Huguenot contraband" smuggled to freemasonry.[7]

To obtain the grade of master it was first necessary that an apprentice show proof that he had fulfilled his apprenticeship. The idea of the masterwork did not yet exist in the thirteenth century, but candidates for mastery were required to show guarantees of another order, such as taking an exam in the presence of wardens of the trade. Candidates were also required to acquit the taxes or fees imposed by royal or manorial authority when the trade was not one that was free and exempt of such obligations. The recipient would then swear an oath on the "saints" to conform to established usages and customs and provide good and loyal work.

It should be noted that women were accepted into the rank of masters in two very specific cases. There were certain trades that were exclusively composed of women (silk seamstresses, silk fabric makers, and so forth). In some other professions, women were accepted to the rank of master just as as men were (they could be fringe makers, linen makers, or poultry breeders). Further, the widows of masters were authorized to continue the trade of their deceased husbands. It was generally assumed that they had acquired sufficient professional experience to do so.[8]

The reception of a new master was occasion for a ceremony, though only the statute of the *talemeliers* [bakers] provides any details of this ceremony. Candidates for master gathered at the door of the trade warden's house. While standing outside, they answered questions asked of them concerning professional customs, and after witnesses gave their approval, they broke a pot of nuts and *oublies**on the wall as a sign of

---

* [These are thin, wafflelike pastries that have been rolled on a cylinder. —*Trans.*]

emancipation. They then entered the house, where a place had been reserved for them at hearth and table. A group meal was served to which all masters contributed one denier, even if they were not attending.

It is probable that similar ceremonies took place in other trades, although Etienne Boileau's book remains mute on this subject. In addition, while this is what could be seen from the outside regarding initiation, it is likely that esoteric rites were also included but were not revealed in public, falling instead under the heading of trade secrets. The practice of these rites eventually alarmed both civil authorities and the Church, which considered them sacrilegious. An interesting allusion to this subject appears in the 1548 arret of the parliament of Paris concerning the Brotherhood of the Passion of Paris. It forbids any staging of sacred texts, mainly the Mysteries, which consisted of episodes from the Passion of Christ. The Officiality of Paris eventually confirmed this condemnation. We will see that this ban was not at all the case in England, where the Mysteries became standardized and where the word *mystery* eventually acquired the meaning of the word *craft*.[9]

A responsibility that the masters had to support in the royal provostship of Paris was also one they found highly irritating: that of the watch. Several trades had obtained an exemption from this duty, notably the stonecutters and mortar makers.

The nominal heads of the trades, as we said earlier, were the craft masters, great officers, or private citizens to whom these trades were pledged. Their role was chiefly honorific while the actual leaders were wardens and sworn members who held and exercised authority in the name of the group. It should be mentioned that trade assemblies were also held, sometimes on a regular basis, and sometimes as an extraordinary event.

The Communities of Masons and Builders

According to the *Livre des Métiers* of Paris, exercise of the trades of carpenter and mason was free in the jurisdiction of the king's provost. Craftsmen were expected to pay a fee only to the monarch. We can understand this point through its application to those professions with francs métiers regulations in the jurisdiction of the Temple.

The masons were dependents of an officer of the royal house, the master of the works of masonry. In 1268, during the time Etienne Boileau lived, this individual was Master Guillaume of Saint Paul. He had under his jurisdiction masons, stonecutters, mortar makers, and plasterers. We do not know to what exactly the trade of mortellier corresponded. This word has long since vanished from speech, but it most likely concerns what are today called dressers—workers who, after the architect and master mason have finished, oversee the cutting and laying of stone, preparation of mortar, and so forth.[10]

This illustrates how far things were then from the specialization of today. For a long time, even extending into modern times, architecture consisted only of this division mentioned by the Canon Hugues de Saint Victor in the eleventh century: masonry *(cementaria)*, which included stonecutters *(latomos)* and masons *(cementarios)*, and carpentry, which included carpenters *(carpentarios)* and joiners *(tignarios)*. One fact should not be overlooked: Until the seventeenth century, private architecture was made of wood—long beams, then short beams after the fifteenth century. Only sacred or public buildings were constructed of stone. Rare indeed were the houses built of stone.[11]

Architects were merely workers of a higher degree, master builders who worked personally either as sculptors or as simple stonecutters. Until the Renaissance, they were designated by the term *master mason* or that of *master of the work, magister aedificans*, or *magister aedificiorum*, when they were the head supervisors of worksites. The word *architect* received scant use during the Middle Ages. Pierre de Montreuil gave himself the distinction of the title *doctor lathomorum*. Like their fellow workers, architects were paid by the day, but benefiting from a well deserved consideration, their salary was higher and included tips as well as gifts (robes, hoods, gloves, pipes of wine, and so forth). These masters of the work were generally men of higher learning. They were in no way technical specialists; rather they worked simultaneously on architectural constructions, war machines, furnishings, and sculpture. Like Villard de Honnecourt, who was quite fluent in Latin and highly knowledgeable about different sciences, and like Tetillon, a monk of Saint Gall Abbey, who was known throughout Germany in the eleventh century as a preacher, professor, Latinist,

Hellenist, painter, architect, carver, and astronomer, they often possessed extensive knowledge of all fields. Proof of the high esteem in which they were held is shown by the many commemorative monuments to the memory of the masters of the works that were erected in the cathedrals and other buildings they built. Among these we can cite figures of masters of the works carved on the medallions of the cathedrals of Amiens and Reims, the inscription carved in 1257 on the portal of Notre Dame in Paris in honor of Jean de Chelles, and that of Pierre de Montreuil in the Chapel of the Virgin in the Parisian church of Saint Germain des Pres.

According to the *Livre des Métiers,* mortelliers and stonecutters were exempt from watch duties. These craftsmen claimed to have enjoyed this privilege since the time of Charles Martel: "The mortar makers have been exempt from the watch and all stonecutting since the time of Charles Martel, as men of integrity have heard it passed from father to son." This declaration presumes an existence of privileges going back to the eighth century, which is an exaggeration if we take into consideration the time-frame of the existence of that actual community. It may have a basis in fact though, to wit the existence of large and influential architectonic associations in Gothic Gaul during the seventh and eight centuries. This assertion becomes even more interesting once we know that, according to the oldest documents of English freemasonry, this art was introduced in France by Charles Martel before he crossed over into England.

The length of the apprenticeship period for masons was six years. The statutes of the community of carpenters in the *Livre des Métiers* are uniquely based on the deposition of an important figure, the king's carpenter, Master Fouques du Temple, who stated that he governed the mastery from the time the king had entrusted him with that responsibility, and this declaration became a craft regulation from that time forward.

Under the unique title of carpenters were gathered all workers who, according to the text, *euvrent du trenchant en merrien,* which means "who worked wood with tools." The different categories under this heading were numerous, amounting to ten in all. They included standard carpenters, *huchiers,** court clerks, coopers, cartwrights, carters,

---

* [A *huchier* is a carpenter specializing in furniture and interior design. —*Trans.*]

house roofers, crochetiers [boatwains], turners, and panelers. The king's carpenter, who was the head of all these specialities, assigned a lieutenant to administrate each one. He himself received eighteen deniers a day for his services along with a livry robe on All Saints' Day (title XLII, art. 1, and 8).

The apprenticeship period for a carpenter was four years. In 1292, according to the Talliage Registry, there were 104 master masons, 98 master carpenters, and 12 stonecutters listed in Paris.

The Extension and Evolution of the Corporative System

The Parisian-type craft community could also be found in a certain number of towns known as "sworn towns." At the end of the fourteenth century Loyseau, in his *Traité des Offices*, explains that the sworn towns are those in which "certain sworn crafts exist, meaning those that have the right to exist as a body and a community in which membership is gained by oath." Up until that time, sworn towns were fairly rare. In the majority of towns throughout the north, central, and Midi regions of France, and even in Paris in the areas of sovereign jurisdiction, including that of the Templars, entry into a profession was free. It was the same throughout Provence until the end of the fifteenth century. In Bourdeaux, franchised trades were exercised in areas called *sauvetes* or *sauvetats*. In Lyon, crafts people were subject only to their own customs and to the police regulation of the municipality or the manorial authority to whom the masters were required to swear an oath of fealty. This last restriction shows that absolute freedom in the trades did not exist anywhere. There were only different systems of rules. An individual could oppose either the sworn trades or the trades governed by municipal or manorial authority. Even the francs métiers, despite the great privileges attached to them, fall into this second category.

In all cases where trades were performed in franchise, there was only one grouping, and it was both religious and professional in nature: the brotherhood. Affiliation with it was obligatory. In addition to its religious and charitable mission, which was led by clerics, the brotherhood mainly concerned itself with its material interests and saw that respect was paid to trade customs. There were officers who were given authority in this matter, such as those known as priors in Bordeaux, for example.

At the end of the sixteenth century, the royal authority in France attempted to extend the system of sworn trades over the entire kingdom. This effort appeared in the measures of an edict issued by Henri III in December 1591 and in another edict of Henri IV in April 1597. These edicts prescribed the entrance of all people into a sworn trade where that form was in common use, and establishment of sworn trades where there were none. But these edicts were applied in a manner that was far from perfect.

According to a 1673 edict, the number of officially recognized state bodies amounted to 73. Another edict of 1691 fixes the number of crafts at 127 and divides them up again, in accordance with their importance, into four classes. At the same time, it establishes the importance of each of these classes with respect to the importance of the king's right during each reception in the city. In the cities where a parliament sat, the masters received in first-class communities paid the king 30 pounds, while those in fourth-class communities paid 6 pounds. The first class consisted of 25 corporations, including those of the masons, carpenters, and sculptors, along with those of the painters, surgeons, apothecaries, booksellers, goldsmiths, and so on. In the fourth class, we find the spike makers, the boatmen, the flower sellers, the *patenotriers,** fishermen, and *maitres fifis* [garbage collectors].

The masons were always placed under the jurisdiction of the master of the works of royal masonry, buildings, and constructions, later called the master general of the king's buildings, bridges, and roadways of France. In the terms of an ordinance of May 17, 1595, they held the right to pass judgement on all transgressions of their statutes. It seems that these mason statutes were the same as those described by Etienne Boileau, which had been confirmed in 1574. The masters continued to be able to ply their trade freely without having to buy that right from the king. But the king, while avoiding any appearance of suppressing this traditional franchise, had restricted its extent by creation of sworn expert masons of the king, veritable public officers whom he designated.

---

* [These are the manufacturers of rosaries, buttons, jewelry, and so forth. —*Trans.*]

These sworn masons purchased their charge and in return they alone were responsible for appraisals, reports, toises, and estimations.

According to the Guilde des Corps des Marchands of 1776, the duration of the apprenticeship period among masons was six years by the terms of their statutes, but was in fact only three years. There was no required period established for work as a journeyman; an apprentice could graduate directly to the status of master.

Like masons, carpenters, too, were divided into ordinary masters and those sworn to the king. Philip the Fair abolished the post of royal carpenter in 1314. It was subsequently restored for a brief time before being definitively terminated. In the terms of the 1649 statute that replaced older statutes dating from 1454, the community was governed by a syndic elected every two years from among those sworn to the king. The elections, reviews, and the settling of business matters took place on March 20, the day after the feast day of Saint Joseph, the patron saint of carpenters.

The examination of an aspiring member consisted of one drawn geometrical design and a masterpiece. The sons of masters and apprentices paid the same rights for master status, 20 pounds total. Six years of apprenticeship were required and journeyman status was intended to last six months. The sons, nephews, and cousins of a master did not count as apprentices. A foreigner to France had to work for an additional four years in Paris before achieving the grade of master.

Carpenters' workshops were known as lodges. An arret issued by Parliament on August 30, 1631, mentions the lodge in its rejection of the appeal of an earlier sentence "that forbade all journeymen carpenters from carrying away from the worksites and even the lodges and workshops of the bourgeois the trimmings, chips, wood ends, and blocks, if it is without the wishes and consent of said bourgeois and carpenters . . ."*

---

* The term *lodge* was contemporaneous with Etienne Boileau's *Livre des Métiers.* Masons also used it: "A document in the archives of Notre Dame de Paris records an incident that took place in the works lodge on the eve of the Feast of Assumption in 1283." [J. Gimpel, *The Cathedral Builders* (New York: Harper and Row, 1984), 77.] Concerning the existence of a lodge in Paris under Louis IX, see Marcel Ollé, *Le Symbolisme,* July/September 1960.

The Brotherhoods

The trade or community remained coupled with a brotherhood, a group that was assembled for religious or charitable purposes, placed under the protection of one or more patron saints, and established in the chapel of a church. The brotherhood was thus subject first and foremost to ecclesiastical authority. Long before the community, it was the first form of trade organization, reflecting the craft's traditional and spiritual elements. While labor retained the supernatural values it had held since time immemorial, religious bonds closely committed the members to God and their fellows in the fulfillment of their daily tasks.

We have seen that in many regions and for a long time there were no trade communities, but only brotherhoods. These also remained the sole professional organizations of the francs métiers. When both groups coexisted, as was the case in Paris, they were no less distinct. They sometimes shared the same directors, but ordinarily their management and resources were clearly separate. Moreover, membership in the brotherhood was obligatory, as was membership in the community.

The Builder Brotherhoods of Paris

In the same city, mainly Paris, a trade would often engender several brotherhoods, who sometimes had different patrons. This was a result of the distance separating some artisans from others. Another consequence was that not all craftsmen were subject to the same statutes. In Paris, some were connected to the community and placed under jurisdiction of the king's provost, while others were dependent on the Temple or some other abbey or sovereign religious order.

In the provostship of Paris at the time of the *Livre des Métiers,* a common brotherhood of masons and carpenters existed, placed under the patronage of Saint Blaise (title XLVIII, art. 2). This patronage had been adopted a good deal earlier and continued to be invoked for several centuries. The seat of this brotherhood was the Saint Blaise–Saint Louis Chapel on the rue Galande near Saint Julien le Pauvre. Another Saint Blaise Chapel, connected perhaps to the same if not to another brotherhood of masons and carpenters, also existed in the neighboring Saint Benoit or Holy Trinity Church on the rue Saint Jacques. It is in fact not out of the question that builders formed several brotherhoods at this time. What is certain—and this is something that happened quite quickly—is that Saint Blaise was not the only saint to have their worship.

Carpenters gladly invoked the patronage of Saint Nicholas and shared his worship with the watermen or water vendors. According to Dulaure, this patronage went far back to the distant past, to a time even before Christianity, for Saint Nicholas simply replaced Neptune. This opinion appears well-founded—simply recall that the Roman builders who settled in Great Britain placed their collegium under the protection of Neptune.

Saint Joseph was also ardently worshiped by the carpenters and seems to have supplanted Saint Blaise. The *Livre des Confréries* indicates that Pope Alexander VII (1655–1667) granted one Brotherhood of Saint Joseph to the carpenters, though it is likely that this was actually a confirmation of a brotherhood that was much older in origin. It was installed in the church of Saint Nicolas des Champs, near the Temple, a parish where builders were numerous, and its coat of arms was an azure field behind a golden image of the infant Jesus holding a compass and measuring a drawing given to him by Saint Joseph.

The *Livre des Confréries* also mentions an organization of stone-cutters: "Brotherhood of the Ascension of Our Lord, erected in the parish church of Notre Dame de Bonne Nouvelle for the brotherhood of journeymen stonecutters, having then in charge Philippe Hubert and Pierre Jouanne in 1663." Its coat of arms "was a compass, triangle, plumb line, hammer, and chisels." The Ascension depicted on the coat of arms of the community of masons ("an Acension of the Son of God, all in gold") compels us to accept the fact that it refers to the craft of masonry.[12]

Certain craftsmen in the building trade, such as roofers, worshipped Saint Anne. In fact, in the Temple there was an altar dedicated to her. Finally, Saint John was worshipped by sculptors and carvers of stone and plaster whose brotherhood had its seat in the church of the Holy Sepulcher near Saint Merri. Fairly recently, according to Cocheris, this brotherhood celebrated Saint John Porte Latine on May 6.[13] Because of their spiritual affinity and their roles as guardians and patron saints of the Templars as well as the Hospitallers, the two Saint Johns—John the Baptist and John of the gospels, the announcer of and the witness to the Light, respectively—were worshipped together by all free and enfranchised craftsmen of the Templar Commandery. This is the reason for the tradition, in existence until the Revolution, of erecting a huge bonfire on the eve of Saint John the Baptist's feast day in the large courtyard of the Temple.[14]

The Brotherhoods in the Provinces

In the north the brotherhoods were known as *bannières*. In the Midi region they were called *charités*. In Montpellier, for example, benevolent institutions that gave assistance had developed rapidly starting in the thirteenth century. Each trade had two ordinary centers consisting of a chapel and an office. Ceremonies and common prayer took place in the chapel, while the office was used for discussing the organization's business activities and for distributing aid to its needy members. The charities had at their disposal the resource of taxes deducted from apprenticeship fees as well as what they took in from various dues. From this fund they gave assistance to the poorer members of the trade and celebrated Masses for their dead. All the trades of Toulouse had their own brotherhoods during the thirteenth century, each established in a different church in which a symbolic lamp, perpetually lit, was placed before the altar.

The community and brotherhood of the carpenters of Angers was undoubtedly of ancient origin. In fact, the statutes of 1487 made mention of the long period of time this craft had been a sworn trade. It elected the two masters that guided it on the feast day of Saint Joseph, and on that same day each master paid the brotherhood the sum of eight sols and four deniers. Each journeyman gave one denier per week to the community. The group's statutes included contingencies for granting brotherhood assistance to indigent foreign journeymen: "For the honesty of said trade, if it should happen that anyone traveling through the region, as long as he is a worker of this trade, finds himself in need and gives his sworn oath that he lacks the wherewithal to meet his travel expenses, the sworn members will be bound to administer to his wants for only one meal and to give him two sols and six deniers."[15]

The same patron saints found in Paris were also worshipped by the brotherhoods of these provincial builders, with the addition of Saint Gregor, Saint Alpinien, Saint Martin, Saint Marin, Saint Etienne, Saint Barbara, and especially the apostle Saint Thomas, who is often depicted holding a square.

Purposes and Traditions of the Brotherhoods

The purpose of the brotherhoods is defined as follows in an edict issued on March 1319 restoring a brotherhood of Saint James and Saint Louis that had been abolished in 1306: "To provide through one's work the gifts of large alms, to feed the indigent brothers, to have Masses said for both the living and the dead, and to busy oneself with various charitable works." But the primary goal, not said outright here yet implied in all that was said and done, was "to elevate man to God and let him earn the Lord's infinite grace."

We know about the organization and life of the brotherhoods thanks to eighteenth-century documents. Each trade community placed under the protection of a patron saint owned a private chapel in a church, where it held its meetings. Each had special officers who were elected to their posts—sometimes a provost and chairman or two sworn masters would share the position. Following Mass every year on its patron saint's feast day, the brotherhood held elections and nominated a collector and a clerk.[16] "The provost would then receive the congratulations and praise of all the brothers, who would lead him solemnly to his home. The chaplain, escorted by choir boys, would then turn over to him, as a sign of his taking possession of the office, the brotherhood's cross, old and new candles, the notes of meetings, and the coffer holding the deniers, property deeds, and the bulls of foundation."[17] The provost alone had the power to convoke the brothers for assemblies, the selection of new members, and the burying of the dead.

> "Sometimes the election of the new chairman would be the occasion for a fairly unique ceremony. Everyone would go to the patronal church and sing vespers. When they reached the verse of

the Magnificat where it says "*Deposuit potentes de sede,*" the chairman who was stepping down from his post would leave his seat, which was located in the center of the choir, and find himself a new seat among the elders. At the same time and continuing through the end of the verse, "*et exaltavit homilies,*" the newly elected chairman would take possession of the baton, the emblem of his station, and sit down on the chair vacated by his predecessor."[18]

Every year the brotherhood sang a solemn Mass, which was followed by a procession in which one member carried the candle and baton of the trade. The following day, another service was celebrated and a Novena was begun for the souls of deceased masters. In addition to this annual ceremony, the divine service with solemn vespers was celebrated on fixed days and a Low Mass was said each day of the year for deceased brothers. At the death of a member, a High Mass was sung and attended by all the brothers.

Despite the persistence of these pious customs, however, the admirable spirit of Christian charity that had animated the brotherhoods during the time of Saint Louis was weakened. Yet it was still considered a matter of honor to give assistance to those craftsmen in the trade who were suffering from misfortune.

The Brotherhoods and Civil and Religious Authorities

The brotherhoods did not always remain inside their pious and charitable provenance. In the beginning of their existence they were often accused, at least under certain circumstances, of degenerating into superstitious practice and belief. There were several cases of this that led to them being banned by town councils in Montpellier (1214), Toulouse (1234), Orleans (1238), Bordeaux (1248), Valence (1255), and Avignon (1326).

A more serious matter was that these brotherhoods were sometimes condemned for fomenting leagues, factions, and disorder. At the beginning of the fourteenth century, they became involved in political agitation and formed federations among themselves, which ultimately led to the temporary abolition of the Parisian brotherhoods in 1306. In 1307, however, the king reauthorized the brotherhood of water sellers and the other brotherhoods reformed shortly thereafter. Following the disturbances and riots of 1380–1382, an ordinance issued on January 27, 1382, suppressed the brotherhoods again, but again, only temporarily.

Through the fifteenth and sixteenth centuries, the brotherhoods seemed to have become merely pretexts for holding feasts funded by monies taken in to assist the poor.* In 1524, the Council of Sens declared that these trade communities existed only to encourage monopolies and base debauchery. On several occasions judicial authorities found themselves forced to intervene. An arret of Parliament enacted on July 28, 1500, forbade the king's provost to authorize any new brotherhoods and ordered him to open an investigation of those that existed.

Another arret of Parliament enacted on July 13, 1501, with the force of legislation behind it, forbade all gatherings of masons and carpenters under the pretext of brotherhoods.

> For several plaintiffs who have come before the Court each day regarding the great faults and abuse that masons and carpenters of Paris, in the provostship and suburbs thereof, have committed and continue to commit as witnessed by said plaintiffs, as by others of their peers and for any other causes for which they are responsible, the Court has suspended and suspends the brotherhoods of masons and carpenters of this city of Paris, and has forbidden and forbids them, under penalty of imprisonment, confiscation of property, and denial of their right to continue in their profession, or otherwise punished as deemed fit in each individual case, that under the cover of brotherhood, or Masses, divine or of any other cause or color, whatsoever it may be, can no longer convoke until this Court has otherwise so ordered . . .

---

* "It is said that these banquets have become the sole reason these brotherhoods exist. It is certain that among the majority of those that remain, if one were to end the feasts held by these artisans and their companions, one would remove at the same time all their devotion and worth." (La Poix de Fréminville, *Dictionaire de la Police Générale*, 245.)

Another arret issued by Parliament on March 15, 1524, went even further, broadly prohibiting all brotherhoods, banquets, and entrance fees; that the holdings thus gathered should be directed toward feeding the poor. Finally, brotherhoods were banned throughout the kingdom by the law passed in 1539, on pain of corporal punishment for those who defied this ruling. The law was initially put into effect and a certain number of brotherhoods were dissolved, but they were not long in reforming. New coercive measures were taken in 1576 and 1579, but the brotherhoods survived all of these condemnations, each of which remained circumstancial at best. Starting with the seventeenth century, the brotherhoods no longer dared rouse the suspicions of an absolute authority and concentrated solely on their charitable aspects.

The Compagnonnages

The compagnonnages* formed another kind of association existing on the margins of the trade communities and brotherhoods.

Historically speaking, the compagnonnages responded to two different intentions. The first, and oldest, seems to have been to group together in a kind of *de facto* federation all the artisans of one craft—master, apprentices, and journeymen—above and beyond all geographical, political, administrative, and jurisdictional divisions. The term *guild* was as of then unknown. Much more than an association, it involved a state of mind, a bond, and a means by which workers sharing a profession could recognize one another and thereby maintain the unity and traditions of the trade.

The compagnonnages therefore fulfilled duties that were never intended for the brotherhoods and communities. By ceasing to be monastic organizations, the brotherhoods simulatenously lost the universal nature thay had shared with religious orders. At best they only grouped together the craftsmen of one city. Furthermore, the trade community did not exist everywhere. As a result, the vast majority of workers in the countryside remained isolated as individuals or small local

---

* [It is preferable to retain the French expression here, for the association has some features that sharply distinguish it from the term *guild*, which is how this word is often translated. —*Trans.*]

groups. The compagnonnage was in fact a response to the necessity of uniting. In this regard it was the continuation of the ancient collegia.

This role played by the compagnonnage diminished in exact proportion to the spread of the sworn community, which maintained the sole right everywhere to represent the trade. With respect to spiritual and moral interests, it was the king and Church's intention to see that these were managed solely by closely supervised brotherhoods. This meant that the original and spontaneous form of the compagnonnage soon lost its reason for existing. As a group whose purposes were self-contracting, and as a de facto association in headlong collision with associations that had the full backing of law and civil and religious authorities, it could only disappear or become almost clandestine.

But economic and social evolution soon gave the compagnonnages a new purpose. More and more, the exercise of a trade was becoming the privilege of masters and their sons. The journeymen could no longer move up to the status of master nor buy their craft. They were constrained to remain salaried employees forever. They also lost what few rights they did have—mainly in Paris, Rouen, Reims, and Arras—to take part in trade administration, such as that pertaining to writing statutes or nominating sworn members.[19] It was then that the compagnonnages transformed from simple de facto connections into veritable organizations whose membership was restricted to valets or journeymen determined to defend their class interests.

This is the reason compagnonnages became more or less prohibited. The sworn or regulated craft, the sole organization of a public nature, had to suffice to promote the legitimate interests of members of the profession. The coalition formed for the sole purpose of increasing prices or salaries was forbidden because it carried the risk of a work suspension that would run counter to the public interest. Beaumanoir, in his Coutumes de Beauvais (written around 1280), considered it a serious crime to ally against the common good for the purpose of demanding a higher salary. Going on strike was punishable by prison and a fine of 60 sols. A law passed on March 18, 1330, mandated the severe punishment of journeymen who, by banding together, had successfully obtained several additional hours of leisure from their masters while still earning the same pay.

In the fourteenth and fifteenth centuries, incidents of this kind were numerous, accompanied even by incidents of collective revolt by journeymen against their masters. These flare-ups, however, involved circumstancial coalitions, not permanent associations. The guild, properly speaking, did not appear prior to the beginning of the sixteenth century and it was immediately characterized by its spirit of protest, as illustrated by journeymen rising up against their masters or by all the artisans of a trade joining together against the authorities.

Even the journeymen brotherhoods transformed into centers of revolt that could incite popular fanaticism. In Lyon, the printers elected a captain, a lieutenant, and ensigns and put together a large league comprised of all the craftsmen in the city. This league was the soul of the revolt of 1539—nor did the repression it unleash stop new plots and new disturbances from occurring. The Villiers Cotterets ordinance of 1539, which prohibited brotherhoods, also banned coalitions. A decree of December 28, 1541, also forbid journeymen from "swearing any oath or monopoly, having any captain or group leader, assembling outside the houses of their masters, or bearing swords or daggers." Despite these general and individual prohibitions, the brotherhoods of Lyonnaise journeymen and others continued to intrigue, as is shown by patent letters from 1561.

More judicial decisions forbidding the compagnonnages were handed down in the seventeenth century, such as the council arret of June 19, 1702, prohibiting journeymen printers from forming "any communities, brotherhoods, associations, or common exchanges."

Despite the general ban on coalitions, however, and taking into account evolution, the police eventually began tolerating the compagnonnages as long as their actions did not pose any threat to public order. The civil authorites were in fact forced to acknowledge that these associations responded to legitimate concerns that were not being satisfactorily addressed in the conventional organizations of sworn crafts dominated by masters.

As a matter of fact, the compagnonnages survived only in certain trades—stonecutters, masons, carpenters, cabinetmakers, and so forth—those organizations in which journeymen were naturally nomadic and loved making the "Tour de France" while they were young, before settling down in a village or town and becoming a master in their own right. It was in the best interests of these itinerant journeymen to organize in order to ensure for themselves the availability of lodging in those various towns and places where they could learn of local job opportunities.

The Church was even more poorly disposed to the compagnonnages than the civil authorities, condemning them under the pretext that their observance of symbols and traditional rites parodied that of holy objects and rites and violated their sworn oaths. There are records of some interesting sentences handed down on May 30, 1648, and on March 14, 1655, by the Theology School (Sorbonne) condemning and at the same time describing the impious, sacreligious, and superstitious practices of journeymen cobblers, saddlers, tailors, cutlers, and hatters.

Some raised the objection that these traditional rites had been practiced for centuries by the former religious brotherhoods who were guided by the clergy. The Church responded easily to this objection, however, suggesting that for the propagation of their art, especially with respect to symbolic teachings and the preservation of their trade secrets, the monks had been under an obligation to preserve them. Furthermore, these rites were traditionally followed and monitored in a sacred and orthodox fashion. These conditions did not apply to the compagnonnages, which no longer included any clerics among their members and which appeared in the eyes of the Church as impious associations when compared to those brotherhoods it once accepted and directed. Finally, and this was the Church's best justification, it is plausible that even if the compagnonnage rites did not disfigure traditional symbols to a great extent, their deeper meaning was nonetheless ungrasped by the humble journeymen. It is merely one step from incomprehension to superstition.

Condemned by royal power and ecclesiastical authority, the compagnnonages still had one safe haven: the Temple commanderies, which, until the Revolution, offered traditional right of asylum to those pursued by the king or Church. We have already seen how the journeyman masons of Paris always maintained their seats—their cayennes—in the censive district of the former Temple commandery. It was only for rather exceptional reasons that the bailiff of the Temple issued a sentence on September 11, 1651, refusing the right of asylum to the compagnonnages condemned by the Sorbonne, which did not include that of the masons.

To conclude our look at French professional organizations, we must note that starting from the fifteenth or sixteenth centuries, neither the trade communities nor brotherhoods could be considered the keepers of the traditions of the ancient collegia. The collegia's regulations were meticulous and their role was limited strictly to matters of the profession. The brotherhoods, for their part, had lost sight of their religious, spiritual, and charitable purposes. They allowed themselves to become too often preoccupied by profane concerns, which served to justify the many interdictions levied against them by royal or ecclesiastical authority. Finally, communities and brotherhoods had become individualistic and more or less local in scope. They no longer held that character of universalism that denoted the Roman collegia or the brotherhoods of the High Middle Ages. Only the compagnonnages remained partially faithful to traditions, ideals, and ancient rites, as well as to this quality of universalism. Their spread, however, was prohibited by the interdictions levied against them and by their activity, which was restricted to the defense of the interests of journeymen. The role they might have played in the transmission of initiatory values would go on to become the prerogative of Scotch and English corporative masonry. These forms not only preserved the ancient legacy but also revitalized and enriched it with contributions from other initiatory sources. Also, by removing masonry from its operative contingencies, it became possible for it to benefit not just masons but everyone whose ambition was to build the ideal temple of Wisdom and Beauty.

9

Builders Corporations in Italy, Germany, and Switzerland

Builders Corporations of Italy

The appearance and development of trade communities in Italy (known as *arti* in Italian, a word that beautifully expresses the medieval and Christian concept of work) were closely bound to the communal movement and its circumstances that were unique to this country.

With the establishment of feudalism, almost all Italian cities had fallen under the authority of the bishops. They were the first to acquire their freedom. The political process, however, was different from the communal movement in France, Flanders, and Great Britain. In these countries liberalization was, from the onset, due to the struggle of the bourgeoisie against the nobles, who often had the support of the king. In Italy, in the absence of any unified central authority, the source and form of communal institutions were first and foremost aristocratic. Transforming these communes into states, which they governed, provided nobles with the means to strengthen their political power. At a very early date, it is true—toward the end of the ninth century—the merchants, who had also become quite influential, had their own seats on the councils alongside the nobles. Toward the middle of the twelfth century, representatives of the arts also gained a council place.

Muratori places the origin of the Italian mastery associations on this side of the year 1100. During the first years of the twelfth century, one was mentioned as already being established in Brescia. It is difficult, though, to precisely date the appearance of these mastery associations. They were not all in existence at the same time and did not all share the same circumstances. In several regions where Roman influences survived, there was probably a continuity in which the collegia gradually transformed into scholoe, or scuole, and mastery associations. This is precisely what occurred in Ravenna, the capital of the Exarchat.

It was possible for mastery associations to attain power by peaceful means on a gradual basis, as was the case in Pistoie, Florence, and Pisa. In some areas, however, they prevailed through violence, as in Milan (1198) and Bologna (1228). Subsequent battles for influence took place between social classes or between noble families whose members sought to gain government positions as either consuls or potentates. In 1165, Emperor Frederic I Barbarossa, when entrusting the earldom of Verona to the count of Saint Boniface, also gave him full jurisdiction over all crafts and trades. Similarly, these professions were subject to the commands of the consuls and nobility in the statutes of Parma.[1] In the flourishing cities of Genoa and Venice, the form of power remained aristocratic and its authority remained in the hands of the patricians.[2]

We should note that this same Frederic Barbarossa, the emperor of Germany who was long at war with the Lombard cities, was finally defeated after many expeditions. Though generally speaking, the emperors, in their political claims to Italy, were in opposition to the sovereignty of the communes, their choice to side either with mastery associations against the nobility or the nobility against mastery associations depended on the circumstances.

The mastery associations were often divided into two categories: mastery associations of the higher arts and mastery associations of the lower arts. Their numbers expanded proportionally with the increased success of industry, leisure, and the multiplication of wants, and at the same time middle arts made their appearance. The mastery associations of the masons *(magistri lapidum, magistri muri, muratores)* were sometimes categorized with the inferior arts and sometimes with the higher ones.[3]

Thus in Florence there were twenty-one corporations divided into seven higher arts and fourteen lower arts. The first included judges and notaries, silk and wool merchants, bankers, doctors, apothecaries, and silk and wool manufacturers. The lower arts included butchers, cobblers, smiths, salt merchants or *regrattiers*, oil sellers, wine merchants, innkeepers, masons and stone carvers, locksmiths, breastplate merchants, leather merchants, wood sellers, bakers, and stocking makers.

Each of these arts had its own meetinghouse and elected syndics and consuls who held places of honor in official ceremonies. Each art also had its own color and its own banner or standard, which was carried at the front of processions.

The standard bearer of the Republic was chosen from among citizens belonging to the higher arts, while those who were inscribed in the lower arts furnished one fourth of the city's magistrates.

There are numerous traces of the builder mastery associations from the thirteenth and beginning of the fourteenth centuries. For instance, we find them mentioned in town and city statutes, such as the masons *(cementari)* of Milan, the magistri murorum of Parma and Plaisance,4 the muratores of Modena, and the magistri lapidum and lignaminis of Florence and Lucca. The Italian mastery associations took on the form of brotherhoods, which is to say they pursued both religious and charitable goals with the same intensity that characterized their pursuits of a more professional nature.

Among the oldest statutes of Italian builders' mastery associations are those of the Venice stone carvers, dating from 1317 and renewed in 1396. These statutes open with a prayer to the Very Holy Trinity and continue on to express a keen desire to contribute "to the glory of God and the glorious Virgin Mother Mary, who is our constant advocate." There is also evidence of the worship of the Four Holy Crowned Martyrs, protectors of the mastery associations.[5] This is quite possibly the earliest mention by builders of the individual worship of the Four Crowned Martyrs, a patronage mentioned in England at the end of the fourteenth century or the beginning of the fifteenth century and in the statutes of the German stonecutters from the sixteenth century. There were also guilds of the Four Crowned Martyrs in Flanders, notably in Brussels and Anvers, that consisted of masons, stonecutters, sculptors, and others.* Given the importance of these patrons to the builders, it is probably helpful to recall the legend of the four crowned martyrs. It varies according to version, but this is how it was recorded in *The Golden Legend:*

> The four crowned martyrs were Severus, Severianus, Carpoforus, and Victorinus, who, by the commandment of Diocletian, were beaten with plummets of lead unto the death. The names of whom could not be found, but after a long time they were shown by divine revelation, and it was established that their memory should be worshipped under the names of five other martyrs, that is to wit Claude, Castor, Symphorian, Nicostratus, and Simplician, which were martyred two years after the four crowned martyrs. And these martyrs knew all the craft of sculpture or of carving, and Diocletian would have constrained them to carve an idol, but they would not carve it, nor consent to do sacrifice to the idols. And then by the commandment of Diocletian they were put into tuns of lead all living, and cast into the sea about the year of our Lord two hundred four score and seven. And Melchiades, the pope, ordained these four saints to be honoured and to be called the four crowned martyrs before that their names were found.†

The feast day of the Four Crowned Martyrs is celebrated on November 8 and churches in some way dedicated to them can be found in a number of locations. There is a Church of the Quatro Santi Coronati in Rome and a depiction of the Four Crowned Martyrs can be

---

* C. Van Cauvenberghs, *La Corporation des Quatre Couronnés d'Anvers* (Anvers, 1889). Deserving special mention is the handsome sixteenth-century triptych that once graced either the corporative hall of the Craft of the Four Crowned Martyrs in Brussels or the altar of Saint Catherine Church in the Chapel of the Crowned Martyrs. Today it is housed in the Municipal Museum and is reproduced in P. du Colombier's book, *Les Chantiers des Cathedrales,* plates XXIV and XXV.

† Jacobus de Voraique, *The Golden Legend or Lives of the Saints,* ed. by F. S. Ellis (Edinburgh: T. and A. Constable / University Press, 1900). The 1942 French translation of this book reproduces an engraving that depicts the saints holding a mallet, rule, square, and prybar.

seen in the Cathedral of Pavia on the front of the monument to Saint Augustine. There they are carved in stone and each figure is named: Claude, Nicostratus, Symphorian, and Simplician (which are not the usual names of the Martyrs). They are holding a hammer, a compass, a chisel, and some other tools and the third figure is holding a label on which can be read "Martuor. Coronatorum." The same patronage of the Martyrs can be found in Sienna, Arezzo, Perugia, Florence, and Palermo in Sicily.

Development of mastery associations in Italy was considerably hampered by the extreme territorial divisions of the country, the political struggles that endured for centuries, and occupation of the country by foreign forces. During the sixteenth century, on the fringes of these mason corporations, academies were formed whose purpose was to emancipate art from the shackles of the association and assert the independence of artists. The most famous is the Accademia del Disegno, the Academy of Drawing, inaugurated in 1563 in Florence under the auspices of Cosmo di Medici. Open to sculptors, painters, and *amateurs* (emphasis mine), it was chiefly concerned with the sciences related to architecture and/or the art of drawing—sciences that art historian Eugene Müntz (Florence et la Toscane) described as "transcendent." This institution went on to become the Academy of Fine Arts, whose palace on Saint Mark's Square now houses some prestigious collections.

Later, when we discuss the birth of speculative Freemasonry, we will learn how these Italian academies indirectly influenced the English Lodges at the beginning of the seventeenth century.

Builders Corporations in Germany and Switzerland

The arts corporations in Germany attained their freedom later than those in Italy but followed their lead whenever possible in the development of their political power. Sometime after the first half of the thirteenth century, trade representatives were admitted into the municipal councils in, for example, Cologne (1259), Frankfurt am Main (1284), Fribourg (1293), and Magdeburg (1294).[6]

The builders communities in Germany are among the oldest. Their origins follow the same pattern as those in France: monastic associations first, followed by brotherhoods whose formation was prompted by the vast groups of craftsmen required to construct the cathedrals. The oldest of these brotherhoods, which were known as *Hütten* (lodges) after the name of the locations in which they held their meetings, is the one in Cologne, which was formed around the year 1250.* Hütten recognized the supremacy of large lodges called *Haupthütten* (principal lodges). In 1275, a veritable masonic congress met in Strasbourg to coordinate efforts toward the continuation of long-interrupted work on the cathedral. There the assembly formed a principal lodge and named Erwin von Steinbach as the head architect of construction and the master who held the chair (Meister vom Stuhl).[7]

In total, there were five principal lodges in the area including Germany and Switzerland. They were located in Cologne, Strasbourg, Vienna, Bern (then Zurich), and Magdebourg. Cologne was the first and foremost among them and the master builder of the cathedral there was recognized as the head of all the masters and workers of Lower Germany. Similarly, the person holding this position in Strasbourg was recognized as the head of all masters for Upper Germany. A central mastery association later established in Strasbourg disputed the primacy of Cologne on the basis that construction was less extensive there than in Strasbourg. The jurisdiction of this central association encompassed lodges from part of France, Hesse, Suavia, Thuringia, Franconia, and Bavaria. Subordinate to the principal lodge of Cologne were the workshops of Belgium and another part of France. The great lodge of Vienna governed the lodges of Austria, Hungary, and Styria, while those of the Swiss were subject to the grand lodge of Bern during the time the cathedral of that city was under construction, and then to that of Zurich when Bern's seat was transferred there in 1502. This principal lodge in Zurich, whose jurisdiction included all the Swiss Hütten, could turn to the Strasbourg brotherhood to resolve serious and tricky questions. The Saxon lodges, which in principle had recognized the supremacy of the grand lodge of Strasbourg, were later placed under the jurisdiction of the grand lodge of Magdebourg.[8]

---

* Findel claims seniority for the brotherhood that was created to build the cathedral of Magdebourg, whose construction began in 1211 (*Histoire de la Franc Maçonnerie*, vol. 1, 57). For interesting information on the Bauhütte, see Franz Bziha's notes published in *Le Symbolisme*, no. 375 and 376, June–September, 1966.

These five grand lodges each held independent and sovereign jurisdiction, and judged, with no possibility of appeal, all cases brought
before them in accordance with their organization's statutes. These
ancient statutes were revised on April 25, 1459, by the Ratisbonne
Assembly under the title "Statutes and Regulations of the Brotherhood
of Stonecutters." The foundations for the revision had been cast in a
preparatory meeting held in Strasbourg in 1452 and the resulting
statutes were subsequently endorsed by Emperor Maximilian in 1498
and confirmed by Charles Quint in 1520 and Ferdinand I in 1588. The
1459 assembly, held in Ratisbonne, the seat of the German Diet, was convoked by Jobs Dotzinger, master builder of the Strasbourg Cathedral.
Those gathered there also dealt with general business concerning architecture and the brotherhood.[9]

The signatures affixed to the revised statutes indicate that the
lodges of northern Germany were not represented in Strasbourg or
Ratisbonne. These lodges added their voice of support to the revision at
an assembly held in Torgau in 1462 by crafting ordinances that were
described simply as reproductions of the Strasbourg statutes established
on the ancient foundations instituted "by the Holy Martyrs crowned in
the honor and glory of the Holy Trinity and Mary Queen of Heaven."[10]

A second masonic assembly, also convoked by the Grand Lodge of
Strasbourg, was held in Ratisbonne in 1464. Along with discussing general lodge business, including reports on buildings then under construction, the assembly gave more precise definition to the rights and
attributions of the four existing grand lodges (in Cologne, Strasbourg,
Vienna, and Bern) and named the master builder Konrad Kuhn to the
high mastery association of Cologne.

In 1469, the grand lodge of Strasbourg convoked a new assembly,
this time in Spire. According to Rebold, the objectives of this congress
were as follows: 1. To share information concerning the status of all completed religious buildings or of those still being built and those whose
completion had been halted; 2. To study the situation of the brotherhood
in England, the Gallic lands, Lombardy, and Germany (which underscores the international nature of the craft); and 3. To examine relationships between the different lodges and their attributions.

In 1535, the bishop of Cologne, Herman, convoked a masonic

assembly in that city to coordinate on measures that should be taken relative to accusations and the dangers threatening free masons. The result would have been a kind of charter, dated June 24, 1535, written in Latin, drawn with masonic characters, and addressed in the form of a circular by the Chosen Masters of the Order of Saint John to all the lodges of their society.[11] But this document would not be produced until 1819 by Prince Frederic of Nassau, who had in mind a reformation of Dutch and Belgian Freemasonry, for which he was the grand master. The resulting charter, known as the Cologne Charter, did, however, indicate the existence of a masonic hierarchy of five grades (apprentice, journeyman, master, chosen master, sublime master) and was meant to serve the prince as the basis for the reforms he contemplated.* It would have been signed by nineteen illustrious individuals such as Coligny, Bruce, Falk, Melanchton, Virieux, and Stanhope. These signatories were all present there as delegates from the lodges of London, Edinborough, Vienna, Amsterdam, Paris, Lyon, Frankfurt, Hamburg, and other cities. They decried the imputations of which masonry stood accused, notably the accusation of seeking to reestablish the Templar Order. They believed it necessary to reveal the origin and purpose of masonry, so that subsequently, when better circumstances prevailed, it could be reconstructed after having been forced to suspend its work on the original foundations of its institution. They specified that masonic society was Christianity's contemporary, and that in the beginning it was known by the name of the Brothers of John. They also explicity stated that nothing indicates that they may have been known under any other name prior to 1440, the year in which they took on the title of the Brotherhood of Free Masons, mainly in the Flemish city of Valenciennes because it was during that time that hospices began to be constructed in Hainaut on behalf of the brothers of this order to care for the poor who had been afflicted with Saint Anthony's Fire.

The signatories went on to list the two guiding principles for all the brothers' activities: "Love and cherish all men as if they were your

---

* This is enough of an anachronism to cast doubt on the charter, unless it was inserted later. It should be added that antiquarian scholars intended to examine the original document produced by Frederic of Nassau. Unfortunately, whatever conclusions they may have reached were never made public and no one knows what became of the document.

brothers and kin; render unto Caesar that which is Caesar's and render unto God that which is God's." It was also noted that the brothers should celebrate once a year the memory of Saint John, the patron of their society, and that this order was governed by a single, universal leader while the various *magisteres* that it was composed of were governed by several grand masters, according to the position and needs of the country.

In 1563, the grand lodge of Strasbourg convoked an important assembly in Basel. This congress endorsed the statutes that had been revised by a commission appointed by the grand lodge of Strasbourg. These statutes, dated Saint Michael, 1563, were printed that same year.[12]

The last large masonic assembly, also convoked by the Grand Lodge of Strasbourg, appears to have been held in Strasbourg in 1564. Its purpose was to definitively iron out all points of contention between the different lodges. The decision was made there that future difficulties would be subjected directly to the grand lodge for final jusgement with no recourse to appeal.[13]

The Statutes of the Stonecutters

The ancient statutes of the Brotherhood of Stonecutters *(Steinmetzen Brüderschaft)* dating from 1459 were not, apparently, the first; there is a good possibility that yet older ones exist. As we have seen, they were revised several times and endorsed by the emperors. Those published in 1563 were the final ones.

The rules began thus:[14] "In the name of the Father, the Son, and the Holy Ghost, and the glorious Mother Mary, and also the Four Crowned Martyrs, their blessed servants remembered eternally." Findel writes that before 1440, the members of the original Strasbourg laborers society bore the name of the brothers of Saint John. He adds that Saint John the Precursor, along with the Four Crowned Martyrs, had always been the special patron saint and protector of the association.

Overall, the statutes of the German stonecutters provide a gripping description of Freemasonry's essential characteristics:

- The associates were divided into masters, journeymen, and apprentices.
- The governance of the organization was entrusted to certain leaders.
- The profane was excluded.
- Privileges extended to the sons of masters.
- Their were conditions governing acceptance into the organization.
- The principals of fraternal equality and mutual aid were primary.
- Procedures were established for specific jurisdiction and how lodge judgments would be handed down.
- Procedures were established for how meetings would be opened and closed.
- There were established initiation rites and forms of greeting *(Gruss)* and customs to be observed at banquets.
- There was a test that foreign brothers were required to undergo.

The guarantee of secrecy was assured by the way brothers greeted one another as well as by how they shook hands *(Schenk)*, although *Schenk* appears instead to designate feast toasts. The ancient statutes make no mention of a "password." The sole time there is any reference to a password is in the rules of the Halberstadt masons, which were filed before the reigning prince in 1693: "The master will tell the worker that he has been welcomed into the order and that he should lock within his heart, at the price of his soul's salvation, the words *(Wörter)* that have been entrusted to him and that by no means will he let anyone else know them, save an honest mason, under penalty of being disbarred from the craft."[15]

The organization did not pursue only professional and social goals. Like the French brotherhoods, it included religious concerns among its objectives:

No laborer or master shall be allowed admission into the order who does not approach the Holy Sacrament once a year and who does not observe the Christian law. If someone who has been admitted into the association refuses to fulfill this precept, may no master form a bond with him and may no journeyman render him assistance until he has renounced his evil habits and been punished by the association. No laborer or master shall bestow his favor on a journeyman who does not go annually to confession and to the Holy Sacrament, in conformance with Christian precept . . .

On the news of the death of an associate [the master] will celebrate a Mass for the comfort of the recently departed soul, and thoses masters and journeymen who are then present will attend this pious ceremony.

The statutes established at Ratisbonne ordered the celebration of four Masses during the year, including the feast day of the Throne of Saint Peter. The tax imposed for this purpose was two large sous for every work performed by the masters and a denier a week for the journeymen. The statutes also prescribed fasts, vigils, and Masses to be celebrated in a chapel in Strasbourg dedicated to the Virgin. The building of churches was to be performed by the associates, by virtue of the same rules, for "the enlargement of divine worship and the salvation of their souls."

The Decline of the German Brotherhoods

The mastery associations in Germany never attained the same level of power that their medieval Italian counterparts did. Their efforts were sometimes opposed by the cities' aristocrats, sometimes by the feudal lords, and sometimes by the emperor himself. The Burgave of Strasbourg had the right to place the masters who headed the arts corporations. In Worms all such associations were suppressed in 1233, with the exception of those of the coin minters and the furriers. The statute handed down by Frederic II to the inhabitants of Goslar in 1219 expressly forbade mastery associations. A decree issued in 1232 by this same emperor from Ravenna banned associations throughout the empire. In 1378, Charles IV put a stop to the training and activities of the arts brotherhoods of Minden, which prompted no intervention by the Episcopal authorities; this decree was later confirmed by Charles V. In all these ordinances no exception was made in favor of the building mastery associations; consequently they were forced to submit, like the others, to temporary or local abeyance, for all these interdictions were generally affairs of circumstance.

In sixteenth-century Germany and Switzerland, the sacrifices made by the populace to erect their churches, coupled with the blatant abuses commited by the clergy and the popes, had chilled their religious fervor, shaken their faith, and made it impossible to complete those churches still under construction. It was at this point that Luther's reformation occurred, which weakened the very foundations of papal authority and halted the construction of the great monuments of Catholic worship. This delivered a mortal blow to the masonic corporations here. By and large, they were greatly dispersed and their remnants were forced to join forces with the mastery associations of the towns' own trades and crafts guilds.

In 1522, the brotherhood in Switzerland was mixed up in matters that were foreign to the building craft, leading to an order for its grand master, Stephan Rülzislofer of Zurich, to appear before the Diet. Because he failed to appear to defend himself, the brotherhood was suppressed throughout the territory of the Heovetic Confederations.[16]

In Germany, those lodges that had not been formally dissolved remained isolated under the guidance of their respective great lodges. After Alsace was made part of France under Louis VIV, the German princes sought to impose limits on the French king's influence in Germany. It was natural that an association whose members were subject to the jurisdiction of French authority—the grand lodge of Strasbourg—would catch their eye. Accordingly, an arret issued by the Diet in March 16, 1707, forbade German lodges from maintaining any relationship with the grand lodge of Strasbourg. The organization of a grand lodge of Germany failed to be realized. Incorrect intelligence and complaints prompted an edict on August 16, 1731, commanding that the grand lodges must henceforth cease being considered in that capacity. In the future, there was no longer to be any distincton between them and the secondary lodges and judgment of any trade or organization disagreement was to be deferred to civil tribunals.[17]

We should end by noting that in Germany, as in France, the initiatory traditions of the builders survived only in the compagnonnages, albeit in a form that was distorted to defend professional or class interests.

10

The Corporative Masonry of Great Britain

I t is in Anglo-Saxon masonry where we witness the birth of modern speculative Freemasonry. While the tradition was dying out on the continent, British masonry was up to the task of transmitting the ancient legacy. We have now looked at the line of descent: from Roman collegia to the Culdees to the Benedictine monks and monastic associations to brotherhoods and guilds. The last of these—the guilds—which first appeared in the northern countries, Normandy, and England, offered an instant legal framework for trade organizations.

The first advantage offered by the guild was that it presented both the professional character of French trade organizations and the pious and charitable nature of brotherhoods. Second, events in Great Britain favored its development. Not only were British guilds spared the strict oversight that French kings strove to impose on the trades, but also they were spared the kinds of restrictions and interdictions that struck the brotherhoods. To the contrary, guilds were encouraged by both royal power and the Church of England. The climate was therefore propitious for maintaining tradition within the guild. According to the law of history, because it remained alive, this tradition was structurally enriched over the course of centuries. Masonry, which had taken the name Freemasonry, now received its principal contribution from Hermeticists and the Rosicrucian Order after it had ceased being purely operative and accepted speculative members in large numbers. We will now take a look at the characteristics and evolution of the British version of operative freemasonry.

The Trade Guilds and Mysteries of Great Britain

Guilds *(ghilds)* were born and grew in Great Britain for the same reasons that prompted this development on the Continent. They were primarily tied to the conquest and defense of municipal franchises.

The first guilds were those of the merchants, which were made up of people of the bourgeois class, all of whom were expected to be members. They controlled commerce and the city insofar as they protected its inhabitants commercially. But over time, a profound change took place. These guilds gradually became aristocracies whose membership was hereditary. At this same time the number of inhabitants of the city was growing due to a constant influx of artisans. Neither villains or serfs, they had been either emancipated or had fled their masters and had dwelled in cities long enough so that their freedom had become a right. Being unable to obtain admission into the merchant guilds, they formed their own craft guilds. Despite the resistance offered by the merchants, these new guilds developed and grew so effectively that by 1735 in London, the city's administration had been transferred from a municipal assembly to that of professional associations, including, notably, the Company of the Masons. At this point no one could benefit from the freedoms offered by the city without being a member of one of these associations that were then known as mysteries.[1]

The word *mysteries,* borrowed from the French in the Norman era, denoted "craft" in old English. Hence the archaic expression *arts and mysteries,* meaning arts and crafts. Etymologically speaking, there was initially confusion among the meanings of the word *ministerium* (a variant of *mistère,* from the twelfth century), meaning "function" or "service" in Latin, *largo sensu,* meaning "craft," and *mysterium,* meaning "religious mystery."

It should be remembered that during the Middle Ages the theater was first religious and that it emerged almost imperceptibly from the liturgy. Starting in some Benedictine abbeys in the ninth century, various episodes from the Passion and Christ's Resurrection were staged in order to more effectively instruct and edify an illiterate populace. The art of stone completed the work of the theater—the theater of the mystery plays was reflected in and finalized by the cathedral—and from this the word *mystery* was born. Etymologically, it summoned up antiquity and the most widespread and deeply rooted rites of ancient times.

The gospel was first transposed into a spectacle by putting to work the magnificent and evocative dramatic resources held in this scripture. This made it possible to present on the stage all the biblical characters who theologians of the time considered to be forerunners of Christ. Through these extensions, the mystery became more and more popular in nature while at the same time recalling the liturgy closest to it.

It is not out of the question that craftsmen, whose brotherhoods and corporations multiplied the mysteries, began to cull from the spectacle both an exoteric meaning—the Passion, literally speaking—and an esoteric meaning related to the trade's initiation rites and their connection to Christ's Passion through the themes of purification, death and resurrection, and the recollection and remnants of the ancient mysteries.

In England these developments took place with the support and instruction of the priesthood and allow us to presume a certain Christianization of a tradition. There were "miracle theaters" that were staged every year by crafts corporations in several cities: Coventry, Chester (1327), York (1350), and Newcastle. We can recall, however, that in France the Parliament of Paris and the Church banned the mysteries during the sixteenth century. While they had been very popular and imbued with faith during earlier centuries, it was determined that they had become incomprehensible and were debasing their original models.

When we turn our discussion to esotericism, however, we shall see that this philosophy, rather than involving impious or hidden secrets or meanings, concerns instead a symbolism that was accepted as pure and perfectly orthodox during the Middle Ages, when it was even even professed by the Church.

The proof of the transmission of these rites in their iniatory and

Christian sense is perhaps discernable in John Pennel's book, *The Constitution of the Free-Masons,* published in Dublin in 1730. For the reception of a journeyman, we find in the invocation that opens the lodge the following characteristic phrases: "We beseech your blessing, O Lord, on our present enterprise . . . Grace [our new brother] with your divine wisdom so that he may be capable of comprehending, by means of the secrets of Masonry, the mysteries of piety and Christianity."

Organization of the English Guilds

Each profession had its guild or mystery in every large city of fourteenth century England. These groups were also known as companies and fraternities. (The word *corporation* was not used during the Middle Ages.) Each guild established ordinances to regulate working hours and the details governing admission into the organization. Some obliged members to make periodic contributions to a common fund and to take part in certain religious ceremonies or feasts and celebrations, such as the public stagings of mysteries.

The Christian spirit of the guilds can be seen in the clauses concerning the reciprocal assistance that members owed each other. All risks and accidents that might occur in life, all cases where aid might be necessary—even those that might befall a departure on a pilgrimage—were anticipated by the statutes.

A solemn oath preceded acceptance into a guild, each of which had a rule calling upon its craftsmen to refrain from revealing the affairs of the organization. Guild members frequently wore special dress and referred to each other as brother and sister. They had the right to establish their statutes with no need of a charter or any other form of permission from the authorities, but they nevertheless had to obtain a license of mainmort when they sought to take possession of lands, which was often the case. In 1389 all guilds filed their ordinances, customs, and deeds and as a result, a great many of these can be found today in the London Public Archives.

The principal officer of the guild was the master, but there were also wardens and sometimes assistants or a committee made up of former officers. Guild members were divided into apprentices, day laborers, and free men. The term *master* was also used to designate any free man who took on an apprentice.

Here we pause for consideration of the term *free man.* It is probably more effective for our purposes to use the ancient French term *franc homme,* with its connotations that we have already established: This is the franc hons who is neither a serf nor villain but has become a free bourgeois, independent of any lord. Going further along these lines, we come upon the free man craftsman called a *free burgess,* which comes from franc bourgeois and means a bourgeois who by feudal law "neither owes nor pays the lord anything for the right to his bourgeois status and is thus free and clear of him."

The sole members of the guild who could become free men were those whose apprenticehip had been satisfactory and who had fulfilled the obligations of their contracts. A penalty was imposed upon anyone who took on a young man and taught him the craft without making him undergo the apprentice stage. A specific ceremony was performed during corporation meetings for the admission of a new apprentice. It was forbidden for any master to take on an apprentice of servile status.

Those who knew the craft but had not undergone the obligatory stages were called day laborers or servants; free men could hire them on condition they their names were inscribed in the company's records. Furthermore, these day laborers could find employment only from a free man. In the Exeter stonecutter guild, men from this class of worker called themselves free cutters. The free men who sought to hire such workers had to acquire a special right of admission for them, and this admission became the occasion for a special ceremony. Day laborers had the right to designate supervisors as their representatives in certain cases. However, these supervisors were not on equal footing with free men.

Finally, there were restrictions concerning the number of servants or apprentices a free man could take on. Sometimes he was not allowed to have any if he himself did not hold a certain position.

The Origin of English Craft Freemasonry

Contrary to what took place in associations in France, in England there was no duplication of duties between the professional association and the brotherhood responsible for religious practices. The guild assumed responsibility for both kinds of duties. Of course, as was the case throughout medieval Christian Europe, the Church kept its hand on the trades and by virtue of this had its own place in the guild. A priest would thus perform the duties of chaplain.

This should not lead us to believe, however, that the guild enjoyed a kind of monopoly and that there were not, outside its walls, autonomous and even rival brotherhoods that were simultaneously professional, religious, and charitable organizations, and that also served as keepers—and sometimes better ones—of the tradition.

In all of this we should not overlook one important fact: During the Middle Ages Great Britain, like the countries of the continent, was subject to feudal law, which was tangibly identical everywhere. All cities freed themselves from their manorial bonds under the same conditions and with the same measures. The guilds, which were the essential cogs in this process, benefited only from the rights and franchises that had been granted to them, and these applied only within the limits of their respective cities.

As in other countries, things went differently for the professional brotherhoods that remained tied to the domain and suzerainty of the religious orders that held all the rights to administer justice. This was the case in the jurisdictional areas of the Benedictine abbeys and the Templar commanderies. The generally extensive franchises that the artisans of these brotherhoods enjoyed extended to all the dependent territories of the suzerain orders and all places where the talents of these artisans earned them summons. This fact is of capital importance in the formation of freemasonry.

There are several documents in England that are quite important to the study of operative masonry but, contrary to what has been previously thought, do not have bearing on modern Freemasonry: In 1212, the court of taxes in London alludes to a company of *cementarii* (masons) and *sculptores lapidum liberorum* (sculptors in free stone)[2] and in the Workers Statute issued in 1351, which was composed in French, there is mention of *mestre mason de franche pere* [master mason of free stone].

Some have deduced from these texts that the term *freemason* may have originally designated a sculptor of stone (*sculptores* in Latin or *latomos* in Greek) working *free stone*, which is to say stone that can easily be carved by hammer and chisel, as opposed to *rough stone* or hard stone. Later, when the decadence of Gothic art had brought about the gradual disappearence of free-stone sculptors, the term *freemason* would have been commingled with *roughmason*, but the first name prevailed. This etymology, which Robert Freke Gould also found dubious, cannot be supported. The word *free* or *franc* does not apply to the craftsman working the stone but to the stone of pure and good quality that is being worked.

In fact, the first use of the term *freemason* appeared in 1376 in the license for the franchise of the Company of Masons of London, where it was used in definition of its members. Its existence should go back to a much earlier time though (the first half of the thirteenth century) and its meaning, applied to the masons belonging to the guild, would have evolved etymologically from its French origins. In 1377 William Humbervyle, designated by the title *magister operis* and *free master mason*, was hired by Merton College, Oxford. A *mason free* appears in the Pershore records of 1381. In 1391, in a license composed in Latin by the archbishop of Canterbury, there is reference to the use of twenty-four *lathomos vocatos ffremaceons,* as opposed to *lathomos vocatos ligiers,* which denotes *liges,* or vassals.

D. Knoop and G. P. Jones[3] also cite fourteenth- and fifteenth-century texts where there is mention together of *freemasons, masouns hewers, masoun setters* [stone cutters], and *masoun legers* [stone setters]. It is these legers with whom they relate the ligiers cited above. It appears their intention is to show the professional distinctions between the first group—freemasons—and the others. In actuality, though, by opposing these terms in this way, the authors introduce an element of confusion to the names of these workers relative to their status and their legal position within their specialization and type of work. It is a bit like referring today to "unionized masons" in one part of a text and in another "cement layers" and "tilers" in such a way that each term appears opposed to another.

Along with this misleading opposition, we should be wary of etymologies. For instance, the word *layer*, from *to lay* or *lay,* could mean someone who lays stone or someone of secular status. The word *setter* could refer to a stonecutter or the member of a set or association, such as a guild. The lay mason dependent upon a guild and subsequently a ligier, lige, or vassal, could then be opposed to the freemason, who is free because of his connection to the Church.

The 1396 text of the archbishop of Canterbury shows that the term *ffremaceons* was then recognized as technically English with no Latin equivalent. It is quite likely that it also confirms that the term *franc maçonnerie* is to be understood as similar to francs métiers, artisans who were not only free but enjoyed certain franchises and exemptions. Originally, these franchises were not the property of the trade itself but of the craftsman's domicile. Only the Benedictines, and especially the Templars, assured trade franchises to everyone throughout the whole of their domains. Recall that the term *franc métier* and, consequently, *franc-maçon* were likely born in the era that witnessed the formation of trade communities, guilds, and brotherhoods. So whereas some had only those rights—limited for *ratione materiae* and *ratione loci*—that their sovereign lords had the power to grant them, others who had emerged from the monastic associations of the Benedictine abbeys, and especially the Templar commanderies from the time they were at the pinnacle of their power, benefited from the largest franchises in the most extensive territories.

Eventually, royal power, inspired by the example set by the religious orders and by the desire to secure the guilds' political support, granted charters and franchises to certain trades. It is helpful here to recall the intelligence agents the English kings kept in the guilds and brotherhoods of Normandy, Flanders, Guyenne, and in Paris itself during their endless wars against the kings of France. It was to the advantage of these kings to support the power and freedom of these professional associations—and it is now easier to understand the reason for the diametrically opposed policy of the French kings regarding them.

The privileges granted by the king to guilds ensured these organizations independence from the framework of cities and allowed them at times to include the profession in all its locations thoughout the entire kingdom. This was the case for the masons of York and London, who became freemasons and whose trade name freemasonry would eventually include the entire masonic craft.

This evolution took shape quickly and is quite visible in the late-fourteenth-century texts cited above. The term *freemason* applied in 1376 to the masons of the Company of London is indicative of the generalization of the term. On the other hand, the license of the archbishop of Canterbury still clearly shows that distinctions existed between the freemason, in the strict sense of the word, and the ordinary vassal mason *(lathomos)*.

Three centuries later a manuscript of the old charters of the masons, the *Melrose Manuscript* dating from 1674, provides the definitive status of the terminology used. The frequently used expression *friemason* is presented as being synonymous with the expression *freeman mason* (master mason) and that of *frie men* with *freemasons*.[4] This was now the common application of the generic term *freeman* or *free burgess* that was used in guilds' statutes to designate masters.

The Statutes of the Masons

English authors, notably Robert Freke Gould, have believed the founding of the Company of the Masons of London could be established around the year 1220. The oldest statutes that have come down to us, however, are the *Ordinance of Workers* and the *Statute of Workers*, which date respectively from 1349 and 1351. These set a maximum salary rate for all kinds of workers, including masons. The statute, written in French, mentions *"un mestre mason de franche-père,"* who draws a higher salary than an ordinary mason.

The Ordinances of the Masons of York (1352) appeared during that same time and was composed in Latin: *Ordinacio facto pro cementariis et ceteris operatis fabrico*. These were revised in 1370 (in a text written in Old English) and in 1409 (in Latin).[5] They concern the construction of the cathedral of Saint Paul, regulating work (referring to an Inspector of the Work) and insisting on respect for customs. They also mention as a meeting place the *logium fabricoe* (craftsmen's lodge) and insist on the need for an oath of loyalty and reliability. The rule in fact mandated a mason *"to swear on the Bible* that he would sincerely and actively work to the best of his ability, without any deceit or secrecy whatsoever, and that he would hold and observe all points of the law thus laid down." Unless this reference was inserted into the text at a later date, it leads to the conclusion that, just like those who followed the *Livre des Métiers* in Paris, the then-Catholic English masons required an oath on the Bible, a point we shall revisit.

Another document, dated February 2, 1356 and known as the *Articles of London,* is a complete, professional, masonic instructional composed in French. The eight rules it lists stipulate that the duration of the apprenticeship period is seven years and that it is the master's responsibility to see that apprentices are justly paid. It also states that infractions are liable to incur penalties involving fines and imprisonment.[6]

One final document of statutes that we will consider from this time is the *Ordinances of the Norwich Carpenters' Guild* (1375), which contains a variety of social and religious directives that all masons were subject to equally. It opens with a plea for protection addressed to the Very Holy Trinity and a substantial invocation to God and all the saints. One of the directives it contains deserves particular emphasis here: that which commands the brothers *and sisters* to gather together on the Saturday following Ascension to give prayers in honor of the Holy Trinity and in favor of the Holy Church, "for the peace and union of the country and for the peaceful repose of the souls of the departed, not only those of brothers and sisters, but those of friends and of all Christians."[7] The mention of sisters here proves that women were accepted as members into the builders associations, an important fact given that modern Anglo-Saxon Freemasonry regards the admission of women with hostility. We should also note that at the end of the seventeenth century, English Freemasonry, which was speculative at this time, still continued to admit women members. Proof of this can be found in the 1693 *Statutes of the Lodge of York.* Here we read: "Hee or shee who would be made a mason, lays their hands upon the Book, [the Bible] and then Instructions are given."*

---

* *Hiram* (May-July 1908). It has been noted that this text contains the original Latin *ille vel illi* (he, singular and plural), words that were incorrectly translated as *Hee or Shee.* See A. Mellor, *Les Grands Problèmes de la Franc-Maçonnerie d'aujourd'hui* (Paris: Belfond, 1971), 108. But is this translation an error or rather an evolutionary translation accepted by custom at that time, with the original Latin reflecting to an earlier time?

The two most important ancient documents on operative freemasonry itself, both of which are now housed in the British Museum, are the *Masonic Poem* and the *Cooke Manuscript*. The *Masonic Poem,* also known as the *Royal Manuscript (Regius)* or the *Halliwell Manuscript,* from the name of its first publisher, dates from around 1390–1400.[8] This poem, 794 verses of rhyming couplets composed in Old English, shows clearly that the mysteries of the brotherhood were practiced in fourteenth-century England. Numerous clues allow us to attribute the work to a priest who had knowledge of various documents related to the history of the organization. He may have held the role of chaplain or assumed the duties of the brotherhood's secretary or, most likely, both in an era when people who knew how to read and write were rare.

Verses 143–46 seem to show that freemasonry was even then accepting members who were not artisans of that craft.

> *By olde tyme wryten y fynde*
> *That the prenes schulde be of gentyl kynde;*
> *And so symtyme grete lordys blod*
> *Toke thys gemetry, that ys ful good.*
> *(By old time written I find*
> *That the 'prentice should be of gentle kind;*
> *And so sometime, great lords' blood*
> *Took this geometry that is full good.)*

The *Masonic Poem* is divided into nine sections. The first concerns the legendary history of freemasonry (86 verses); the second is fifteen articles related to corporate labor (173 verses); the third consists of fifteen articles concerning the constitutions and underscores the fact that the order is religious and moral (209 verses). We should note that the *articulus quartus* [fourth article] and the *tertius punctus* [final point] mention the lodge *(logge).* The fourth section of the poem provides the procedure of the annual general assembly (25 verses); the fifth presents the legend of the Four Crowned Martyrs, the protectors of the Order (37 verses);* the

---

* The legend of the Four Crowned Martyrs also entered England at a very early time. It is said that a church of the Four Martyrs was built in Canterbury in 597 (Gould, *A Concise History of Freemasonry,* 238).

sixth concerns the construction of the Tower of Babel (33 verses); the seventh discusses the liberal arts (19 verses); the eighth dwells on religious instructions (111 verses), and the ninth section is an outline of expected social graces and civility (101 verses).

The *Cooke Manuscript* dates from 1410–1420 but is a transcription of a compilation that was at least a century older. It is divided into two parts. The first, consisting of nineteen articles, is a history of geometry and architecture. The second is a "book of duties," including an historical introduction; nine articles governing the organization of labor, which were allegedly promulgated at a general assembly that took place during the time of King Athelstan; nine counsels of a moral and religious nature; and four rules concerning the social life of masons. The word *speculative* actually appears in this document: "the son of King Athelstan was a true speculative master." The *Cooke Manuscript* served as the foundation for the work of George Payne, the second grand master of the grand lodge of London, who ensured that this organization adopted a first rule to Saint John in 1721. It also appears to have been the principal source from which Anderson drew his *Book of Constitutions.*

In addition to the *Masonic Poem (Cooke Manuscript),* we also have the texts of old charters and statutes concerning corporative Masonry. There are a great many versions of these, which are known as old charges, and none of them dates earlier than the end of the sixteenth century,[9] yet their language seems to indicate that they are copies of much older documents. The most significant Masonic archives and documents were destroyed in an auto-dafé initiated by Désaguliers, grand master of the Grand Lodge of London, on June 24, 1719. The motives for this destruction are still unknown.

The oldest of these charges are those known as *Grand Lodge Manuscript no. 1,* kept at the Grand United Lodge of England, which dates from 1583, and the *Lansdowne Manuscript,* which goes back to the second half of the sixteenth century. The last to convey some important additions was the document known as *Harlejan 1942,* which dates from approximately the mid-seventeenth century. We should also mention the two *Sloane Manuscripts* (1646 and 1649), the William Watson version (1687),* the four manuscripts from the old Lodge of Dumfries (1675–1710),[10] and again, the *Melrose Manuscript* (1674).

The Legendary History of Freemasonry

All the ancient charters, despite their various distinguishing features, follow the same general outline. They open with an invocation to the Trinity and more or less continue as follows: "Good Breathren and Fellows, our purpose is to tell you how and in what manner this worthy craft of masonry was first begun." A memorandum declaring that geometry is the oldest of the sciences and the greatest of the seven liberal arts follows this. These are the essential points it covers:[11] After the Flood, Hermes found one of two pillars† in which the scriptures containing all the sciences had been hidden. He absorbed all the knowledge that he rediscovered, taught it to humanity, and became the father of all sages.

The legend goes on to state that Nimrod (or Nimroth), king of Babylon, provided his masons with a "rule" stating that they should be loyal to each other and love each other. It is said that he also gave them two other rules concerning their science, though it is not known what these were.

The next major figure in the narrative was Abraham. He left his native region on the Euphrates River for Egypt, where he taught the Egyptians the seven sciences. One of his students was Euclid. During this time, the nobility were giving birth to so many children that they were at a loss as to how to find uses for all of them. It was Euclid who, with the king's permission, taught the noble children geometry (and it was during this era that this science was given its name) and then saw to it that they built temples, churches, and castles. Euclid also granted his masons a charge or license stating a number of directives, among

---

* In a history of Staffordshire published in 1686, Dr. Plott included a history of the freemasons. The legendary story he recounts is clearly based on a version of the ancient charters that closely corresponds to William Watson's document, which is written in the style of English that was commonly used at the end of the fifteenth century.

† According to the *Cooke Manuscript*, Pythagoras found the second pillar after the Flood.

them that the masons owed the king their loyalty, that they should render assistance to each other and call one another "brother," that they should deserve their wages, and that they should designate the most skilled among them as director of the work and call him "master." Finally, Euclid ordered his masons to hold an annual assembly.

The legend next speaks of David, who loved and cherished the masons and gave them licenses. His son, Solomon, gathered together 80,000 masons, including 1,000 masters, and finished the construction of the Temple. Hiram, king of Tyre, who greatly loved Solomon, provided him with the wood he needed for the construction and sent him an artist who was the very spirit of wisdom. This man's mother was of the Nephtali tribe and his father was a man of Tyre, and his name was also Hiram. (Some versions of the story describe him as the son of King Hiram; others give his name as Amon or Aymon.) There had been no one like him in the world before his time. A master mason of great nobility and refined knowledge, Hiram was master of the construction, all the builders of the Temple, and all the carved and sculpted works in the Temple and the surrounding area.

The legend then leaps ahead several centuries and recounts how Namus Graecus,* who had taken part in the building of Solomon's Temple, introduced masonry into France by teaching it to Charles Martel, who then instructed the men of France in its mysteries.† The tale then arrives at Saint Alban, the patron saint of masons, who granted them a personal charter.‡ Subsequently, masonry suffered from a series of wars until the era of King Athelstan, who greatly esteemed the masons, and his son Edwin, who himself became a mason. It was Edwin who issued the Charges of the Masons during an Assembly held in York in 926. At this point the story abruptly comes to a halt.

This briefly describes the legend that was reproduced, with different

---

* It should be noted that this name simply replaces a Greek name that a former copier was unable to decipher. For that reason we do not know which historical figure this might be.

† We have already discussed the grounds on which this legendary role attributed to Charles Martel is resting and how firm it might be.

‡ The *Cooke Manuscript* also mentions a Saint Amphibal, who converted Saint Alban.

variants and details, by the ancient charters and can be found in the *Masonic Poem (Regius Manuscript)*, the *Cooke Manuscript*, and so forth. There is no need to point out its anachronisms and historical fantasies; these in no way detract from its importance from an esoteric point of view.

It is important to note the abrupt ending of the legend with the Congress of York in 926 when all the existing versions of the ancient charges are dated to after the end of the fourteenth century. Why was there no effort made by the compilers to update the legend, at least to the year 1400? We have to assume that either the original legend was drawn up shortly after the last event it mentions, which is to say around 926, and was then copied by craftsmen who gave no thought to any continuation; or that it was the result of a later compilation by some writer who had a special reason for stopping the story at the time of Athelstan and Edwin.

The first assumption is not supportable. Historically, it is impossible to speak of a corporation or crafts guild from the beginning of the tenth century. The mention of Euclid in almost all of these texts, however, gives us a means to set the earliest possible date on which the legend was crafted. The works of Euclid were most likely completely unknown in England before they were introduced there by Adelard of Bath in 1130.[12]

In favor of the second hypothesis, we have the fact that in 1389 Richard II requested that the corporations file their statutes, indicate the origins of their formation, and provide an inventory of their property. It was completely in a corporation's interest to produce a charter because it would strengthen its position within the city and could serve to show its seniority. It was also advantageous to trace seniority back to Athelstan, who was the last Angle king and was both the first and the last to hold uncontested domain over his entire kingdom. He was also, as noted earlier, a great legislator, and he granted various charters to certain cities that referred to guilds that, if not professional, were at least religious.

The Masons' Obligations

After the conclusion of the legendary history, the ancient charters listed the obligations imposed upon the brothers, indicating that they had been agreed upon by several assemblies of masters and journeymen. These rules consisted of a varying number of general charges followed by a series of special obligations.

Concerning these obligations, it helps to examine first the requirements that were of a religious nature. All of these documents stress the profoundly Catholic nature of the fraternity: "The mason's first duty is to be faithful to God and the Holy Church, and to flee from heresy and error"; "Whosoever exercises the art of masonry should honor God and his Church. Whosoever wishes to learn this art, must first and foremost love God, the Holy Church, and all the saints"; "Each of its members humbly beseeches All-powerful God and his mother, the gentle Virgin, for the grace of being faithful to his duties." The statutes also require that the feasts ordained by the Church be sanctified. They also stress that in order for each worker to behave decently, all must observe certain rules, which are described in meticulous detail.

Following the obligations, the ancient charters provide a clue concerning the oath of the "new men who have not yet been received," by which are likely meant the masons who have recently completed their apprenticeships and become qualified workers. The *Harleian Document* (circa 1650) provides a detailed formulation of an oath that could be equally appropriate for a speculative Mason. This is also true for the text of the statutes published by the Masonic Assembly of December 8, 1663. This is the text of article 7 of these statutes:

> That no p'son shall be accepted a Free Mason, or know the secrets of the said society, until he hath first taken the oath of secrecy hereafter following: —I, A. B., doe in the presence of Almighty God and my fellows and brethren here present, promise and declare that I will not at any time hereafter, by any act or circumstance whatsoever, directly or indirectly, publish, discover, reveale, or make knowne, any of the secrets, priviledges, or counsells, of the fraternity or fellowship of Free Masons, (559) which at this time,

or at any time hereafter, shall be made knowne unto mee. So helpe mee God, *and the holy contents of this booke* [emphasis mine].[13]

This oath is also significant. The last phrase, which I emphasized, indicates that the oath was made on the Bible, most likely on the gospels. We have observed this earlier in France, in Etienne Boileau's *Le Livre des Métiers*, and in England in the 1352 *Regulation* of the York masons. Closer to the present, this instruction can be found in the 1683 *Statutes of the York Lodge* cited earlier. This statute specifies that "One of the Elders takes the Book; he or she who would be made a mason places his or her hands upon the Book, and then the Instructions are given." The text goes on to say, "It is a matter of great peril for a man to perjure himself upon the Book." We shall see, when studying masonic ritual, that the Bible, the square, and the compass were considered to be the three symbolic "pillars" of the lodge.

The revised statutes of 1639 remain perfectly Catholic, or at least follow Catholicism to the letter. Nevertheless, one doubt may cross our mind. The text commands masons to be "faithful to God and the Holy Church," but it so happens that this statute was published under the reign of the Protestant William of Orange, who had shown his approval of freemasonry and even joined it in 1640. So what Holy Church did the writers have in mind? Was it the Roman Church of the Anglican Church? We shall see that the problem was quietly addressed by the publication of new masonic statutes in 1694 from which the reference to the Holy Church was simply removed.

Whatever the exact form of worship the authors of the statutes may have had in mind, the statute of 1693 clearly confirms the overall Christian character of freemasonry.

Operative Freemasonry in Scotland

In Scotland there is important information on masonic history provided by the statutes (the *Schaw Statutes*) that were signed and promulgated by William Schaw, master builder of the king and overseer of the masons toward the end of the sixteenth century. These statutes consist of a series of articles or rules stripped of any legendary history and dissertation on the seven sciences. They are essentially practical rules established by the masters of the corporation gathered in Edinburgh and set as mandatory for all masons to observe. The first date from 1598 and, on the whole, correspond to the rules of other crafts corporations. These concern the election of lodge officers, restrictions concerning admission of apprentices, and other purely operative matters. The first two articles command obedience and honor and anticipate a masonic initiation about which no details are given. Included are simply a mention of the taking of the oath and the transmission of the "mason's word."* Characteristic in this regard is the manuscript known as the *Edinburgh Register House,* dated 1695, which explicitly states that the oath is made on the Bible and that the candidate "swears by God, Saint John, the square, and the compass." This gives the strong impression that the oath in Scotland was made on the Gospel of Saint John.

Another series of statutes dating from 1599 was certainly set out by the Old Lodge of Kilwinning. The Lodge of Edinburgh is mentioned in these as the first and primary lodge of Scotland, Kilwinning as the second, and Stirling as the third. The statutes define the lodge's jurisdiction and establish its mandatory taxes. The warden had the power to verify the qualities and aptitudes of the fellows, as well as to expel those found wanting. It is also said that he could appoint a secretary. These statutes employ the terms *apprentice, journeyman,* and *master,* which proves the existence of these three grades in Scottish operative freemasonry, whereas things are much more vague in the English craft.

The Mason Companies and the Authorities

As indicated above, the guilds, notably those of the masons, as a general rule benefited from the favor of British civil and religious powers.

---

* Robert Kirk, an Aberfoill minister, writes in 1691: "I have found five curiosities in Scotland, not much observed to be [known] elsewhere . . . 2. The Mason's Word, which though some make a Mystery of it, I will not conceal a little of what I know; it is like a Rabbinical tradition in [the] way of comment on Iachin and Boaz, the two pillars erected in Solomon's Temple, with the addition of some secret sign delivered from hand to hand, by which they [the Masons] know and become familiar with one another." Quoted by Gould, *A Concise History of Freemasonry.*

Of course, we can certainly cite arrangements that were made against them, but these were particular cases due to very specific circumstances.

An example of this rare animosity occurred in 1360–1361, when the *Statute of Workers* was published again. This text included a measure according to which all alliances and associations of masons and carpenters, as well as assemblies, chapters, ordinances, and oaths that could be established between them, would be annulled. It might seem, at first glance, that all of this was directed against the obligations and meetings of the masonic order. This seems even more obvious by the existence of an array of many intermediary statutes of the same kind, such as an ordinance from 1389 and the bill crafted by Parliament in 1425 at the urging of the bishop of Winchester, tutor of King Henry VI, who was then still in his minority. This bill states that the assemblies of masons imperil the law and that consequently they would no longer be allowed to convene. Prison and a fine, according to the king's good pleasure, would punish those who violated this ban.

In truth, it seems that the actual scope of this bill has been exaggerated. What it suppressed, or proposed to suppress, was not at all lodge meetings or the yearly assemblies held by the order, but those gatherings, comparable modern strikes, that were organized with the intention of forcing the hand of the authorities or the masters.

Proof of this can be seen, according to Rebold, in the great assembly that was nonetheless held in York on Saint John's Day in 1427, which protested against the 1425 bill that otherwise would have remained of no consequence.[14] Similarly, an entry in the Latin register of William Mollart, prior of Canterbury, shows that in 1429, while King Henry was still a minor, a lodge was held in Canterbury under the sponsorship of Archbishop Henry Chichery and attended by Thomas Stapylton, master; John Morris, described in Franco-Norman as *cultos de la Lodge lathomorum,* or "warden of the masons lodge"; fifteen fellows; and three apprentices, whose names are also listed.[15]

The importance of the restrictions imposed by the 1425 bill ought to be viewed in their proper proportion. These interdictions were, at most, local matters by virtue of the independence of the corporations and lodges of each city during a time when the idea of multiple obediences did not exist. They were certainly merely matters of place and opportunity, which is the reason they can be found periodically repeated in specific and varying circumstances, proof that they were quickly forgotten. As an example, in 1436–1437, an edict was issued restricting the privileges of the brotherhood of English masons; in 1495 King Henry VII banned the use of signs of recognition by masons and confirmed the edicts of Henry VI.[16]

It is perhaps risky to mention the legend according to which Queen Elizabeth, because she was ineligible to be admitted into knowledge of the mysteries, harbored suspicions of the masons, which their enemies did not fail to encourage. Things reached such a point that orders were given on December 27, 1561, day of the annual celebration of the York Order, presided over by Sir Thomas Sackvill, to send soldiers to break up the assembly. Complaints lodged by some of the most eminent national figures convinced Elizabeth to end her opposition to the gatherings of members of the order. The queen eventually became a protector of the masonic brotherhood and confirmed the choice of Sir Thomas Sackvill as master.[17]

In contrast to the occasional interdiction, facts indicate that companies of masons enjoyed a good deal of consideration at this time. The *Articles of London* (1356) describe the corporation as "an enterprise quite apt for leading (the work) to a successful conclusion." In 1417, the Company of London received its official arms.[18] In 1427 and 1429, the assemblies of York and Canterbury, respectively, received arms, with the latter group held under the sponsorship of an archbishop.* In 1472, a new coat of arms was granted to The Hole Craft and Fellowship of Masons of London, a privilege that it was the first among guilds to obtain.[19]

On June 24, 1502, the same Henry VII who had renewed the 1425 bill presided over the holding of a grand lodge in London on the occasion of the laying of the first stone of Westminster Chapel.[20] This is the second historical event, following the Saint John's day Assembly of 1427, where we find Saint John invoked.

A century later in 1586, at the dawn of speculative Freemasonry,

---

* It has even been claimed that King Henry IV was initiated into the masonic brotherhood in 1442. His example would have been followed by all the lords of his court. (Rebold, *Histoire générale de la Franc-Maçonnerie*, 673.)

the Durham Charter was promulgated in which we see freemasons holding the principal position among all the most important trades.[21]

From all this evidence, we can draw the conclusion that the development of freemasonry in Great Britain was never hindered by royal power or religious authority. The situation here was thus completely different from the one that prevailed in France, where the ancient brotherhood found itself divided between the strictly regulated trade, which was controlled and confined to a professional role, and the *stricto sensu* brotherhood, which was quite often banned and often suspect in the eyes of the Church.

In England, the companies or fraternities of craftsmen retained the unity and traditions of the earlier brotherhoods. Restrictions imposed upon them by the king were limited only to specific periods of time and for specific purposes. Furthermore, the corporations were to a large extent the masters of their rules. Finally, they never collided with the hostility of the clergy. In fact, there is no visible instance of any condemnation laid upon them by the Church. When the bishop of Winchester stepped in in 1425, it was not as a pastoral figure but as a holder of temporal power. It was only following the Reformation and the dynastic changes that Freemasons—not only the Scots but the English as well—because they remained faithful to the Catholic religion, or at least maintained traditional rites and customs, incurred the wrath of the Anglican clergy. Later we will see how they skirted this danger by creating the Grand Lodge of London in 1717.

The Masonic Bond

Outside of those connected to religious orders, guilds and brotherhoods alike retained a local character because of the way they originated. Their organizations and activities were confined to particular cities, which was as true for the companies or brotherhoods of masons as for any. Despite the widespread movement of their statutes and franchises into general use, thanks to the favor of public officials, their authority was limited in each instance to the city in which the craftsmen grouped together. Because of the unique aspects of the builders trade, however, it was impossible for their organization to remain strictly local. The construction of cathedrals, churches, and castles led to large numbers of masters and workers moving about and gathering in different places. Work needs and manual labor conferred an itinerant character to masonry. There was constant intercommunication between lodges; not only was each brother expected to be admitted into the lodge of every city where his work took him, but larger construction projects necessitated the collective travel of lodges and the ability to work together. It was therefore necessary for masons to possess or employ signs of recognition. Equally crucial were the existence of a single technique and common practices. In general, it was necessary to preserve the procedures and secrets of the craft.

The defense of these common interests, the maintainance of traditions, the need to make certain that lodge statutes conformed to these traditions, the necessity of spreading and teaching the science and techniques of the order—all of this led to the creation of a higher organization, which was regional at the least, but to a certain extent national, if not international. This organization displayed itself in three ways:

- In the holding of periodic assemblies to expedite matters of general interest
- In the recognition of regulating lodges, known as ancient lodges or mother lodges
- In the nomination of a common protector, called master or grand master

This same unifying phenomenon is what we saw earlier in Germany. An important observation must be made, however. This organization was strictly limited to the defense of common interests and to the respect of charters and traditions. It was not at all a precursor of a permanent legislative and administrative body or a prefiguration of the different obediences, which did not make their appearance until 1717, with the formation of the Great Lodge of London. The assembled freebuilders proceeded from their own personal authority, with no thought of soliciting authorization or of placing themselves under the control of a masonic central authority. Individual lodges were not subordinate to the mother lodge as they are today to the modern grand lodge.

In England, the role of mother lodge was long held by the Old Lodge of York, which could demonstrate seniority based on its earlier organization. Its legend states that its constitution goes back to the charter of Edwin in 926, which is why the Old Lodge of York refused to recognize the authority of the Grand Lodge of England, when the latter was instituted in London in 1717.

Considerable progress toward organization was achieved at the beginning of the sixteenth century. In 1509 Cardinal Wolsey, then chancellor, united the corporations of masons and other associations of the building trade into a grand guild for which Saint John would be the patron saint.[22]

In 1567, after Sir Thomas Sackvill resigned as master of the masons of York, the confraternity formed two branches, one for northern England that was dependent on the York Lodge, whose master was the earl of Bedford, the other for the south, which recognized the jurisdiction of the London Lodge and its master, Thomas Gresham.[23]

It was only after the meeting of the Masonic Assembly of York on December 27, 1663, a time in which Freemasonry had already become speculative, that the title of grand master was sanctioned, although it conferred no administrative authority on the figure thus designated. In fact, the person in this role could be only a "protector," granting his patronage to the corporation. The powers of the grand master were not actually created until 1717, with the Grand Lodge of London.

According to legend, the first grand master or "protector" was Henri Jermyn, earl of Saint Alban, who at the same time was named to and decorated into the Order of Bath during a session over which King Charles II presided. His successors were Thomas Savafe, earl of Rovers (1666); George Villiers, duke of Buckingham (1674); Henri Benoît, earl of Arlington (1679); Sir Christopher Wren, the famous architect (1685); Charles Lennox, duke of Richmond (1695); and Christopher Wren again (1698).[24] In 1702, the same year he resigned his duties as superintendet of the royal buildings, Wren ceased to play the role of grand master and was not replaced. Nonetheless, he alone, undoubtedly because of his position and duties, exercised direct professional authority over the masons, though it seems he had only just been initiated as a Freemason in 1691.

In Scotland, the two lodges in Edinburgh, Mary's Chapel and Kilwinning, held the privilege of forming new lodges. Kilwinning was given the significant title of "mother lodge" and practiced a unique rite that has become known as the Rite of Kilwinning.* There are a number of lodges in Scots Freemasonry that grew out of the Kilwinning Mother Lodge and formed in various locales throughout the region, even in Edinburgh. These daughter lodges added the name of Kilwinning to the names of their own locations, becoming Canongate Kilwinning, Torpichen Kilwinning, and so on.

The *Schaw Statutes* make mention of another lodge, that of Stirling, which also held authority over a certain number of workshops. A fourth very old Scottish lodge, one which the *Schaw Statutes* does not mention but which can be found in city documents of 1483, is the Lodge of Aberdeen.

The Scottish lodges had as their judges and hereditary patrons, who would now be called grand masters, the Saint Clairs, the Barons of Roslyn, and the Earls of Orkney and Caithness.[25] This hereditary privilege went back to the Scottish king James II who, in 1438, granted the right of jurisdiction to the masters of the Scottish lodges. They were authorized by him to establish personal tribunals in all the large cities, using the proceeds from a four-pound tax levied on each mason graduating to the rank of master, so that the privileges of freemasons would be protected. Furthermore, the lodge masters were authorized to impose an admission fee on each new member. In 1439, James II named William of Saint Clair, lord of a family of French origin who came to England with William the Conqueror, to the dignity of master of the Scottish lodges. A document delivered by the masons of Scotland in 1628 and signed by all the lodge representatives confirmed to William Saint Clair's successor the dignity and hereditary rights of this same position. Although the extent of these rights was subsequently contested, the Saint Clair family invoked them until 1736.

We can still find a trace in Scotland of other officers exercising

---

* While discussing the Templars, we learned the legend of the creation of this rite as well as that of the foundation of the Order of the Thistle of Saint Andrew. Whatever the validity of this legend, it does appear that a Kilwinning Rite definitely did exist, at least after 1685.

jurisdiction over several lodges. For example, a charter granted by King James IV on November 25, 1590, conferred upon Patrick Copland of Udaught the right to exercise the office of first warden of the freemasons in the districts of Aberdenn, Banff, and Kinkardine.

In summary, we have observed that in Great Britain as on the Continent the necessities of the mason's profession created a bond between different lodges. But this bond often went beyond a national context. During the era of great construction, a veritable liaison was imposed between one country and another. It is this international organization that we shall now examine.

11

Universal Freemasonry

Over the course of the preceding chapters, we have seen how builders went from country to country and spread their science and art. The master builder monks of the Carolingian and Romanesque eras traveled widely, some emigrating from motherhouses to found new monasteries in far places while maintaining close relations with their home abbeys. These relations often included sending monks with artistic expertise. The minor abbeys sent their novices to study in those monasteries that were famous for their inhabitants' knowledge of science. Monks, like laypeople, often went on pilgrimages to Rome, Compostela, and the Holy Land. While journeying, they made numerous stops where they would learn much, thus benefiting from their foreign experience. Often the title of master builder was enough to earn a place in the retinue of lords who made expeditions to distant lands.

Later, lay artists, like monks, traveled great distances. French artists could be found in all the countries of central Europe. During the twelfth century, Guillaume de Sens traveled to Canterbury (1174–1179) and in the thirteenth century, Pierre, served as master builder of the cathedral of Toledo, while Villard de Honnecourt traveled to Hungary, Etienne de Bonneuil to Sweden, and Pierre d'Agincourt to the court of Naples. In the fourteenth century, Mathieu d'Arras worked on the cathedral of Prague and Jean Mignot, in 1400, traveled from Paris to Milan to correct and continue work on the Duomo. Until the Renaissance, architecture —in fact, culture as a whole—retained a very international character. Freemasons were part of this, forming a truly catholic, universal group that traveled ceaselessly from one country to another to employ the secrets of their craft, their art. This international movement is why it is often difficult to speak of schools as defined by their geographic location.

It is important to comprehend how this international understanding manifested itself on the spiritual and religious planes as well as on the operative plane of labor unity, which means we must discover how this unity was guaranteed among builders and between builders as a group and the profane and temporal powers of the time.

The Christian Character of Freemasonry

Their religious foundation was the essential glue of all the builders groups of the Middle Ages. For the monastic brotherhoods, the propagation of the faith was the direct impulse for the construction of convents and churches. The vast brotherhoods that built the Gothic cathedrals responded to this religious inspiration. It was an era when "man looked up at the heavens with faith, in search of hope and consolation. He entrusted his misery to she who should no doubt understand it best, because she was weak and she was a woman, and she could best speak to He who could do all, because she was the Mother of God. He built for the Lord of Lords; he built for Our Lady . . . [1]

It was a time when Christians could be seen "leaving their native land to devote themselves wholeheartedly to the construction of a cathedral rising on the banks of a foreign river . . . and then, after twenty or thirty years of laboring in complete obscurity, the cross would shine from atop the sanctuary built by their hands, and they moved on, without leaving their names, to die in peace, in the blessed thought that they had made something for God." [2]

This enthusiastic faith continued to animate the craft communities as they began forming. Over the centuries, religion permeated the lives of men and their work itself could not be separated from its sacred nature. It was the ascetic path of the Christian life that led to God. Craft associations could not be solely professional in nature, for if they were, as was the case in France, a religious brotherhood claimed the same members as the trade group. Thus in these associations, priests played a mandatory leader's role.

It is beyond doubt that religion and metaphysics were a part of the lodges' practices, all the more so as they gave shelter to artists and scholars as well as simple craftsmen, and as study gradually turned on a philosophy that was identical to theology.

Though it would seem that the religion of the builders was Roman Catholicism, it is still frequently claimed by Freemasons and their adversaries alike that this was and is not so. Cited as evidence of this are their pagan traditions, their skeptical attitude that grew from constant travel and contact with diverse peoples, and the sculptures they used to adorn the portals of the churches they built.

The most extreme theory that has been presented in this regard claims that Freemasonry was the supplier of Manichean and Cathar propaganda. This theory was triggered early on by Abbe Barruel in his *Mémoires pour servir à l'histoire du Jacobisme* (1798). The Germans Krause and Eckert espoused it again during the nineteenth century.* The theory is based on the notion that the leaders of Manicheism, the quintessential Gnostic sect, joined forces to wage all-out war against the Catholic Church. Because Rome was the center of the Church's strength that flowed out in all directions, the Manicheans resolved to make it the headquarters of their apostles. During this time, the Church's monasteries were bringing up the flower of youth and educating citizens in the arts. Hence, the necessity for the Manicheans to feign a fervent piety and devote themselves to the monastic profession, where, through teaching, they could win the credit and authority of both nobles and craftsmen and converts to their sect. The Manicheans did not hesitate to set their hearts on the builders associations as being the most likely to play into their intentions. Among themselves they soon formed an organized group and founded a grand lodge in Rome. Its adherents took on the name of the Johannite Brothers and established themselves as an association

---

* See also Abbe Lecanu, *L'Histoire de Satan* (1861), which detects numerous Manichean, Gnostic, and Cathar influences in Romanesque symbolism. This hypothesis was picked up by a majority of Mason authors, whose secular tendencies it flattered. See especially F. L. Lachat, *La Franc-Maçonnerie opérative* (Lyon: Derain-Rachet, 1934), 162.

whose purpose was to obtain religious glory through the construction of churches and to give service through their labor to whoever asked for their services. Their renown spread throughout the Church; France, England, and Germany enviously requested their support.

Of course, this hypothesis is merely based on legend; not one historical element nor even any probability exists to accredit it. The same can also be said of similar theories suggesting that in connecting the Templars to the freemasons, the alleged heresies of one group are imputed to the other. Yes, the builders associations were subject to Templar influence; this was clearly demonstrated in chapters 6 and 7. But there is no sound supporting evidence that these influences could have caused builders, masons, and carpenters to deviate from the orthodox Catholicism of that time—especially given, as we have seen, that the Eastern, Muslim, and Gnostic influences absorbed and transmitted by the Templars did not provide grounds enough to label them heretics. Although it is reasonable enough to assume that tendencies that are not considered heretical in one era can be considered so in another, it is easy to see that the associations or brotherhoods of builder craftsmen that were created and nurtured under the aegis of the Templars continued to live, with their rites and symbols, traditions and franchises, under the protection of the Templars' successors, the Hospitallers and the Knights of Malta, whose religious orthodoxy has never been in doubt.

In order to dispel any misunderstanding, it is helpful to emphasize here how the medieval mind conceived of religious orthodoxy. In the Middle Ages and up until the Reformation, though theology was the chief topic of debate, freedom of expression was quite considerable. While not more expansive, the notion of orthodoxy was much more flexible than it is today, for the essential dogmas hadn't varied over time. Certain systems that today may appear daring, at least to Catholics, were never suspected by Christians of being heretical before the Council of Trent. The reasons they were now considered suspect arise from the counter-reformation that shrouded the division of the Christian world. The apparent paradox concerning dogmas also stems from the evolution—or rather, change—in the modes of reasoning: Today's logic finds it difficult to find a place in the framework of the dogmas and theories that medieval logic found entrance to with no difficulty.

This was the era when Raymond Lulle reconciled the Jewish Kabbalah and Christianity; when Abelard, Saint Bernard, Saint Thomas, Roger Bacon, and Gerson gave new life to the theories of Aristotle; when Arab works spread throughout the University of Paris. It was also the time when Marsilio Ficino, perceiving the philosophical continuity connecting the systems of Zoroaster, Hermes, Orpheus, Pythagoras, and Plato, developed them further with the assistance of the Kabbalah and Christian philosophy. Meanwhile his colleague, Pico della Mirandola was kabbalistically analyzing Genesis and declaring that no science proved Christ's divinity better than Magic. Another Renaissance scholar, Pietro Pomponazzi, was denying, in the name of Aristotle, the immortality of the soul, or the immortality of consciousness; and was establishing that everything occurs in the world through generation, in accordance with necessary laws; and was daring to found a morality that was based on its own merits, one that was disinterested in either hopes or fears of another life. Not one of these philosophers was accused of heresy. The only one of those mentioned here who ran afoul of the authorities, Roger Bacon, was imprisoned for sorcery, not heresy.

The fable that the Middle Ages were the Dark Ages must be abandoned. With respect to certain crimes of intolerance, such as the Albigensian Crusade, or the condemnation of the Templars, medieval motives are much more easily explained as originating from politics rather than from any impulse to combat heresy. Heresy merely served as a pretext for seeming intolerance. True intolerance was born with the Reformation.

When we grasp the ferment of ideas and freedom of expression that was truly characteristic of the Middle Ages, it is easy to imagine how metaphysical questions would have been the natural subject of study for the elite of the master masons, both clerics and laypeople. Their language was the symbol, which was expressed by carved stone in the time before printed books were available. The mischievousness expressed in certain sculptures—which were sometimes erotic, to boot—the depictions of bears and foxes wearing clerical garb, cardinals and popes suffering in the fires of hell, and the couplings of clerics and nuns, should not be cause for surprise. During the Middle Ages, it was the clerics and ecclesiastics who oversaw the building of the churches and who paid the masons. How likely is it that they would allow themselves to be insulted to their faces in this way and immortalized in this fashion on buildings intended for posterity?* These representations correspond instead to the mores of a time when what constituted the borders of license or convention were not at all the same as our own.

It is most important to avoid viewing the audacious sculpture of the gargoyles and tympanums as merely a liberal manifestation of somewhat satiric artists who have seen behind the scenes and grasped more than others what was actually going on there. These fantasy depictions show that the freedom of the stone had been in practice for many centuries before that of the press. What was attacked were the mores of the clergy and not the religion itself. Such art reconciled with religion in perfect piety. The clerics themselves were not scandalized by it. They may have viewed it as hell's due, but they also saw it as serving a moral purpose: The depiction of these improprieties served as a means of punishing and correcting the more vicious clerics. It was a test of humility, the reflection of the *sum indignus* of the divine office, to have such art included in monuments to the faith.† Recall that the beloved Fra Angelico of Fiesole included popes, cardinals, and monks among the damned in his famous painting of the Last Judgement. It would be thoughtless to believe that he was displaying his total disdain for the highest authorities of the Church. What he wished to express was a basic Christian truth: that in Christ's judgment, everyone will receive what he or she deserves, whether good or bad. The same could be said of the workers who carved stone.

---

* Recall that the Second Council of Nicea (787) decided that the composition of religious images should not be left to the artists' initiative but should originate in the principles established by the Church and religious tradition. "The Art alone belongs to the painter, its placing and arrangement belong to the Fathers."
† It should be noted that these depictions are generally placed outside the church, and on the portal facing west, which is to say, outside and in opposition to the light.

Craft Secrets

The international unity experienced by freemasonry was clearly displayed in the practice of its craft. The brotherhoods and communities fulfilled an educational mission insofar as each master instructed journeymen and apprentices in the craft.

Rather than being merely technical, this instruction assumed a basic minimum knowledge of geometry and art in an era when work was not at all specialized and the master builder was simultaneously architect, entrepreneur, mason, carpenter, stonecutter, and sculptor. He had to possess all the knowledge that Vitruvius demanded of the architect during Augustus's century, namely mathematics, arithemetic, geometry, physics, history, astrology, music, and even jurisprudence, rhetoric, and medicine. Perfection in the art of building implied a quintessence of the sciences and human talents: "This art, which consists of giving proportion to the different parts of a monument, to raise those bold spires and audacious belltowers, to curve those vaults beneath which sound, far from diminishing, will take on a more harmonious fullness, would seem to be a magic art."[3] It was the first and noblest of them all; it was the Royal Art.

To builders it was so incomprehensible that science could be excluded from their areas of expertise that in 1401 the Parisian master Jean Mignot unleashed a controversy involving the Milanese artists who had reproached him for the fact that his arguments were in the domain of science and not art because, they insisted, the two were entirely different. Mignot indignantly responded: "Art without science does not exist *(Ars sine scientia nihil est)*."[4]

Of course, such vast knowledge could be the privilege of only the most gifted individuals. But even the least of masters had to possess a minimum of equally developed skill and culture. So there is nothing surprising in the fact that the time of apprenticeship for masons and carpenters was six to seven years. Its duration eventually decreased as technical and social advancements brought about a greater divison of labor and a greater emphais was given to specialization.

In an era when teaching in general and mathematics in particular were barely developed, the builders, more than any other craftsmen, possessed true secrets. Teaching in part came in the form of a professional initiation that included the knowledge of natural forces, the properties and effects of these forces, the science of numbers and measures, geometry, and arithmetic. Because the science and practice of this speciality had to remain the privilege of craft masters, it was necessary to avoid at all costs divulging anything to "laypeople" or to competitors. It was forbidden to teach the art of building to simple manual laborers. In order to maintain their monopoly, all builders were enjoined to jealously use secrecy.* The necessity of prudence also dictated the impossibility of writing down the principles of the art, which explains why we have no architectural treatises from the Middle Ages except for the album of Villard de Honnecourt, which is unintelligible to the noninitiated.†

Because of the sacred nature of anything related to work and the secrecy explicit in their oath, any builder's revelation would have been tantamount to sacrilege. To gaurantee the international unity required by their craft, it was necessary that freemasons own privileges and franchises that transcended the temporal and were valid in all lands. Fulfilling this need was the role of the Church. It was also necessary that builders share common signs and a universal language by which they could recognize one another. Esoterically, this need was fulfilled by the use of symbols; exoterically, it was met by use of the French language.

International Privileges

The Church was the sole power capable of granting and guaranteeing to builders a privilege of internationality that earned them "freedom of passage." Generally speaking, the Church was a constant presence in the performance of work. In this instance, its intervention was given even more justification because the work consisted mostly of the con-

---

* According to Etienne Boileau's *Livre des Métiers,* masons, mortar makers, and plasterers could have "as many assisitants and valets of their trade as it pleased them, provided they revealed to none of them any information about their craft." Article 13 of the statutes of the Ratisbonne stonecutters from 1458 listed similar prescriptions.

† C. Enlart, 68. "In the Middle Ages artistic or industrial property was understood and protected differently from how we envision it. It was not the monopoly of a single model for the benefit of its inventor but the monopoly of a kind of labor for the benefit of a corporation."

struction of religious buildings. Spiritual authority and unity were interrelated.

This was why builders communities identified with monastic associations. Their ecclesiastical quality conferred upon craftsmen the privilege of internationality. The builders, both lay and clerical, who belonged to the Benedictine, Cistercian, and Templar brotherhoods could circulate freely, build, and settle anywhere in the whole of Christendom. Their freedom was guaranteed by the immunity and sovereignty of the Church to which they belonged.

Later, because of feudal bonds the communities that had turned secular would continue to enjoy the same privileges and franchises they assumed when they were religious dependents. More important, all craftsmen had the right to asylum and the free exercise of their trade in the domains of the Templar commanderies and the popes maintained these privileges for domains held by the Knights Hospitaller or Knights of Malta until the time of the French Revolution. When we recall that the Temple numbered some 900 commanderies, many of which were extensive, and 10,000 castles, we can see how operatives, especially masons who traveled widely, could be assured of finding hospitality, security, and work everywhere they went.

The popes also conferred these privileges, valid throughout the Catholic world, to the lay masons that built churches.[5] Boniface IV granted these craftsmen the first diploma of franchises in 614. During this time, however, there were not any true lay communities or associations and such franchises could have concerned only Benedictine builders.

Mention has been made of the briefs that Popes Nicholas III (in 1277) and Benoit IX (in 1334) crafted with regard to mason corporations, confirming their status as a monopoly that encompassed the entire Christian world, granting them protection and an exclusive right to construct all religious edifices, and conceding to them "the right to direct authority from only the popes," who freed them "from all local laws and statutes, royal edicts, and municipal regulations concerning conscript labor or any other obligatory imposition for all the land's inhabitants." These popes ensured that members of the corporations had the right to set their own salaries and to regulate exclusively, within their general chapters, "all matters pertaining to their internal governance." It was forbidden for "any artist who had not been accepted into the association to establish any competitive endeavor at the expense of the association and for any sovereign to support his subjects in such a rebellion against the Church." Finally, all were expressly enjoined "to respect these credentials and to obey these commands, under pain of excommunication." The pontiffs signaled their approval of these absolute methods by citing "the example of Hiram, King of Tyre, when he sent architects to King Solomon to build the Temple of Jerusalem."

On reading these privileges, it is difficult to believe, like Clavel (who accepts them), that the members of these corporations were opposed to the pope. While we may accept the authenticity of these briefs, the originals of which are missing, it is necessary to measure their scope. They were applicable only within the framework of canon law. They addressed only the construction of religious buildings. The pope held no temporal power that allowed him to grant anyone private privileges that would constitute a departure from the rules of feudal or manorial law or to strike a blow against the power and competence of those administering high or low justice. With the exception of canon law, the Church could act only in the temporal sphere and within the limits of its own jurisdiction. The pope's authority in this regard did not extend beyond the borders of his states. It was because of this and in the roles of lords high justice that the Benedictines, Cistercians, and Templars could act within the immense extent of their thousands of abbeys, houses, and commanderies.

Symbolism

The use of symbolism on its own constituted a universal language. Symbols were used by builders as much for spiritual teaching as for the transmission of operative craft secrets. "During the Middle Ages," Victor Hugo states, "the human race formed no important thought that it did not set down in stone." All form was, as Emile Male put it, the clothing of a thought.[6] This was the case for the general design as well as the proportions of churches and cathedrals, for the figures sculpted on the portals and capitals, the gargoyles, and the composition and color of the stained-glass windows. Until the fourteenth century, everything in Romanesque and Gothic art was invested with meaning. Purely decorative whim and chance were merely exceptions to this basic rule.

It was mainly the excess of motifs drawn from flora and fauna during the Romanesque era that earned Saint Bernard's condemnation. These should be seen as copies of ancient originals from Celtic, Byzantine, and Oriental cultures, which is not to say that these are the source of art that is lacking in symbolic meaning, just that it is sometimes difficult to pronounce an accurate opinion on this meaning and its Christianization. Strictly decorative flora and fauna can be found in much Gothic art, a charming expression of a deep and tender love for nature. It's main Christian teaching could be summed up as this: All God's creatures have their place in the Church, sheltered from the world.

Some English authors such as E. W. Shaw and A. F. A. Woodford, who have studied exclusively the simplest forms and professional intention of their symbolism—masons' marks—believe that while these were originally simply alphabetical and numerical, they subsequently took on esoteric and symbolic meaning. They feel that, at least during the Middle Ages if not during all eras in the history of building, the marks constituted the external signs of an occult organization. Drawn from geometry, they form a kind of universal alphabet, which, outside of some international variations, was a language that all workers could understand.[7]

The symbolism in architecture, sculpture, and stained glass, which was the work of artists under the direction of the clerics, was the expression of science and philosophy, akin to that of alchemists and Hermeticists. Throughout the Middle Ages and the Renaissance, philosophy, metaphysics, alchemy, and Hermeticism were closely commingled and these disciplines were inseparable from theology. The means of expression were the same in all these areas, for, in the final analysis, they could all be boiled down to the formulation of fundamental metaphysical truths. It is easy to cite famous alchemists who were also master builders, such as Gerbert, who was pope from 999 to 1003 under the name of Sylvester II, or Nicholas Flamel, to whom Sauval attributes the contruction of the southern side of the ancient Parisian church Saint Jacques de la Boucherie.[8] This same Nicholas Flamel gave two paintings to this church in 1413, one of which is called *An Image of a Misericorde of Our Lord,* whereas the other depicts the Passion and the Resurrection.[9] It so happens that the coat of arms of the Parisian masons and stonecutters depicted the Resurrection and Ascension of Jesus Christ. Another famous architect and Hermetic philosopher from a later time is Philibert Delorme, the builder of many "dwellings for philosophers," who was "general master of the masonry of the kingdom as well as the king's chaplain.[10]

It is important to underscore that the immense symbolism, the true thought of the Middle Ages, was not only the philosophical province of great doctors and scholars; it had a universal teaching power and the Church understood how to impart it to the masses. This is why there exists such perfect unity between different works—though of course the artisans who crafted it, be they ever so humble, were admirable artists.

That masons may have benefited from outside contributions to their repetoire of symbolic expression is beyond doubt. But the terrain was prepared beforehand to receive them. Traditional symbolism was a framework that was ready to accept these diverse influences. A vital force fully aware of its own universal nature, it did not hesitate to create the synthesis and transmutation of everything it found valid in its inheritance from the past. Hence it is legitimate to detect the most diverse influences in traditional symbolism, but it would be erroneous to view it as debatable syncretism, or even heresy. Furthermore, during the Middle Ages everything, even that which seems most profane to us, remained within the universal Christian vision, marked by a connection between the visible and invisible. Our modern mind, habituated as much to a strictly logical method of reasoning as to crystalized dogmas, often finds it difficult to perceive such a mentality. Convincing evidence exists, however, that from the times of earliest antiquity to the time of Descartes, the modes of expressing thought were essentially esoteric and symbolic. At the risk of perplexing our Cartesian, habit-trained minds, it is not rash to state that such a system of logic equally deserves the label of rationalist, because it simultaneously addresses the two poles of thought (discursive and intuitive). Modern scholars, moreover, have recovered from many of the preventive measures taken against symbolism, notably that displayed against the alchemists since the time of Lavoisier. They have grasped the hidden meaning of their writings and have understood that the symbol is a suitable kind of approach and even an expression of the truth. Accordingly it is *a priori* of the transcendent.

In the next chapter we will see that the organized implementation of symbolism occurs through ritual in order to transmit the profound and traditional teachings of freemasonry.

Signs of Recognition

We can divide the symbols intended to preserve the craft secrets of masonry into the categories of ritual "words, signs, and touches." We have already come across the masons' word in our discussion of the statutes of the Scottish lodges. Reverend George Hickes wrote on this subject in 1678: "They [the Freemasons] were obliged to receive the Masons' word, which is a secret signal that they possess to identify each other throughout the whole world. He who holds it can bring his brother mason to his side without hailing him and without your seeing the signal."[11]

Although this testimony dates from an era when Masonry had become largely speculative, it is probable that it refers to a very old craft tradition.

French: Language of the Crafts

Although often given to excessive imagination, Péladan justly noted that from the twelfth to sixteenth centuries, the language of the crafts was French:[12]

Before the idea of internationalism had been expressed,* the high dignitaries of the corporations had established between themselves and their colleagues a diplomatic understanding that concerned

---

* It was an expression of Christianity.

working methods as well as the economic situations of the artists. The language of esoteric use until the threshold of the sixteenth century was French. Its use was so extensive that in order to comprehend the so-called rebus writing, the language of heraldry, or what Ménage called "the ambiguities of the painting of the word," it was into the French language that these esoteric and allegorical hieroglyphics so frequently found on ancient monuments and edifices must be translated."

This role of French was an important one in the building arts. Isn't Gothic art, with its distinction between Old Gothic or Romanesque and "modern" Gothic, primarily a French art? Both the building arts of the Middle Ages and Gothic art were born in France. The one that first saw the light of day in the Benedictine monasteries of the old Goth provinces remained permeated with Roman traditions, while the other arose in the brotherhoods on the Ile de France. We saw how they spread into foreign lands, mainly England, which eventually became the birthplace of modern Freemasonry. It so happens that the French language exerted a very unique influence in England. Imposed by the Norman monarchs following the Battle of Hastings and the conquest of the land in 1066, it remained the official language for three centuries. As noted earlier, the *Statut des Ouvriers* (Statutes of the Laborers) of 1351 and the *Articles de Londres* (London Articles) of 1356 were written in French.

According to Péladan, the builders of the Middle Ages assumed the name of *gaults* or *coqs* [cocks], because of the homonymy between *galli*, meaning "Gauls,"—that is, Frenchmen—and *galli*, meaning "cocks" or "roosters." Their symbol was the rooster as well as the pobjoy, popinjay, or parrot.[13] it is beyond doubt that the rooster figured in seals or coats of arms of master masons. In 1438, Jehan Lambert, master mason of Paris, had a rooster with three stars added to his shield.[14]

The rooster also had a profoundly esoteric significance. Without examining too deeply its symbolism, which would necessitate moving well outside the concerns of this book, we can say that this animal was always considered a solar bird. The great initiate Rabelais informs us, in *Pantagruel*, Book I, chapter 10, that "the presence of the powers of the sun, which is the organ and storehouse of all terrestrial and sidereal light, is symbolized and represented by a white cock." Subsequently, the rooster came to symbolize daybreak and by extension the Resurrection. Today it still figures in the initiation skit of the apprentice Mason.

The Decline of Masonic Universalism

The universalism of the medieval builders was closely connected to the Catholic religion and the building of its churches. A breech had already been torn in this universalism by the communal movement, when purely local brotherhoods formed without any solid bonds to another brotherhood or ties of origin to the monastic association and, through them, to tradition. The Renaissance and Reformation dealt a fatal blow to this universal character.

The sixteenth century was marked first and foremost by a serious decline in the art of religious construction. The essentially religious Gothic art disappeared to make way for the essentially secular Renaissance art. The Christian symbolic language, vehicle of the tradition, was erased with the same stroke. Despite the efforts of the Italian academies and the most prestigious artists, such as Leonardo Da Vinci and Michelangelo, the return to antiquity was accompanied by little in the way of understanding and quickly became widespread solely as a visual and decorative art. It contributed no compensation for the spiritual values it replaced. Finally, the encroachment of the Reformation upon Western Europe and the army of iconoclasts that emerged from it brought a complete halt to the construction and maintenance of the magnificent monuments to piety on which so many master builders had collaborated.

Other contrasts contributed as well. The Gothic building technique was quite difficult and exacting, whereas that of the Renaissance proved to be much simpler and more flexible. We should also note that with the development and vulgarization of the arts and sciences, the number of artists multiplied. Each country had its own reserves of personnel from which it could draw to meet construction needs. Cosmopolitan artisans had far fewer opportunities to meet their foreign colleagues.

Finally, from the weakening of the Christian mind brought about by the intolerance and fanacticism of confessional conflicts, social bonds withered away while individualism experienced a rebirth. The master became more egotistical and distant. Secure in his position, he monopolized all the posts of the mastery association; at the top of the corporation and with his peers, he tended to form a band apart. Soon artists and artisans, masters and journeymen, had more and more difficulty understanding each other; a moat was slowly being dug between them. The disappointed, discouraged, and sometimes rebellious journeymen grouped together separately. This was the time when the modern form of the compagnonnage was born, retaining the signals of recognition, the rites, and the symbols passed down by tradition. Their secrecy allowed the journeymen to protect the quality of their work and the identity of the worker. This was also the era when, finally, the brotherhoods, which had lost sight of their pious and charitable goals, degenerated into excess, causing alarm for both religious and civil authorities, who banned them in both France and Germany.

All of these factors brought about a rupture of the bond that united the freemasons not only from one country to another, but also within each kingdom. This period marked the decline of operative masonry. The universalism, prestige, and power of the builders died with the fracturing of the Christian world and with the slackening of faith. They would be reborn, however, with speculative Freemasonry. In the transition from one form to the other, continuity was compensated by a subrogation: The connection between operative freemasonry and speculative Freemasonry was the language of symbol and the thought beneath it. Symbol, which had served to maintain professional and religious unity, changed design and now served to create a scientific, philosophical, and spiritual unity. This universalism was no longer, alas, a widespread transcendent and social fact. Henceforth, for only an initiated elite, it would be the key to an ideal.

12

Speculative Freemasonry

The Speculative Nature of
Craft Freemasonry

It is customary to oppose modern speculative Freemasonry and ancient operative masonry. In reality, the masonic organizations we have studied—the collegia, monastic associations, brotherhoods, craft communities, compagnonnages—were never invested with a strictly professional nature. All of these associations pursued religious, charitable, and social goals as well as those pertaining to the defense of their craft interests.

In this chapter, we will not revisit the initiatic, religious, and cultural character of the craft brotherhoods and communities, particularly those of the masons. For these workers, they could claim the pure quality and perfection of their work only by integrating it into the creative work of God, the Great Architect of the Universe, the sole dispenser of the Good and the Beautiful. It is up to humans, through their conduct and effort, to earn the essential grace of this assistance from on high. All the old statutes expressly mention the religious, moral, and social duties imposed upon the association's brothers. It was a requirement that the initiate had been born free (meaning he was not from a servile or vassal status), and that he was a legitimate son of good moral character who was religious, honest, and of calm temperament. Those who failed to perform their duties, led a libertine or unchristian life, or were known to be unfaithful to their spouses could not be admitted into the organization or, if already members, would be expelled.

The *Masonic Poem (Regius Manuscript)* contains a veritable treatise on civility. It stipulates that an individual should attend to his own education and that of his family to attain courteousness, distinguished manners, good morals, and self-mastery. The *Cooke Manuscript* attests to masonry's enduring desire to require its members to display a character of rectitude and uprightness. It was forbidden to keep a "night crawling" apprentice, for he could not effectively perform his duly appointed tasks and would give his fellows cause to complain. No master should seek to supplant another. If a mason has a quarrel with his journeymen, he should submit to the judgment of the master or warden who rules in his stead and reconcile with his journeymen on the next feast day of the calendar. A master or journeyman who has transgressed any article should be judged before a general assembly of the lodge. If he does not acknowledge his misdeeds, he will be expelled and handed over to the sheriff or lord mayor to be imprisoned.

Philibert Delorme, in his *Treatise on Architecture*, advises the reader that in addition to the science required to perform his craft, the qualities of probity, openness, and scrupulousness "should distinguish the mason; he must neither be mad, nor vain, nor proud, nor presumptuous."

Finally, we should recall that brotherhoods and craft associations pursued social objectives that were not confined merely to providing charitable assistance to brothers in need. All craft communities had a much larger target in mind. They often played a truly political role and were unfailingly the basis of the municipal franchises. Particularly in the northern countries, Italy, and England the mastery associations remained the instruments of the municipal administration, taking part in basic policing, finance issues, urbanization, and even the defense of the city, especially with regard to the levying of troops. Consequently, it is superfluous to emphasize how questions of a political and social nature could be the subjects of discussion in these organizations. Nor should we look elsewhere for the reasons they sometimes incited—especially in France—the distrust of royal authority, all the more so because they often had eminent figures among their membership, which made them seem even more dangerous in the eyes of the crown.*

This means simply that the operative concerns of the trades were always combined with concerns of a speculative nature. They were inseparably joined, at least in their original forms, when it was difficult to draw a line of demarcation between the temporal and the spiritual, between the craft and the sacred. This fact was of vital importance to the mason's craft because of the knowledge and skills it required and because its purpose touched on matters of primordial importance concerning life and human destiny.

This profound and truly initiatory teaching of masonry appeared in the ritual for works and ceremonies that was practiced in the lodge and in the analysis of the rites and symbols it gave as means of instruction.

The Ritual

For a long time there has been little at our disposal regarding the ritual in masonry. The reason for this is easy to grasp: Rituals and instructional catechisms were not created to be written; their practice and transmission were purely oral. It was strictly forbidden to put them into writing, even as a memory aid. Fortunately, research undertaken by English Freemasons at the beginning of the twentieth century has led to the discovery of revealing documents. Douglas Knoop, G. P. Jones, and Douglas Hamer have gathered together these texts in their book *The Early Masonic Catechisms,* which first appeared in 1943. These works, though few in number and sometimes incomplete, provide enough information to show us the essential elements of the ritual followed by operative masons. The word *ritual* in the singular is used here on purpose, for all these documents, despite their varied origins, display identical elements that reveal a shared symbolism and esotericism.

---

* To get a sense of the political role played by corporations in France, it is enough to recall their interventions during the times of Etienne Marcel [the leader of a failed revolt against royal authority in Paris during the fourteenth century], the Caboche [members of the butcher and skinner guilds who briefly seized power in fifteenth-century Paris and undertook radical reforms before being ousted; their name comes from the word for skinner], and the League [the Holy League in France, which fought for Catholic interests during the wars of religion that wracked France in the sixteenth century].

The time of their writing stretches from 1696 to 1730, but it seems obvious that they are simply transcribing a traditional ritual whose origin reaches back far into the past, although we are not able to precisely identify this genesis.

The fact that this operative ritual is so old can be supported on the one hand by crosschecking the texts against the contents of the statutes and old charges, which are greater in number and which date back to the fourteenth century, and on the other hand by comparing them to the customary rituals of other organizations, which, although different from those of freemasonry, shared the same common root. For instance, the French Compagnonnage and the German Bruderschaft shared masonry's symbolic themes.

Perhaps one of the best proofs of the age of the masons' ritual has been overlooked until now: the nature of its symbolism, which is the key to its iniatory and esoteric meaning and which can be illuminated as an overall value only through its Christian explanation such as that doctrine was professed in medieval times.

Comparison of the symbols of the ritual to those expressed by Christian religious thought during the thirteenth and fourteenth centuries allow us to grasp the high scope of the ritual and to establish, albeit approximately, the time of its birth. It is significant that, starting at the end of the fourteenth century, all the symbolism that had been used in previous centuries to formulate the Christian truths that experienced an apotheosis in the thirteenth century gradually fell into disuse and became incomprehensible. Without renouncing them, the Renaissance that occurred from the fourteenth century in Italy to the beginning of the sixteenth in France, the Low Countries, and Great Britain replaced it with a symbolism restored from antiquity, even though it may have led to the same traditional values. After around 1530, this tradition became blurred and the symbolic thought employed in religion, art, and philosophy became foreign and eventually disappeared altogether from popular thought. It no longer had any deep roots. How could the people have any genuine interest in those who took the place of the saints—Jupiter, Mars, Apollo, Ceres, and Proserpine or the ancient heroes of Greece and Rome or the Caesars? Even if this new art, especially prominent in the plastic arts, still recalled the tradition, it no longer faithfully translated the civilization and life of that time. The cathedral no longer took the place of all the books. It was no longer the symbol of the faith, of love, of all. The peak of this evolution would be Versailles. Its strongly emphasized symbolic conception converges toward the unity of the Solar Majesty, image of the king and no other, who personally embodies grandeur and the perennial. This is a completely different world.

Based on this shift, it seems incontestable that a ritual continuing to express traditional values in a thirteenth-century Christian form, especially occurring as it did among craftsmen, could be nothing less than a teaching that had been passed down from an earlier time.

The esoteric character of the operative ritual can be boiled down to the general symbolism of the building of Solomon's Temple, which was one of the most popular myths of the Middle Ages. This popularity reveals an interpretation of the story that reaches far beyond the tale of the magnificent temple, which David began and Solomon completed in order to provide a dignified place to worship the Eternal One and house the Holy of Holies, the Ark of Covenant containing the Tablets of the Law. To the medieval mind, Solomon's temple was the replica of God's true temple and must be visualized on two planes: that of the Universe and the Divine Creation and that of Man, the reduced form of the Universe to which Christ's incarnation had conferred a level of grandeur or some value sequal to it. The temple was the symbol of both the universal macrocosm and the human microcosm.

This is the basic model of the Christian church. No other religious edifice has as simply and eloquently expressed the immemorial symbolism of the temple consecrated to the godhead. Its perfection was reached in the Romanesque church, in the outline of its basic plan in squares and cupolas, sacred architecture's classic vocabulary for symbolizing the union of heaven and earth, the the uncreated and the created. It is easy to see how the instruments used to depict the circle and the square, the compass and the square, were invested with an identical symbolic meaning.

It is in this very broad sense that the reconstruction of Solomon's Temple was understood. Likewise, Jerusalem was not merely the city in Palestine where the Crusaders gathered. This was simply its geographical and historical meaning. As for all interpretation of scripture, it required in accordance with the methodology of Church scholars the perception of its allegorical, tropological, and anogogical meanings. In the allegorical sense, Jerusalem was the militant Church; in the tropological sense, it was the Christian soul; and in the anagogical sense it was the celestial Jerusalem, the land above announced by Saint John in the Apocalypse.

With respect to Kings David and Solomon, both of whom were extremely popular, they were regarded, curious as this might appear today, as signs or portents of Jesus Christ. The same was true of Hiram, the founder of the Pillars of the Temple, and Adoniran, Solomon's high official and head of the conscripted labor. *Hic et Christus,* said the Venerable Bede in the eighth century, meaning that it is Christ who guides the workers of the Temple and provides the measures of the construction. This was repeated in Walafrid Strabo's *Ordinary Gloss,* which, from the ninth to the sixteenth century, accompanied all editions of the Bible.* Emile Mâle describes this book as one of the most valuable to come down to us from the Middle Ages.

This view of the figures of the Hebrew Scriptures as those who heralded the coming of Christ was traditional among the Fathers of the Church. The same perspective held true for Adam and Noah; for the patriarchs Abraham, Isaac, Jacob, and Joseph; for Melchizadek, the pontiff king; and for the prophets Moses, Ezra, Aggee, and Zerubbabel. As disorienting as this may appear to our modern logic, the people of the Middle Ages did not understand the Hebrew Scriptures in solely their literal sense, as the record of a historical and chronological process (which would be too narrow and anti-Christian). Truth for them was intemporal, not merely a question of historical contribution. Truth was what was primarily and clearly expressed in the New Law as taught by Jesus, the Verb Incarnate.

For the Church Fathers, the literal sense of the Hebrew Scriptures was clearly sacred in nature. According to the symbolic exegesis, the

---

* W. Strabo in Kings III, 7, 13 for Hiram and Kings III, 5, 28 for Adoniram (Kings I in modern editions of the Bible, in which the former Kings I and Kings II have become the Book of Samuel). This reference comes from the Latin Bible of Froben (Basel, 1498; Bibliothèque National, Res. A 807.) See also Emile Mâle, *L'Art religieux du IIIième siècle en France,* vol. 1, 23 ff.

historical foundations of the scripture should not be disregarded; Abraham, David, Solomon, and all other biblical characters truly existed. But God made these men the heralds of his Son yet to come upon the earth. Therefore, it is necessary to search through all they said and did, and in doing so, we will find Christ. "The Old Testament," Saint Augustine said, "is nothing other than the New Testament covered with a veil and the New Testament is merely the old one unveiled."

The Divine Plan transposed into the tangible figure of Christ helps us to move from the macrocosmic symbolism of the temple to its microcosmic symbolism. Even more, in giving resonance to the millenary symbolism of this point, Christianity gave it new life.

The Romanesque church, inspired by Solomon's Temple and the image of the cosmos, is constructed on human measures such as they most notably were given in Saint Hildegard von Bingen's *Liber divinorum operum simplicis hominis*. Of course, the form of a cross, man's image, was an ancient symbol used for the blueprint of a temple, the most grandiose example of which is perhaps the Temple of Luxor in Egypt. But never was the harmonic correspondence of Universe-Temple-Man invested with such high significance as it was in Christianity, for while the Romanesque church offers the image of man, it also presents, first and foremost, through the perfections of its measurements, the symbol of the Perfect Man, meaning Christ, Incarnation of God.

This brings us to the foundation of Christian teachings. Man is the true temple of God, for which Solomon's Temple is a symbol. "Know you not," Saint Paul asked, "that you are the temple of God?" (Corinthians 1, 3:16.) "Are you not aware that your body is the temple of the Holy Spirit within you?" (Corinthians I, 6:19) It is the same truth, an affirmation of God's immanence, that Saint Bernard would proclaim in his second sermon devoted to the dedication of the church. He makes an allusion there to the visible temple built to shelter humankind, but in which God dwells not as he resides in his image, meaning within man.

The oldest known mention of Solomon's Temple as origin and container of the art of masonry is found in the *Cooke Manuscript* from the fourteenth century.[1] Most of the later versions of the old charges repeat and develop this same theme. One noteworthy fact is that the same symbolism can be found in both French compagnonnage and the German Bauhütte, in which there also occurs specific mention of the two pillars, Jachin and Boaz, important elements of symbolic masonic language. What sense did operative masons attach to this symbolism of Solomon's Temple? Once we understand how set and professed the Christian interpretation was during the Middle Ages, it seems obvious that beyond the similar connections this symbolism forged with their professional concerns and the model it provided for their work, the masons of that time would have been incapable of seeing it from any other perspective or deducing from it an esoterically different teaching inside their Church-controlled brotherhoods.

Eloquent proof of this is provided by the ritual itself. The best articulation of it is *Dumfries Manuscript no. 4,* dating from around 1710 and belonging to the Old Dumfries Lodge (now Dumfries Kilwinning no. 53).[2] It provides a fairly complete record of the entire ritual that was followed at the time of the transition that preceded the construction of the Great Lodge of London. This manuscript provides characteristic clues related to the symbolism of Solomon's Temple. It takes the form of a question-and-answer catechism:

Q. How high is your lodge?
A. Inches and spans Inumberable.
Q. How Inumberable?
A. The material heavens & stary firmament.
Q. How many pillars is your lodge?
A. Three.
Q. What are these?
A. Ye square, the compass, & ye bible.

This is the affirmation of the cosmic and sacred meaning of the Lodge. Following is the Christian meaning of the temple:

Q. What ladder had they . . . building of ye . . .?
A. Jacobs . . . between ye heaven [ ] ye earth.*

---

* Words are missing from this part of the manuscript.

Q. How many steps was in Jacobs ladder?

A. 3.

Q. What was ye 3?

A. Father, Son & Holy Spirit.

Q. What meant ye golden dore of ye temple, Qr (where) the went in to sanctum sanctorum?

A. It was another type of Christ who is ye door ye way and the truth & ye life by whome & in whom all ye elect entreth into heaven.

Q. What was ye greatest wonder Yt seen or heard about the temple?

A. God was man and was God. Mary was a mother and yet a maid.

Q. What signifies the temple?

A. Ye Son of God & partly of the church ye Son soffered his body to be destroyed & rose again ye 3 d day & raised up tu us ye Christian church we (which) in ye true spiritwal church.

Q. (What signifies) the ark of the covenant?

A. It represents as weel our saviour Christ as ye hearts of ye faithfull for in Christs breast was ye doctrine both of law & gospel so is in ye faithfull though not in ye measure he was ye true manna yt descended to give life to ye world ye table of ye law move us to love & obedience Aarons rod flowrishing wt blossoms signifies ye swetnes of ye gospel & ye glory of our High priest Jesus Christ of whome Aaron was a figure.

The entire medieval Christian doctrine can be found reinforced in this text: the immanence of God in man, the realization of the law by the Incarnation of Christ, the construction within man of God's true temple by obedience to the Law and by Love, the symbolic figure from the Hebrew Scriptures as a sign of the gospel. This interpretation was very familiar in the Middle Ages. Developed as early as the eighth century by the Venerable Bede in his work *De Templo Salomonis,* it can be found everywhere in Strabo's *Ordinary Gloss* of the Bible.

The end of the ritual makes a long allusion to the two pillars of the

Temple, Jachin and Boaz: "where (was) the noble art or science found when it was lost." This is the meaning it gives them: "For ye present ye sons of God have received strength inwardly, for ye time to come God will stablisch so with his spirit of grace yt they shall never wholly depart from him."*

The Legend of Hiram and the Initiatory Myth

The legend of Hiram is particularly significant with regard to the sacred scope of the masonic ritual. For the masons, who made him both their master and model, Hiram was a mythical figure who was the brilliant builder of the Temple. Haloed by glory and talent, he is a synthesis of two biblical figures: Huram or Hiram Abi, and Adoram, Adonhiram, or Adoniram.

According to the Kings III (5:13, 14, 15), King Solomon fetched Hiram out of Tyre.

> He was a widow's son of the tribe of Naphtali, and his father was a man of Tyre, a worker in brass; and he was filled with wisdom, and understanding, and cunning to work all works in brass. And he came to King Solomon and wrought all his work. For he cast two brass pillars . . . that of the right was Jachin, and that on the left, Boaz.

According to the Chronicles II (2:14 and 4:11), Huram Abi was sent by King Hiram of Tyre to Solomon.

> He was the son of a woman of the daughters of Dan, and his father was a man of Tyre, skillful to work in gold, and in silver, in brass, in iron, in stone, and in timber, in purple, in blue, and in fine linen, and in crimson; also to grave any manner of graving . . . And Huram made the pots, and the shovels, and the basons. And Huram finished the work he was to make for King Solomon for

---

* This explanation conforms to the etymology of these two names. Jachin means "he will establish" and Boaz means "in strength."

the house of God. To wit, the two pillars, and the pommels, and the capitals which were on the top of the two pillars.

Adoram, Adonhiram, or Adoniram, son of Abda, was one of Solomon's high officials, the head of the conscripted workers (Kings III, 4:6). It was he who, in this capacity, directed the works of the temple, but we know that in reality the true architect of the Temple was God himself. When King David gave his son Solomon the plans for the building of the Temple and the models of the tabernacle and all the tools, he declared: "all of this was written by the Lord's hand which gave unto me the understanding." (Chronicles I, 28:19). Solomon and Hiram were merely executing (albeit perfectly) the will of God.

In the commingling of Hiram and Adoniram, the masons followed the customary interpretation of all the medieval commentaries and interpretations of the Bible. But the masonic legend—a major theme of the initiation of the mason to the grade of master—invented the tragic death of Hiram, who was said to have been killed by three evil journeymen to whom he had refused to give the master "word." He was then transfigured and resuscitated in the person of the newly initiated master.

In this story, the masons embroidered upon the Bible. What's more, as we shall see, Adoniram was killed in circumstances that bear resemblance to Hiram's death through their sacred and spiritual significance.

Hiram is mentioned in the old charges (see the Tew manuscript, circa 1680, which describes him as the son of King Hiram; see also the Inigo Jones manuscript from the same era). But the legend of his death, with its initiatory and therefore secret character, appears in documented form only with modern Freemasonry, specifically in Prichard's exposé *Masonry Dissected* (1730). The ancient provenance of this legend seems accurate, however, for it seems its full meaning and the source for its inspiration could be found only in a medieval reading of the Bible, a mind-set that was completely lost with the arrival of the Reformation and Counter-Reformation.

We may invoke additional arguments in support of this legend's age. The creation of legends based on biblical themes was a widespread practice during the Middle Ages. It was encouraged by popular fervor and a taste for the marvelous. The Church itself, far from condemning these glosses, encouraged their creation to a certain extent. We may recall how similar legends were transposed into apocryphal texts and were spread through sculptures and the images in stained-glass windows. Some of these were Christianized forms of ancient beliefs and stories—depictions of myths that were eternal bearers of the Transcendent. As described in the image of Isidore de Seville, Holy Scripture was a lyre whose strings had infinite resonance.

Thus, all the patron saints and fabled figures who were the protectors of the crafts had their own legends. Those of Saint Christopher, Mary Magdelene, and the Three Magi, which remain extremely popular today, shared the same sources. Outside of these particularly deep-rooted cases, however, other similar innovations woven from the scriptures were no longer accepted by Christian churches—either Protestant or Catholic—after the Reformation and the Council of Trent.

In the masonic rite of initiation, Hiram, projection and adaptation of the tradition, is the embodiment of Christ in the form of a minor deity. The Church itself declared as much for eight centuries through Bedes and Strabo's commentaries on the Bible. In them, Hiram and Adoniram are seen to be combined in a single figure: the image and figure of Christ. As we learned earlier, *Hic est Christus* is written in the text about Adoniram (*Ordinary Gloss* in Kings III, 5:28).

The comparison gains more strength when we recall that Adoniram was executed by stoning at the hands of the northern tribes of Israelites who rebelled with Jeroboam against Solomon, King of Judea and Jerusalem, and then against his son Roboam. To Roboam the Israelites declared, "What have we to do with the son of Jesse?" (Kings I, 22:16–18). These are words fraught with significance, for according to Saint Matthew, who based his position on Isaiah (11:1–10), Jesse, David, and the kings of Judea were the source of Christ's genealogy:

And there shall come forth a rod out of the stem of Jesse, and a branch shall grow out of his roots. And the spirit of the Lord shall rest upon him, the spirit of wisdom and understanding, the spirit of counsel and might, the spirit of knowledge and fear of the Lord. And shall make him of quick understanding in the fear of the Lord. And in that day there shall be a root of Jesse, which shall stand for an ensign of the people.

No other prophecy exists that influenced the art of the Middle Ages in such enduring fashion. According to Emile Mâle, the motif of the tree of Jesse seems to have been conceived by Abbot Suger, for the oldest known image of the Jesse Tree can be found in Saint Denis in a stained-glass window that dates to a time earlier than 1144. Jesse Trees were numerous in the twelfth and thirteenth centuries and can be found in stained glass (for example, in Chartres, Saint Denis, Le Mans, and Sainte Chapelle) and in the archivolts of portals (in Senlis, Mantes, Laon, Chartres, Amiens . . .). Starting at the end of the thirteenth century, the Virgin began appearing at the top of the tree, holding the Infant Jesus in her arms. She is the rose, the flower that blossoms at the tip of the stem.

How illuminating and eloquent Hiram's legend becomes when placed alongside Christ's Ascension, which was so often celebrated by stone sculptors, masons, and carpenters.

All the prophets and seers of Israel, all those heralds of Christ, all those figures who gravitated around the scriptures and the Apocrypha and oral tradition or the books of legends such as Jacques de Voragine's *Golden Legend,* Comestor's *Historia Scholastica,* and Vincent de Beauvais's *Speculum Historiale* [Mirror of History]—all of these were common figures to the people of the Middle Ages. Each year at Christmas or on Epiphany or other religious feast days and commemorative celebrations, these figures and their retinues paraded in costume. The processions they formed entered the church or cathedral and each of them, at the call of his or her name, stepped forth to give witness to the truth, reciting a verse or a monologue. Religious dramas and mysteries emerged from these kinds of processions and the same thought behind them provided the same lessons everywhere. It permeated all of life's circumstances.

Using an understanding of the amphibological meaning of Christ's Passion with respect to the French and English crafts of the Middle Ages, this is a good time to revisit these mysteries. The Passion was certainly the subject that aroused the greatest enthusiasm in the medieval imagination. In truth, it was the preferred study of the Middle Ages, inspiring men such as Saint Francis of Asissi to push love to the extreme until it was impossible for them to make any distinction between themselves and Christ. It was expected that these figures, who had served as heralds, would also be illustrations of the Passion in accordance with the indications of their gestures as related by the scriptures and various legends. All of this served as a departure point for the elaboration of the Mysteries, which in this way rejoined and continued the traditions of the ancient mysteries.

The masons' legend connected to Hiram belongs within this general framework. The circumstantial and fixed death of Hiram, followed by his resurrection within his own person as well as in those who emulated him, is a reflection of the Passion in the fullness of its lesson. It is also a continuation and the Christianized spiritual finality of the ancient mysteries: the attainment of immortality and understanding through by incorporating the divine substance within oneself and through this, becoming a god. In simpler terms, the legend, without its pagan overtones defiling its harmony, is the glorification of Christianity: finding the road to salvation and eternal life by building within the ideal and undying dwelling of the Lord.

A final observation may prove helpful in explaining the symbolic meaning of these narratives. The majority of ancient Bibles provide a lexicon that interprets Hebrew names. In Franciscus de Hailbrun's Bible (Venise, 1480; Bibliothèque nationale, Res. A2331), for instance, we can read: "Adoniram = *dominus exaltatus, vel dominator sublimes; Hiram = vivit excelsus, aut vivens est excelse.*" The word *abi* means *pater,* father, which lends even more support to the identical nature and unity of the two figures. *Adon (dominus)* is the precursor to the name Hiram, which is the explanation that Vuillaume gives in his *Masonic Tiler.* Lord the Father, Lord most high, Lord of Life—we find the same amphibology on the initiatory legend. These were commonly taught during the Middle Ages, connections that everyone understood in the theophany in which the world lived.

To measure the importance of the legend for which Hiram's legend is central, it is important to note that despite the existence of three levels in masonry—apprentice, journeyman, and master in Scotland, England, and on the Continent—we cannot assume that three separate rituals existed for initiation at these three levels. The initiation ritual among the operative masons should be viewed as a single entity marking the true entrance of the apprentice into the craft—in other words, his graduation to journeyman when he had successfully completed his apprenticeship. In addition to this initiation ceremony, there would be ritual forms of practice. We can see, then, what must have become two traditional rituals practiced during the time of transition from operative to speculative Freemasonry. One took place in the lodge of apprentices (for general trade meetings), the other in the lodge of journeymen and masters (meetings concerning the intrinsic secrets of the craft). The private ritual of the masters only appeared later and the speculative or "accepted" masons divided the rites of masters, initiation, and practice into three differentiated rituals.

"Accepted" Masons

The speculative character of operative masonry was transmitted and maintained but certainly softened since the time of the Reformation with respect to the spiritual and traditional perception of its rites and symbols. It was reinvigorated—though with certain adaptations—when freemasonry began admitting "accepted" members, meaning accredited individuals who were foreign to the actual craft of masonry. These new members were attracted to the order for three reasons.

First, masonry, along with all other corporations and brotherhoods, offered the only possible form for associations in the society of the time. In France, illicit assemblies were ranked as capital crimes until the end of the Ancien Régime. In his *Somme Rurale,* Boutillier defined an assembly as illegal when it exceeded the number of three people. Second, the nature of masonry, including its privileges, the renown of its masters and artisans, the kinds of matters that could be discussed in that company, and the protection offered by powerful patrons, must have had a seductive effect on studious and contemplative minds seeking to increase their knowledge and share their ideas without arousing suspicion. Finally, because of the nature of its work, masonry was the sole corporation not tied to one locale. Thus it maintained connections between cities and even countries that offered protection and welcome to brothers away from home. In this regard it played a significant and unique role in the exchange and spread of ideas.

The admission of "accepted" members is a very old practice in masonry. Clerics were always to be found in the association because of the religious foundation of mastery associations and brotherhoods. This was how a priest initiated into the order was the one to draft the famous *Masonic Poem (Regius Manuscript)* at the end of the fourteenth century. This priest most likely held the duties of chaplain or secretary or perhaps both. In the seventeenth century, Atcheson Haven Lodge shows these duties entrusted to a notary who was intentionally initiated as a mason so that he could write apprenticeship contracts.[3]

Over time many other figures were given access to masonry, whether because they themselves were drawn by the institution's prestige or because their support was sought by the organization. This was how King Henry IV and the nobles of his court were initiated into the brotherhood in 1442.[4] Indeed, the *Regius Manuscript* mentions apprentices "with the blood of high lords." It is obvious that this does not refer to the sons of high nobility who were actually plying the craft of masonry. The *Cooke Manuscript* is the first to employ the word *speculative*. The son of King Athelstan, it states, was a true speculative master.

In these older times, the professional or operative element was more prevalent in the order. But an era eventually arrived when the external element, the accepted, prevailed over the operative element, first in quality then in actual quantity. This occurred when artisans confined to their professional tasks considered all that had constituted the grandeur and prestige of the order to be nothing more than an old, worn garment. This old clothing, deemed to be more or less anachronistic by humble craftsmen, was, however, quite suitable for the needs of others.

For various reasons, the task of achieving this transformation—this subrogation, to use a legal term—belonged to the lodges of Great Britain.* The Scottish lodges preceded the British lodges down this

---

* Although L. Vibert claims the contrary, the German Hütten included accepted members. We need only refer to the stonecutter statutes for proof of this. Further proof can be found in the well-known sign of the interlaced square and compass with the letter G at its center, which served as the logo of Strasbourg publisher Jean Grieninger in 1525, a time when the corporation was still enjoying the height of its prosperity in that city (Clavel, *Histoire pittoresque de la Franc-Maçonnerie,* 86; B. E. Jones, *Freemason's Guide and Compendium,* 299).

path. In fact, we have already seen that since 1439 the Scottish lodges had hereditary grand masters in the Lords Saint Clair.*

Under the reign of James V (1513–1542), husband of Mary of Lorraine and father of Mary Stuart, the wind of a new era was blowing through Scottish high society. The king was a fervent humanist as well as an admirer of the ideas and masterpieces of the Renaissance. Did he inspire this interest? The fact remains that Lord Sinclair resolved to visit Italy. He returned full of enthusiasm and immediately decided to entrust to Italian artists the construction of a chapel inside his domain at Roslyn. This chapel is still standing today and is admired by its visitors for the high quality of its architectural décor, in which shines all the masonic symbolism of the time. Not content merely with building a chapel, Sinclair invited additional Italian masons, put them together with Scottish masons, organized them into a brotherhood, and granted them a charter. From that time, under the protection of the king, this brotherhood's prospects soared.[5]

It appears that we can trace the origins of the transformation of operative masonry to this era. During this time, through the infusion of new blood, it was given a new impetus that could be seen on both the cultural and artisitic planes.

The first historic trace of a nonoperative Mason who was neither a powerful patron nor a cleric is provided by the minutes of a meeting of the Mary's Chapel Lodge in Edinburgh on June 8, 1600. This "accepted" mason was John Bosnel of Auchinlek, but it is certain he was not the first. On May 20, 1641, the members of this same Edinburgh lodge, who were then in Newcastle with the Scottish Army, admitted as an accepted mason the honorable Robert Moray, the general quarter master of the army. Interestingly, it had been long-standing practice to form lodges within Irish and Scottish regiments. In chapter 13, we will see the important role this played in the establishment of modern Freemasonry on the Continent, especially in France.

---

* [Saint Clair was eventually Anglicized to Sinclair. —*Trans.*]

In 1670, more than three quarters of the members of the Aberdeen Lodge were not professional masons and the Laws and Statutes specified that this speculative membership was exempt from the collecting box, the mark, the banquet, and the pint of wine. They paid no fees.*

The cohabiting cultural and social differences and differing objectives of the two groups did not fail to cause problems at times. The freedom and independence of the lodges as a whole led to the formation of certain lodges composed solely of nonoperative members. The first such case cited is the lodge constructed in 1702 by eight land owners in the village of Haugfool, near Galashiels.[6]

In England, the situation began to change noticeably after 1607, the year in which James I named Inigo Jones the General Intendent of the Buildings of the Crown, a title that gave him authority over the entire corporation of masons. Just like Lord Sinclair, Inigo Jones had been smitten in Italy by the style of Andrea Palladio and had taken to heart the desire to transplant it to England. To achieve this, he organized lodges on the model of the Italian academies, where skilled instructors could give lessons in architecture based on the principles of the school he championed.

These novel events produced two noteworthy results: First, the number of unschooled masons gradually diminished. Second, prestigious figures seeking culture requested admission into the corporation. This was how the doors of the lodges began opening wider and wider to people who were not professional masons—but their admission rested on the express condition that they use their social influence and knowledge to benefit the masonic community without receiving in return the privileges of working masons. It then became fashionable for nobles and the rich to be received as masons. In 1620, a group of accepted masons gathered in London under the auspices of the Company of Masons. At this time, seven individuals who were not part of the company were confirmed as accepted masons in return for a special tax.[7]

When the large embellishment projects that had been undertaken to

---

* Nonoperative members, generally gentlemen of higher birth, who were accepted in the seventeenth-century Scottish Lodges were customarily referred to as Geomatics, while professional masons were known as Domatics. (See Gould, *A Concise History of Freemasonry.*)

incorporate the new architectural style were completed, working masons were forced to disperse in order to seek employment. The same was not true for the accepted masons, who gained strength through the admission of new brothers. This fact and the social position of these lettered individuals ensured that the accessory portion became the principal part and took the corporation's business into their hands. The statutes published on the occasion of the large masonic assembly held in 1663 establish evidence of this.

Philosophical and Mystical Influences

It is important to understand the spiritual influences freemasonry was subject to during this transformation, or at least to comprehend those that facilitated this transformation.

An accepted fact of history is that from the end of the fifteenth century in Italy through the sixteenth and seventeenth centuries in Europe as a whole, there was a strong inclination among educated individuals to join together in more or less secret societies. The desire to create these kinds of groups, their organizational plan, and their goals arose in large part from the reading of certain books published in different forms by the illustrious authors of that time, principally Thomas More, Rabelais, Andrea, Francis Bacon, and Robert Fludd.

In his famous work *Utopia* (1516), Sir Thomas More (1477–1535) puts into practice a program of democratic reform on the imaginary island of Utopia. In this society, the chief concern of government is to furnish the material needs for individual and public consumption. Each individual is given as much time as possible to free him- or herself from the servitude of the body, freely cultivate his or her mind, and develop his or her intellectual abilities through the study of the letters and sciences. The civil organization of the Utopians is republican and all religions are tolerated. Here we should note an important point as observed by A. Lantoine. "It was Sir Thomas More who created a word that until that time was unknown: tolerance."

In his rule of the abbey of Theleme, Rabelais (1494–1553), who was certainly an accepted mason, has left us with the constitution of a society of free men. The sole rule of the Thelemites was this:

Do what you will, because people who are free, well-born, well-bred, and easy in honest company have a natural instinct that drives them to virtuous deeds and deflects them from vice—and this they call honour. When these same men are depressed and enslaved by vile constraint and subjection, they use this noble quality, which once impelled them freely towards virtue, to throw off and break this yoke of slavery. For we always strive after things forbidden and covet what is denied us.[8]

Johan Valentin Andrea (1586–1654), abbot of Adesberg, was the unintentional founder of the Rosicrucians. In 1610, he published *Fama fraternitis,* or *Discovery of the Honorable Order of the Rosy Cross,* a work inspired entirely by his imagination. In this fictional work, he recounts the fabulous story of a certain Christian Rosenkreuz who discovered a secret, concealed for centuries, that could ensure the happiness of humanity. To enable the success of his propaganda, he founded a secret college (lodge) whose purpose was doing charitable works and promoting internationalism and the advancement of true morality and religion. The members of this society were required to swear to the strictest discretion. The book enjoyed great success and its readers, particularly in England, believed the Order of the Rosy Cross genuinely existed. Andrea followed up his first work with others, notably *The Universal Reformation of the Entire World* (1614) and *The Chemical Wedding of Christian Rosenkreuz* (1616).

Robert Fludd (1547–1637), whose works enjoyed considerable success, established himself as a defender of the Rosicrucian Order. Rosicrucian societies were formed in London under his influence and adopted his philosophical doctrines. These ideas were inspired by those of Paracelsus, Cornelius Agrippa of Nettesheim, and Jacob Boheme and consisted of a synthesis of alchemy, the Kabbalah, and Neoplatonic and Hebraic traditions collected from the writings of Hermes Trismegistus mixed with the ambitions and mysticim of the Rosicrucians.

Francis Bacon (1560–1626) chancellor of James I, is the famous author of *La Nova Atlantis*. In this fictional work, Bacon depicts a republic headed by a secret society consisting entirely of intellectuals from the fields of both letters and sciences. The members of this order, who called each other brother, devoted themselves in complete freedom to philosophical discussion and to working to improve the conditions of the lower classes and advance true religion and morality.

One final avatar whose plans for an ideal society offer many analogies to the tenets of modern Freemasonry is the famous Czech pedagogue Jan Amos Komensky. The persecutions suffered by reformers in Catholic countries during the Thirty Years' War and the sight of the bloody collisions among races and religions had inspired in some noble souls the conception of a humanitarian mysticism for which Komensky was an eloquent spokesman. He dreamed of the reconciliation of the principal Christian factions. In his *Pansophia Diatyposis* (1643) and his *De rerum humanarum emendatione catholica,* whose first parts were published in 1666 under the titles *Panergesia* and *Panaugia,* he proposed the founding of a society with the purpose of spreading the ideas of tolerance and respect for the individual. The objective of this society would be the construction of a Temple of Wisdom, similar to the Temple of Solomon, built upon Mount Moriah (in other words the Temple Mount). Komensky also proposed the creation of a large international organization, the Collegium Lucis, which would be a Wisdom school to provide an education for those seeking to enter the Celestial Academy. All steps taken in this regard had to be taken secretly and Komensky's full treatise was to be shared only with those participating in the undertaking. All the academies and societies throughout Europe were to be encompassed within this vast organization, which would take London as its hub.

From the end of the fifteenth century and throughout both the sixteenth and seventeenth centuries in Europe, we can observe the creation of associations of thought that enjoyed the indispensable backing of sovereign authority. The goals of these associations, the oldest of which first saw the light of day in Italy, cradle of the Renaissance, corresponded more or less to those of fiction's imaginary societies.

Marsilio Ficino founded a Neoplatonic society in Florence as early as 1460. It was certainly no secret association—its patrons were the Medicis—nor an initiatory one. But it was still novel for its time. The philosophy Ficino taught there would leave a significant mark on the next generation, influencing Cornelius Agrippa, Thomas More, and

Rabelais. It was Ficino's contribution to develop a syncretic philosophy inspired by the systems of Zoroaster, Hermes, Orpheus, Pythagoras, Plato, the Kabbalah, and Christian philosophy. He wrote:

> God appeared in eternity, creating or rather luminously emanating from the center of the circumference, which radiates outward from being and good to nothingness and evil. As men, who are intelligences, finite lights within the abode of time and movement, we aspire toward that motionless light for which we are its mobile emanantions. Death, by delivering us from the body, draws us close to it and its other angelic lights, pure spirits whose bliss is found in rest. Death is therefore a pleasure and it is death that the philospher dives into each day when leaving the body to soar on the wings of the soul.[9]

In 1512, Florence would also witness the creation of an original organization, the Company of the Trowel. This society appears to have emerged from the operative masonry that preceded it, although it left behind its material purpose to embrace its mystical intent. Consisting of scholars and prominent figures of the civil society of the time, it employed symbols such as the trowel, the hammer, and the chisel and chose for its patron saint the same one who watched over the Scottish masons: Saint Andrew.[10] We know the great influence the Italian academies had over the English and Scottish Freemason lodges. Undoubtedly the Platonic Academy and the Company of the Trowel, whose members were the same as those of the academies, exerted a similar influence.

Another important society that likely had an effect on masonry, however indirect, is the Guild of Mages. It was founded in 1510 by Henri Cornelius Agrippa when he arrived in London and was modeled on the organization he had already created in France. The Guild of Mages was a secret society consisting of masters of alchemy and magic. Its members, who used personal identification signs and passwords, founded corresponding organizations—*chapelies*—in other European countries for the purpose of studying the "forbidden" sciences. If we give credence to a manuscript by Michael Meir (1568–1622), conserved in the Leipzig Library, this Guild of Mages gave birth in Germany to the Brothers of the Gold Rose-Cross in 1570, which was earlier than Valentin Andrea's *Fama Fraternitatis.* *

The Rosicrucians represent the most direct influence on the transformation from operative masonry to speculative Freemasonry. At the beginning of the seventeenth century, there existed in Holland, Germany, and England various groups of learned men who formed secret societies in conformance with the principles proclaimed by the books we have already mentioned, but particularly Andrea's *Brotherhood of the Rosy Cross*. Not surprisingly, these same men were drawn to freemasonry. In fact, Sir Robert Moray, who, as we have learned, was admitted as an accepted mason in the Lodge of Edinburgh in 1641, was a Rosicrucian.[11]

Because of its symbolism, masonry provided an especially propitious environment for this influence. The first proof of a relationship between freemasonry and the Rosicrucian Society can be found in a poem published in Edinburg in 1638: *Muses Threnodie*. Its author was Henry Adamson, master of the arts and citizen of Perth. In it we can read this verse:

> *For we breathren of the Rosies Cross*
> *We have the mason work and second sight.*

Rosicrucianism's most profound effect on Freemasonry can be observed in London. Toward the end of the first half of the seventeenth century, one Rosy Cross Society was a powerful organization in the capital. Alchemy was then at the height of its popularity and its adepts played an important role—as paradoxical as it may appear—in the

---

* The Agla, an association of book craftsmen, is another example of a sixteenth-century esoteric society whose influence on the creation of modern Freemasonry is less obvious but no less significant. The collective "glyph" of this vast organization was the number 4, which figured in the personal mark of every master of this brotherhood, frequently drawn atop a secondary figure representing an internal group to which the signatory belonged. For example, a hexagram, "Solomon's Seal," the planetary sign of Saturn, or the monogram of Mary designated a group concerned with alchemy and hermetic studies, whereas the heart, such as the one found on playing cards, indicated a branch in which mysticism, particularly that of the Kabbalah, was studied and practiced. See Amberlain, *Le Martinisme* (Paris: Niclas, 1946), 48 and 55.

founding of that great scholarly association known as the Royal Society.[12] One of the most active members of London's Rosicrucian society was Elias Ashmole (1617–1692), known by the nickname "the English Mecuriophile." After performing well in his studies, he became a solicitor in 1638 and in 1641 returned to his native Litchfield. There he became a staunch supporter of the Stuarts' cause in 1644 and was named a commissioner of the king. Some have maintained that Ashmole was an Israelite, but in actuality he was an active member of London's Catholic circle and was buried in the Catholic church of South Lambeth.[13]

Ashmole was introduced to the Rosicrucian Society by William Backhouse and on October 16, 1646, according to his own journal, was admitted as an accepted mason into the Warrington Lodge. Here he found himself in the company of the Warton brothers, Thomas and George; the mathematician William Oughteed; the doctors of theology John Herwitt and John Prarson; and the astrologer William Lilly.

With these men he founded a society whose purpose was to build the House of Solomon, the ideal temple of the sciences, in imitation of the models imagined by Sir Thomas More and Francis Bacon. He persuaded the masons to allow them to meet on their premises. We should note that the society formed by Ashmole, like those of More and Bacon, was meant to remain secret.

In 1724, a manuscript of ancient masonic constitutions was printed under the title *The Secret History of the Free-Masons*. Its preface presented the Rosicrucians and masons as "brothers of the same fraternity or order." Similarly, the Daily Journal of September 5, 1730, indicates that the modern Freemasonry was an offshoot of the Rosicrucian Society.

Political and Religious Influences

Just as it was practice in Germany for factions to seek the support of the rich, organized, powerful guilds and corporations during divisive times such as the election of emperors or the religious wars, in England, when the struggle broke out between the Stuart royal family and Parliament and later between the Stuarts and the House of Orange or Hanover, political parties sought to enlist the corporations to their side. It seems that the Stuarts, from James I to Charles III, likely employed such measures, at least with respect to the freemasons. It is also certain that they intensified the establishment of masonic lodges inside the regiments in order to create political auxiliaries. In 1689, Scottish and Irish regiments landed in France with their military and masonic staffs. According to scholar Gustave Bord, these military staffs were the executive agents while the masonic personnel were the administrative authority.

When James II was dethroned in 1688, the corporation of masons was under the authority of Christopher Wren, superintendent of the royal buildings and an ardent Jacobite. He nonetheless held this position until 1695 and regained it in 1698, exercising this authority until 1702 and the ascension of Queen Anne, who reinforced the Protestant factions. Freemasonry was still so Jacobite at this time that the masons refused to continue work on the construction of Saint Paul's Cathedral, which would not be completed until 1710, despite the orders of William Benson, inspector of the Queen's buildings.[14]

It is likely that the Catholic influence on the freemasons remained significant under the Protestant monarchy of William of Orange. The text of the 1693 *Charter of the York Lodge,* which reproduces much older statutes, states that "the first article of your Instructions is that you will be faithful to God and the Holy Church, to the Prince, to his Master, and to the Lady he serves." The same structure is found in statutes dating from 1704. The term "Holy Church" could refer here to the official Anglican church, rather than the Catholic church, but it is likely that in the minds of numerous masons the traditional expression continued to mean the Holy Catholic Church.

This likelihood seems to be supported historically. It is a fact that the Orangemen tried to make use of masonic lodges and sought to change their traditional Catholic orientation. It appears fairly well established that William III of Orange was initiated as an accepted mason in 1694 or, more exactly, that some English masonic lodges put themselves under his protection at that time and that in this role of protector, he presided over several assemblies held at Hampton Court. This branch of masonry published new statutes in 1694 in which Article I was redrafted: "Your first duty is to be faithful to God and to avoid all the heresies that misinterpret him." This masonry, whose allegiance was pledged to the Protestantism of William of Orange, simply omitted the reference to "the Holy Church" to which masons had always been expected to swear fidelity. This omission appears to show that the expression "Holy Church" was not assumed to refer to the Anglican church. The Orangemen deemed it preferable simply to suppress a dangerous connection to a Catholic tradition.

In the next chapter we will revisit these incidents of religious interference and the controversies they raised with the formation of the Great Lodge of London and with Scottish Freemasonry.

The Decline of Operative Freemasonry

At the same time that speculative and "accepted" Freemasonry was developing under the effect of philosophical, religious, and political influences, the corporation of professional masons was undergoing a slow death.

In 1666, a terrible fire destroyed 40,000 houses and 86 churches in London. Given that there were only seven lodges at that time in London, nine tenths of whose members were accepted masons, it proved necessary to summon masons from all the counties of England to rebuild the city. These masons and architects put themselves under the authority of the Company of the Masons of London and the architect Christopher Wren. Seven years earlier, under the direction of Wren, construction on Saint Paul's had begun, with King Charles II laying the first stone. At that time, the count of Arlington was the protector of the corporation, but operative masonry was nonetheless in full and obvious decline.

In 1703, the Lodge Saint Paul made a decision that reveals how Freemasonry had gradually transformed: "The privileges of masonry will henceforth no longer be reserved for construction workers alone, but, as it is already a practice, they will be extended to persons of all estates who would wish to take part therein, provided they be duly presented, that their admission be authorized, and that they be initiated in the usual manner."

The history of speculative Freemasonry had begun.

13

The Grand Lodges and Modern Freemasonry

The Grand Lodge of London

On June 24, 1717, Saint John's Day, four London lodges with names borrowed from the taverns where they gathered—The Goose and Gridiron, The Crown, The Apple Tree, and The Rummer and the Grapes—formed a unified organization under the name of the Grand Lodge.[1] Anthony Sayer, a gentleman, was elected grand master and was given authority over all his brothers. On June 24, 1718, he was succeeded by George Payne, who ordered work begun to gather together all the charters in England having to do with Masonry. Replaced the following year by John Theophilus Desaguliers, Payne again assumed the office of grand master in 1720. The Grand Lodge first became a regulatory body in 1721 at the same time the Duke of Montaigu was elected grand master.

The Scottish pastor James Anderson was given the charge of drafting the *Book of Constitutions,* published in 1723 under the grand master the Duke of Wharton and containing both the legendary history of the fraternity and the obligations of Freemasons. Other authors have noted that Anderson, an intellect of small scope, was almost certainly not the true author. The better part of the material and the thought behind it was likely supplied by Desaguliers. The son of a pastor of

New Rochelle who emigrated to London following the revocation of the Edict of Nantes, Desaguliers had a brilliant and supple mind that was universal in scope and was himself a pastor, doctor of law, physician, mathematician, member of the Royal Society, friend of Newton, and chaplain to the Prince of Wales.

We do not know the official reasons for the creation of the Grand Lodge of London, which was fairly modest at conception. Emphasis has been placed on a possible need for a regulatory power over the lodges. As long as freemasonry remained operative, rather than speculative, this power belonged to the guild or company, which supervised the lodges to ensure their members adequately met the duties of their craft. The situation changed when lodges were formed by "accepted" masons. The danger became a potential influx of external contributions and innovations invading the institution and distorting the spirit of the organization as a whole. Religious and political quarrels have also been mentioned as a possible impetus. Men in positions of power could, for the purpose of pacification, impose their views and discpline over the workshops that, under the practice of the old customs, were somewhat independent and autonomous. All of these probable reasons for the formation of the Grand Lodge more or less mesh with one another and can be justified, with inflexions and nuances, by the events that took place not only in Great Britain but on the Continent as well.

The British Reactions

Article 1 of the *Obligations* of 1723, an accessory document to the *Book of Constitutions,* concerns God and religion:

> A mason is oblig'd, by his Tenure, to obey the moral law; and if he rightly understands the Art, he will never be a stupid Atheist nor an irreligious Libertine. But though on ancient Times Masons were charg'd in every Country to be the Religion of that Country or Nation, whatever it was, yet'tis now thought more expedient only to oblige them to that Religion in wich all Men agree, leaving their particular Opinions to themselves; that is, to bee good Men and True, or Men of Honour and Honesty, by whatever Denominations or

Persuations they may be distinguish'd; whereby Masonry becomes the Center of Union and the Means of conciliating true Frienship among Persons that must have remain'd at a perpetual Distance.

This is a magnificently literal declaration of tolerance, which seems to put an end to the conflict dividing Catholics and Anglican Protestants on the subject of the "Holy Church." In the silence that surrounds the actual intentions of the text and in order to discover what they may precisely have been, quite a few highly debated interpretations have been offered. At the outset it is important to note that it would be an exaggeration to claim, as some in France have done, that the tolerance this document displays is akin to a proclamation of free thought.[2] This would be the equivalent of declaring that modern Freemasonry no longer has anything whatsoever in common with operative freemasonry. But this is a highly partisan form of reasoning and completely ignores the climate of the time and environment in which the *Book of Constitutions* was written.

In 1943, Knoop and Jones, in their study *Freemasonry and the Idea of Natural Religion,* which was presented before the Quatour Coronati Lodge of London,[3] have emphasized the evidence that the 1723 constitutions involved a kind of deism, but they did not push their analysis more deeply. In 1965, another member of the Lodge Quatour Coronati, J. E. Clarke, went much further. Under the title *The Change from Christianity to Deism in Freemasonry,*[4] he maintained the theory that the *Book of Constitutions* deliberately rejected Christianity and replaced it by simple deism as the religious basis and profession of faith in Freemasonry, despite the order's apparent monotheism. He did not explain, however, what meaning could thus remain invested in what remained of the rituals and ancient symbolism of operative masonry.

Akin to Clarke's theory, but reaching a different conclusion, was the hypothesis put forth by Albert Lantoine in 1925 in his book *La Franc-Maçonnerie chez elle.* It is interesting to note that Lantoine had little inclination to center his interpretation of Freemasonry on its symbolism. In his opinion, the liberal deism of 1723 was assumed as a ploy until Anglican Protestantism should emerge triumphant and that this is proved by later editions of the *Book of Constitutions* in which theism took the place of deism.

The best argument J. R. Clarke provided to support his contention that deism became the rule is that Jews were accepted into Freemasonry shortly after 1723. First mention of this is in the *Daily Post,* September 22, 1732, and *Fog's Journal,* October 7, 1732, which announced the admission of Daniel Delvalle.[5] How could Jews who remained orthodox utilize the Christian symbolism of traditional freemasonry? And why would the lodges have admitted them if they had renounced Freemasonry's principles?

In his missive *Anderson's Freemasonry not Deistic,*[6] E. Ward responded by showing, with the support of precise facts, that English Freemasonry had actually retained Christian objectives following 1723. Thus the admission of Jews into Freemasonry could amount to only isolated instances corresponding to particular circumstance, much like the admission of several Turks into the lodges of Smyrna and Aleppo in 1738.

Ward also thought it wise in regard to the dispositions of Pastor Anderson's mind to quote two sermons, one of which was published in the very year of 1723: *"Refutation of the Errors of the Socinianus, Pythagorians, Papists and Others."* The other, *"Unity in Trinity against Idolaters, Modern Jews, and Anti-Trinitarians,"* was published in 1733. Besides the rejection of the Jews, Freemasonry's apparent rejection of "papists" and "idolators" reinforces Lantoine's sentiments. The tolerance of the *Book of Constitutions* barely conceals the struggle against the Catholics as a means for Anglicans to defend Christianity.

But we should also look at the contemporary reactions of London and Great Britain as a whole to the founding of the Grand Lodge of London. Tolerance, even if it was a ploy, was nonetheless seen as being in tune with rituals and the formulation of oaths, invocations, and prayers using any word or expression that might irk anyone or cause controversy, no matter the form of Christian worship. Many saw tolerance as a renunciation—if not an outright denial—of Christian disbelief.

For a long time, the influence of the Grand Lodge of London remained constricted because its jurisdiction was confined only to the cities of London and Westminster and their suburbs. The majority of lodges, especially those in the provinces, were reluctant to abandon their independence and they continued to respect the ancient obligations of the craft. In 1722, the same time that Anderson was writing his text, the edition of *Ancient Constitutions* cited earlier appeared in London, with this first article: "I am to admonish you to honour God in his holy Church; that you use no Heresy, Schism and Error in your Understandings, or discredit Men's Teachings."[7] Could these words be read as an answer to the views like those of Anderson and Desaguliers?

One of the principal centers of resistance to the Grand Lodge of London was the Old Lodge of York. The oppositional workshops, called *antients,* were not grouped in any kind of denominational format, although in 1725 the Old Lodge of York adopted the title of Grand Lodge of England, which corresponded more with its ancestral role of mother lodge than to any demoninational power. This grand lodge existed until 1792 and in the interim, in 1779, it even gave a charter to another grand lodge that lasted a dozen years, the Grand Lodge of England South of the River Trent.

It was only in 1751, with the struggle unrelenting, that the opponents of the Grand Lodge of London, resolved to fight against it in force and by using the same weapons, formed a veritable rival organization, the Grand Lodge of the Free and Accepted Masons According to the Old Institutions.

The Antients reproached the Moderns for having omitted prayers, dechristianizing the ritual, and no longer honoring the holy days (the feasts of the two Saint Johns). To them at stake was the tradition inherited from the craft—at least what had survived of the tradition, for the terrain had been altered for a long while and the transcendent perception of this tradition had been watered down or transformed under the pressure of outside influences. The best proof of this evolution lies in the differences that existed between "traditional" seventeenth-century rituals of the Antients, on the one hand, and what we now know about the ritual of the operative masons, on the other. In any case, when respect for Christianity was invoked in the seventeenth century, little remained in either Catholicism or Anglicism of what had expressed and given life to Christian expression in the thirteenth or fourteenth centuries. Disuse had scuttled the traditional.

In Scotland, the lodges long retained their independence with respect to customs. In 1736, however, they too decided to form an independent overseeing authority—the Grand Lodge of Scotland—but its spirit was different from that of the Grand Lodge of London. While the Scottish masons used English Freemasonry as their model for a centralized denominational organization, they remained solidly attached to the traditional rites, leaning more to the side of the Antients and opposing the Moderns. It is significant that they named as their first grand master William Saint Clair of Roslyn, last in the line of the family of the hereditary protectors of the Scottish lodges. The Scottish distinction was further emphasized by the undying fidelity of many to the house of Stuart and the Catholic religion, the sole "Holy Church" for them in the terms of the old obligations. Despite all this, a number of Scottish lodges did not rally to the new denominational form. Their resistance found a cohesive structure in 1743 when the old Mother Lodge of Kilwinning established itself as a single grand lodge, like that of York or England.

But staunch Scottish resistance to masonic modernism did not only occur in Scotland. It was also taking hold, perhaps even more strongly, on the Continent, primarily in France.

Scottish Freemasonry in France

It is commonly believed that modern French Freemasonry was an offshoot of English Freemasonry and that the first French lodges were created if not directly by the Grand Lodge of London, then at least on the model of those lodges it established.

This opinion conforms to the claims of the Grand United Lodge of England, which, although formed in 1815 by the merger of the Antients and the Moderns, dates its founding to 1717 and by virtue of this feels it should be recognized as the Grand Mother Lodge of the World as well as guardian of the masonic tradition. Many French Freemasons are receptive to this viewpoint with one major distinction: They place this modern tradition with Anderson's 1723 *Book of Constitutions,* where, as they read them, theism and deism gave way to free thought. This of course does not result in atheism so much as nondogmatic attitudes. We know that this interpretation is strongly rejected by the English, who today are clearly in support of a theism that leaves each brother the freedom of his faith.

It should be noted that in this debate made obscure by sectarian attitudes, the question is not one of explicitly defining the tradition and its temporal formulation, but rather of knowing if a tradition—truly, two traditions—might not have been substituted for another one. Everyone might thus be either correct or mistaken and find themselves on a path that has been substituted for the Christian tradition of the operative masons and its initiatory path.

Perhaps it is best to stick to the historical data. In actuality, speculative Freemasonry was imported into France by Scottish Catholics and the Stuarts. According to the book *Annales Maçonniques des Pays-Bas*,[8] which cites a sixteenth-century document, there were two Scottish lodges in France in 1535: one in Paris and the other in Lyon. While this is debatable, we do know that as early as the sixteenth century, Scottish craft freemasonry was admitting accepted members. The Scots had already long been in the habit of forming military lodges, so it is not gratuitous to assume that the Scots—who had been part of the French court for some time where they notably formed one of the king's noble guard units (the Ramsays were part of it in the fifteenth century)—had introduced the customs of their own country into their adopted land. The ties between the Scots and French were strengthened further during the sixteenth century when Mary Stuart I, Queen of the Scots from 1542 to 1567, became Queen of France through her marriage to François II (1558–1560).

The ancestral role played by Scottish Freemasonry in France is confirmed by the knight Ramsay in his famous *Discourse* of 1737: "By degrees our Lodges and our rites were neglected in most places. This is why of so many historians only those of Great Britain speak of our Order. Nevertheless it preserved its splendour among those Scotsmen to whom the Kings of France confided during many centuries the safeguard of their royal persons."

The presence of Scottish lodges in France was more evident when the Stuarts were forced into exile following their reign in England. In 1649, following the beheading of Charles I, his widow Henrietta of

France, daughter of Henri IV and Marie de Medici, accepted a royal refuge in the chateau of Saint Germain en Laye from King Louis XIV. She was soon joined there by numerous members of the Scottish nobility.

Without delay, they organized anti-Cromwellian activity with an eye to promoting the restoration of the heir, Prince Charles II. To protect themselves from English strangers or those hostile to their side and to lead Cromwell's police astray, they acted under the cover of the masonic lodges, of which they were honorary members. Under the protection of so-called trade secrecy and without too much risk of commiting an indiscretion, they could thereby communicate with their brothers who had remained in Great Britain to plot the overthrow of the "dictator."[9]

In 1661, on the eve of ascending the throne of England, Charles II formed a regiment in Saint Germain called the Royal Irish, whose name was soon changed to the Irish Guard. Under the orders of Lord Colonel William Dorrington, this regiment, which outlived the Stuarts, landed in Brest on October 8, 1689, as part of the surrender terms of Limerick. Until 1698, it maintained a garrison in Saint Germain but remained independent of any French units, although it was maintained by Louis XIV. On February 27, 1698, it was incorporated into the French Army under the name of its colonel, still Lord Dorrington. This regiment of the Irish Guard seems to have had the oldest lodge recognized by the Grand Orient of France. In fact, on March 13, 1777, the Grand Orient acknowledged that the original constitution of the Guard dated from March 25, 1688.*

It is likely that this Scottish lodge in Saint Germain had no distinctive title originally and bore only the name of its colonel. After 1752, the name Perfect Equality appears, but it is possible that it existed under this name earlier. It is the sole French lodge of the seventeenth century that has left any sign of its existence, but it is conceivable that the Scots and Irish founded other lodges in France, notably inside a second regi-

---

* Ibid., 491. See also Loucelles, *Notices historiques sur la R. L.: La Bonne Foi à L'Orient de Saint Germaine en Laye*, (1874). F. Chevalier, *Les Dycs sons l'Acacia* cites a 1737 letter of Bortin du Rocheret that, when speaking of Freemasons, states: "Ancient society of England . . . introduced into France following King James II in 1689."

ment.* We are somewhat better informed about the Scots and Stuart lodges founded at the beginning of the eighteenth century. Unfortunately, as their appearance is coincident with that of the English lodges created under the aegis of the Grand Lodge of London, their distinctive quality has not always been noted, nor has the fact that until 1738, the date when the Duke d'Antin was named grand master of the masonic order in France, there were two categories of lodges in Great Britain: Scottish lodges and English lodges. The latter were dependencies and creations of the Grand Lodge of London while the former continued to live and spread based on the traditional rites of freemasonry. Among these Socttish lodges were the famous Lodge of Saint Thomas, named in memory of Saint Thomas à Becket, the saint most worshipped in Stuart England. This lodge was created in 1726 by a famous partisan of the Stuarts, Lord Derwentwater, about whom we will earn more.

Another Scottish lodge worth mentioning is the famous Lodge of Aubigny, established on August 12, 1735, in the castle of the same name owned by the Duke of Richmond, Lennox, and Aubigny, who had recently inherited his estate from his grandmother, Louise de Keroualle, the duchess of Portsmouth.[10] In her youth, Louise Renée de Penancoët de Keroualle had been considered the most beautiful woman in France. To serve King Louis XIV with the sole weapons she possessed, her beauty and taste for intrigue, she left France for the court of London, where she became the mistress of Charles II, who made her Duchess of Portsmouth. In her older years, she had become a deeply bigoted Catholic. Repenting of her past errors, she adorned the churches that sat on her lands with offerings of her piety and even installed a convent of Hospitaller nuns in her chateau. But her brilliance at intrigue had not abandoned her. Although she remained a fervent partisan of the Stuarts, she also frequented the other side, which paid more attention to her grandson, the Duke of Richmond. He had converted

---

* G. Bord, *La Franc-Maçonneries en France, des origins à*, 489–90. Most of this author's assertions are open to doubt although his scientific integrity is never in question. What is most disappointing about his work is the absence of references. L. Berteloot, who I knew well and who utilized Bord's line of argument in his own study, told me on several occasions that he knew the identity of the references justifying Bord's thesis, but because they were private sources, they could not be revealed.

to Anglicism from Catholicism but still enjoyed great credit in Catholic milieus. Just like his father, who had been sponsor in 1695 of a freemasonry that mixed operative and speculative members, he was grand master of the Grand Lodge of London in 1724, a time when this lodge, in the midst of a full crisis of growth, sought, under an apperance of tolerance, to take control of the lodges that remained independent and orthodox, both English and Scottish.

Before it was housed in the duchess's chateau, the Lodge of Aubigny had operated in its Parisian manor on the rue des Petits Augustins (Rue Bonaparte) or rue des Saints Pères (on the corner of the rue de Verneuil). It was established on August 12, 1735, by Lord Weymouth, grand master of the Grand Lodge of London. Hence its affiliation with that institution. This reveals how the opposition between the two versions of Freemasonry was not completely black and white. In fact, there was quite a bit of grey, evidence of the great spirit of tolerance solemnly proclaimed by the Orangemen and Hanoverians as well as by the Stuarts. This does not mean, however, that a spirit of competitive bidding and self interest was not also evident.

From the beginning, which was around 1728, the Scottish Lodges of France recognized as grand master Philip, duke of Wharton, former grand master of the Grand Lodge of London, and supporter of the Stuarts. At his death in 1731, Charles Radclyffe, Lord Derwentwater, assumed the status of grand master, followed Hector MacLean, Baronet of Scotland, from 1733 to 1735, and then Lord Derwentwater again in 1736.

The Radclyffes belonged to a very old family, which remained faithful to the House of Stuart and to Catholicism until the extincton of its line. It seems that Charles Radclyffe was inititiated by Sir Charles Ramsay. In attempting to return to England in 1746, he was captured and imprisoned. Condemned to death, he was executed on December 8, 1746. These were his final words:

> I die a true, obedient, and humble son of the Catholic Apostolic
> Church in perfect charity with all mankind and a true well-wisher
> to my dear country as I desire that it know no happiness until he
> treats with justice its king, the best and most slandered of sover-

eigns. I die with feelings of gratitude, respect, and love for the king of France, Louis the Beloved, a glorious name. I commend my family over to His Most Christian Majesty. I repent from the bottom of my heart for all my sins and I hold firm hope of being forgiven by all powerful God, by the grace of his blessed son Jesus Christ, Our Lord, to whom I commend my soul.

This declaration of faith provides an eloquent illustration of the state of mind of the Catholic Scots and Stuarts who had introduced Freemasonry into France from their land. This Scottish Freemasonry has certainly undergone a political divergence, but still remained true to its traditional principles of Catholicism and independent lodges. This mind-set is also asserted in the lines of a letter addressed by Ramsay to the Marquis de Caumont and dated April 1, 1737:

The unfortunate discord of Religion that set Europe ablaze and rent it apart during the sixteenth century ensured the degeneration of our order from the grandeur and nobility of its origins. In compliance with the usurping parricide, Elizabeth, who viewed our lodges as nests of Catholicism that needed to be snuffed out, the Protestants altered, disguised, and degraded several of our hieroglyphs, transformed our Agapes into Bacchanalias, and defiled our sacred assemblies. Milord, the Count of Derwentwater, Royal and Catholic martyr, wished to bring everything here back to its source and restore everything on its ancient footing. The ambassadors of Holland and George, the Duke of Hanover, by taking offense and blaspheming against what they do not know, imagining that the Catholic, Royalist, and Jacobite Freemasons are one and the same with the heretical, apostate, Republican Freemasons, first condemn us then cover us with Praise, shouting everywhere that we seek to raise a ninth Crusade to restore the true monarchy of Great Britain.[11]

Following the publication of Jerome Lalande's *Mémoire historique sur la Maçonnerie*,[12] it was generally accepted that Lord Derwentwater would have transferred his powers around 1736 to his friend Lord

Harnouester. But because this name could never be found listed in the Bristish peerage, the grand mastery of this lord ceased to be mentioned. The figure was either identified as Lord Derwentwater, his name being considered merely a corrupted form, or was simply labeled "Clodion of the Masonry."* In 1934, during a conference held by the English research lodge Quatour Coronati, W. E. Moss offered the opinion that the name Lord Harnouester could be a deformation of Count Charles Arran Wester of the Butler Family of Ormond, a title that appears in Scottish nobility and the Irish peerage and was held by zealous Stuart partisans.[13]

A letter dated August 2, 1737, from Ramsay to the Jacobite Carte[14] seems to confirm this opinion. Speaking of his *Discourse* of the previous year, Ramsay writes: "I sent the discourse I wrote for the various receptions of eight dukes and peers and two hundred officers of top rank and the highest nobility, to his Grace, the Duke of Ormond." Is it possible that this figure to whom Ramsay submitted his text was the grand master of the Scottish lodges of France?

Scottish Innovations

It has been claimed that the Scots, who allegedly created the grade of master, used it for political ends and instituted the high grades for the same purpose. It has also been argued that English Freemasonry originally recognized only the grades of apprentice and journeymen. The term *master* was used by English Freemasons only to designate the patron or elder of the lodge. Things were different in Scotland , however, where the grade of master was part of the craft hierarchy. This had been true for a long time as is demonstrated by the *Schaw Statutes*.

During this era of religious and dynastic struggles, it is said that the Scots tried to use this distinctive feature as a means of dominating the lodges. At this same time they were developing the symbolism of the master grade. In particular, the legend of Hiram, the brilliant builder of the Temple who was murdered by three evil journeymen and was res-

---

* [Clodion refers to the Merovingian king whose brother, Fredemundus, was claimed as an ancestor by the Stuarts. —*Trans.*]

urrected in the person of the newly initiated master, was used by the friends of Charles I to avenge his death and set his son upon the throne. English Freemasons, it is claimed, adopted the grade of master in the years 1723–1725, when the thinking that had inspired its development and application had faded from memory.

Similarly, some say the Jacobites combined their knightly titles and decorations with Freemasonry and that this served as the origin of the Scottish higher grades, which were intended to serve the political purpose of dominating Freemasonry and placing it in the service of the dynastic interests of the Stuarts.

We have covered the legend of Hiram at length and it seems it has an ancient origin that cannot be traced to any single location and retains a sense that is strictly traditional and Christian. We have also seen that the English craft did not overlook the grade of master, but that it was simply less differenciated in their practice than it was in Scotland. During the era of the transistion between the two forms of masonry—operative and speculative—lodges of both England and Scotland followed two rituals, those of the apprentice grade and those of the journeyman grade. It is conceivable, though, that masters in Scotland had, if not their own ritual, then at least signs of identification—words and customs reserved for their use alone. By virtue of circumstance, Scottish master masons were able to take advantage of these distinctive features for purposes of superiority and management, which were not always purely initiatory.

It was only starting in 1723 that the English masons of the Grand Lodge of London instituted a clearly separate grade of master similar to that in Scotland. In the domain of ritual, a replica of the journeyman ritual and the gradual impoverishment of its symbolism accompanied this creation. There is nothing in their adoption to suggest, however, that they were able to integrate the unique Scottish features to reverse this impoverishment. Further, remaining within the strict concerns of the order, the grade of Scottish master could continue to be considered as a veritable extra grade with its own secrets. This would explain the nomination of "Scots master masons" that took place at that time, chiefly at the Lodge of Bath (Somerset) on October 28, 1735. Yet we should not jump to the hasty conclusion that "Scots master mason" refers to the Scottish master, the first of the high "Scottish" grades in the way the term is currently understood. But this could well have been its seed. It seems its growth took place in France and Germany. Properly speaking, these high grades did not make their first appearance until 1734 under the names of Scots and Architects. The first knighthood grade, the Knight of the Orient, did not appear until 1749.

In some of my other books, I have dealt at length with the formation and development of the high grades that are called "Scottish" and have found nothing to suggest that the dynastic concerns of the Stuarts brought them, or any other aspect of modern Freemasonry, into being.[15]

Nonetheless, it has often been said that the Stuarts, despite the decline of their political fortunes, ceaselessly took advantage of the high grades of Freemasonry to facilitate their undertakings. The Jesuits are said to have been their most active allies at infiltrating these higher grades. At the same time, members of this religious order would have acted in their own interests, especially after 1762 during the Seven Years' War, at which time the Society of Jesus was dissolved in France and the order found its principal haven with the chief adversary of the king of France, Frederic II of Prussia. Later, in 1773, Pope Clement XIV decreed the complete suppression of the order. It was not restored until 1814 so that all its activity in between those two dates was more or less clandestine.

While there is a telling lack of any historical certitude about the Jesuit–Stuart alliance, there are certainly strong arguments supporting assertions concerning efforts made by the Stuarts and the Jesuits through Freemasonry. All of this, however, held only an episodic place in the history of the high masonic grades. What is primary and indubitable in the propagation of these grades and the constitution of the systems they embodied is their ritual and symbolic contents, which made them the vehicles of choice for mysticism and all the esoteric and Hermetic doctrines that were popular during the eighteenth century. This is clearly where the new focus of the tradition occurred and the question that arises is how this harmonized with the sources of craft freemasonry.

The Pope and the Condemnation of Freemasonry

The pope was never alarmed by craft freemasonry. Quite the contrary; the Church always had a presence within it, which made it easy to address a situation if particular circumstance called for steps to be taken. The Church took no greater concern regarding the admission of "accepted" members into the lodges.

When religious and dynastic conflicts broke out in Great Britain, Church leaders quite naturally took an interest in the situation, decidedly from the side of the Stuarts. They supported them through their misfortunes with words of encouragement, always a good thing, and with financial assistance, which is even better. James III visited the Pope on several occasions, especially following the Treaty of Utrecht, and when Louis XIV was compelled to expel the Pretender from France, it was to Rome that he went in search of consolation and support.

How is it imaginable that in their intimacy with the Stuarts the popes would remain ignorant of the activity of the Scot Lodges? Their long silence leads us to believe that they thought well of them. As noted by P. Berteloot, "if they were not assured that they pursued political secrecy that was favorable to the interests of Catholicism, they would not have failed to raise their voices against it." Their silence lasting half a century takes on greater significance when compared to the numerous condemnations that were lodged against Freemasonry once the new impetus given the institution by the Anglicans gained the upper hand. The first Bull of Excommunication against the Freemasons was not in fact fulminated until May 4, 1738, the date on which it was issued by Pope Clement XII.

1738 is a date to remember. It truly marks the formation of modern Freemasonry and the organization of the grand lodges. It was the year the *Book of Constitutions* was revised to carry a Protestant meaning and when Article I of this text was altered. In its new form it echoes the charter allegedly issued by Edwin I in 926: "A mason is obliged by his tenure to observe the moral law like a true Noachid . . . and to the three great articles of Noah," to wit, the prohibition on worshipping idols and false gods, and committing blasphemy and murder.

Before this publication, the pope was already aware that the Scottish school had lost its chance to triumph over the Anglicans in the lodges. The political and religious usefulness of the "Scots" Lodges had become quite weak with respect to the new impregnation they had taken on.

It is true that the papal bull of 1738 makes scant mention of doctrine and faith. It notes that the Freemasons should be regarded as "strongly suspect" of heresy for reason of masonic secrecy and its corollary, the oath. If Freemasons were not doing evil, it seems to contend, they would not have such hatred of the light. There were additional reasons for suspicion of heresy added to this primary one, reasons described as "just and reasonable, known to Us," though it appears these were of a temporal nature and touched on the danger Freemasonry posed to the order and peace of nations.[16] This papal condemnation was confirmed on several occasions, but it was not until Leo XIII delivered the *Humanum genus* encyclical that it truly took on a doctrinal and theological basis. It was at this time that the doctrine of modern Freemasonry was declared to be incompatible with that of the Catholic religion.

The Autonomy of French Masonry

What was to happen in France in 1738, the eldest daughter of the Church ruled by the descendent of Saint Louis and the land where the Scottish lodges, faithful to Catholicism, remained in the majority? Not what we are likely to imagine. The kingdom of France ignored the pope. The king, after all, received his crown from God. All justice issued from him. The papal bull was not registered by the Parliament of Paris as required by the fundamental laws of the kingdom in order for it to be applicable in France. *Lex non promulgata non obligat.* The bull remained a dead letter for the French lodges.

It was determined that French Freemasonry should be independent and Catholic. So it should therefore come as no surprise that it was also in 1738, for all these reasons, inluding that Gallic pride found its voice and had its own role to play, the French lodges of English origin openly freed themselves from any oversight on the part of the Grand Lodge of London. It was true that the preparations for this had been laid well in advance. Indeed, it was not until 1732 that "English" lodges with a direct connection to the Grand Lodge of London were established in France. In 1735, these lodges drew up plans to form a provincial grand lodge, sending their request for a constitutional charter to the Grand Lodge of London, which turned them down. To avoid a second refusal, they decided to go outside the organization and that following year, in accord with the "Scottish" Lodges, they founded on their own authority a provincial grand lodge. Two years later, on June 24, 1738—in other words, six weeks following the issuance of the papal bull—a peer of France, the Duke d'Antin,* was named the Perpetual and General Grand Master of the Masons of the Kingdom of France.

The creation of this Grand Mastery Association, entrusted to a peer of France, dissolved the bonds of French Freemasons to the Grand Lodge of London, much to the irritation of their British brethren. "These ingrates forget that the splendor they enjoy comes to them only from England," was the bitter English response recorded in the 1738 edition of Anderson's *Book of Constitutions.* French Freemasonry thereby escaped Protestant nationalism, as has been noted by Albert Lantoine.†

There was no room for any ambiguity concerning the religious domain of French Freemasonry. On December 27, 1776, the very Catholic Lord Derwentwater, grand master of the Freemasons of France—in other words, of the "Scottish" lodges—approved and signed the *Devoirs enjoints aux maçons libres des loges françaises,*[17] which is simply a version of one of Anderson's *Constitutions,* in which the phrase "It is now considered more appropriate to compel [the masons] only in that religion on which all men are in agreement," was replaced by this one: "It has been deemed more appropriate to require of them the religion appropriate to all Christians." This was the tolerance, limited to Catholics and Protestants, that was then deemed politically expedient to proclaim by both the Stuarts and the Hanovers. The target was hit more precisely following 1738. In *Les Statuts en usage dans les Loges de Frances,* published in 1742 but established earlier, we

---

* He was the great-grandson of the legitimate line of the Marquis de Montespan and the beautiful Françoise Athenaise de Rochechouart.

† In 1771, there were not even ten lodges in France who drew their authority from the Grand Lodge of London (Bord, *La Franc-Maçonneries en France, des origins à,* 490).

find the following: "None will be received into the Order, who has not given solemn oath or promise of an inviolable attachment to Religion, King, and Morals. Any merchants of shoddy goods peddling their skepticism, who will have spoken or written against the sacred dogmas of the ancient faith of the Crusaders, will be forever excluded from the Order." It is added that "these statutes are expressed in terms that are quite appropriate for the lands in which they should be observed."[18] The profession of the Catholic faith—for no other was legal in the kingdom of France—was substituted for the idea of tolerance implicitly targeted by the Bull of 1738.

Lodges of both English and Scottish origin remained imbued by Catholicism during the course of the eighteenth century, even within their sometimes heterodox nature. They thus rebuffed the principal reason for the papal condemnation, which, now rendered meaningless, caused little worry among the French lodges to which the ecclesiastics aligned themselves in Mass. Interestingly, in 1781 half of the members of the L'Amitié à l'Epreuve Lodge of the Orient of Narbonne were members of the clergy[19] and in 1780 there were twenty-six lodges headed by priests.

In Search of the Tradition

French masonic unity appears to have been ensured by the integral respect for tradition that was general practice. This put it out of step with the times, however. During the Age of Enlightenment, when the Reason of Philosophers triumphed, faith was questioned if not outright shaken and demanded fortification. A vast mystical current arose then in reaction against the skeptics and the libertines. Freemasonry, faithful to religion, helped to nurture this current. It could claim to respond to all doubts and to unify the faith, which it would do in the name of the religion it embodied. It was thus a matter of some importance that it formulate its principles and establish its forms, that it go further than the Church, or at least second that institution's efforts, which were no longer capable of convincing the growing number of freethinkers.

Ramsay had written Cardinal Fleury as early as March 22, 1737: "I have only ever attended them (Freemason assemblies) with an eye to spreading those maxims that will gradually render incredulity ridiculous, vice odious, and ignorance shameful. I am convinced that if one placed at the head of these assemblies wise men chosen by Your Eminence, they could prove quite useful to the religion, the State, and to letters." It seemed Ramsay had not forgotten his conversations with Fénelon in Cambrai. He concluded his letter by recounting these discussions with words borrowed from his interlocutor: "One cannot be sensibly a Deist without being a Christian, and one cannot be philosophically a Christian without becoming a Catholic."[20]

This was both a well-intentioned and laudable beginning. Still, it was necessary for Freemasonry to act as the centralizing factor of Deist sentiments and the catalyst of their transcendental unity around aspirations for betterment. Eventually, a surprising development occurred within this presumptuous objective: Excess acted as compensation for doubt. Under the pretext of reforging its bonds with the order's origins, this spiritualist Catholic Freemasonry fabricated during the eighteenth century and beyond a veritable swarm of degrees and rites. Every historical or legendary delusion of mysticism found a home therein. This movement was followed next by Protestant and Catholic Germany and ultimately supplied a source of inspiration for Romanticism. This was in turn relayed to the Americas in the form of the dreams of chivalry held by Caribbean colons.[21] The Light became the *selva oscura* of Dante. Everyone was to seek a clear view of this in order to discover the origin and goals of the Masonic order—that is, its tradition.

The more pragmatic English, who were closer to the sources of Freemasonry, knew full well that this tradition was to be found among the builders of an earlier era. Brother Preston asserted this fact in 1722 in his book *Illustrations of Masonry*. But no one took it any further. The quarrels between the Moderns and the Antients were based on a heavily obscured tradition. The authentic ritual passed down by a necessarily oral tradition had become lost over time and the way it was received, even by self-declared Christians, had ceased to be comprehended and perceived, thus it could no longer be fully preserved in its form or in thought.

The more serious Masons on the Continent, however, did not fail to demonstrate curiosity about the origins of the order and its tradition.

The most notable displays of their interest were the Congress of the Gauls held in Lyon in 1778 and the Wilhelmsbad Congress held in 1782. Primarily under the impetus of J. B. Willermoz, who was perhaps the best informed and most active Freemason of that time, the research arrived at the conclusion that Freemasonry was related to the Templar Order, such as it was at the time of its founding. The Rectified Scottish Rite and the Order of the Benevolent Knights of the Holy City emerged from these conclusions. Freemasonry was therefore oriented toward chivalry in the best sense of the word, but the rituals of the new rite approved in Wilhelmsbad showed proof, unfortunately, of an almost complete misunderstanding of the operative tradition. The implementation of this system was not negligible on the spiritual and philosophical planes, however, especially in Germany. But Freemasonry nevertheless continued to evolve primarily in a state of disorder and at the whim of unbridled imaginations.

The famous Philalethan Congress held in Paris from 1785 to 1787 provides the perfect picture of the complete confusion to which all eventually succumbed. It called upon eminent Freemasons from all lands and all rites to convene "to discuss and clarify the most essential points of the doctrine, the origin, and the historical affiliation of the true masonic science." Each of these seasoned brothers, who came from all points on the horizon, brought with him his own pertinent opinion. The resulting understanding generally agreed upon was that Freemasonry was the "original religion" handed down from such diverse sources as King Arthur, Richard I, Ramon Lulle, the Gnostics and the School of Alexandria, the Templars (as instructed by Judas of Galilee, disciple of the hermit Banon), Pythagoras, Plato, Jesus Christ and the Apostles, the Persian philosopher Each-Ben-Mohammed-Eleansi, Ormus, the Egyptians, the Benedictines, the Rosicrucians, Zoroaster, Abbaris, Channondas, Eudoxus, Hermippis, Hermes Trismegistus, Porphyrus, Plotinus, Proclus, Jamblique, the priesthood schools of India, the Gauls, the Hebrews, the Essenes, and the Persian magi.[22] The Temple of Solomon had been transformed into the Tower of Babel.

Only a single brother, one of the most eminent in attendance, Baron von Gleichen, made any allusion to operative masons—but only for the purpose of disdainfully rejecting any such vulgar association: "The charters cited by Preston are not relevant to the Free Brothers of Modern Masonry but to practical, material masons. Preston has no doubt confused the former with the builder masons." This citation clearly shows that the initiatory sense of traditional masonry had been lost. After two years of such distractions, it was not necessary to be a magician to prophesize with Cagliostro, who had refused to have anything to do with the Congress and whose anthology of stories moreover would have been enriched if it included his opinion: "Miserable Philalethans, you sow in vain, you will reap naught but weeds."

Starting in the nineteenth century and continuing right on into the present, these erring ways persist by staking claims to the respect of imaginary sources. This has caused an amplification of both a trend of pseudospiritualism and occultism and a modernist trend combining free thought, scientism, agnosticism, and politics. This highly diffused situation has noticeably permeated the majority of rituals for the higher degrees such as the Ancient and Accepted Scottish Rite, despite the fact that its motto is *Ordo ab Chao* [Order out of Chaos].

What path should be taken to restore the unity—in other words, the truth—of the operative tradition created by the cathedral builders?

In 1938, in his book *Qui est régulier?*, Oswald Wirth discussed the problem of knowing what remained faithful to *pure Masonism* under the regime of the grand lodges inaugurated in 1717. In his appraisal of this book René Guénon rightly observed that the authentic expression of pure Masonism could apply only to the craft masonry of a bygone era. He noted that if speculative Freemasonry would one day acknowledge this, it would be logically led to the integral restoration of the old operative tradition. But, he went on to ask, where were those capable of achieving such a restoration, a task that was most likely impossible?[23]

The Survival of Operative Masonry

An integral restoration (and the necessary search for it beforehand) of the ancient operative tradition: This is the primary concern that has guided the writing of this book. There is an important aspect of this subject that we have overlooked up to now: In our examination of the appearance and development of modern speculative Freemasonry, we have assumed that since the time when modern Freemasonry was constitutionally formulated in 1717, operative masonry was for all intents and purposes finished.

Along with many contemporary authors, we can certainly deny the validity of the theory of a transition—at least for England but not Scotland. Many believe that modern Freemasonry has nothing in common with the craft of masonry and that the people who made up its membership after around 1690 had quite simply decided to adopt the rites of masons to make their meetings more interesting. It is plausible that this may well have been the case for the four lodges that formed the Grand Lodge of London.

This line of reasoning, however, cannot escape the fact that in 1717 there were still a large number of lodges whose origin was incontestably operative. But wouldn't these lodges also have consisted exclusively of speculative members? There is one other fact that is certain. In modern Freemasonry lodges there was not a word mentioned of operative members. Did they just leave everywhere of their own accord? Why did they become invisible and mute? These craft masons nonetheless continued to practice their profession. Did they all simply and unanimously renounce their rites and customs? Raising such questions does sow some doubts.

It is reasonable to assume that an operative masonry continued to exist and more or less continued to practice its traditional rites. It is the trace of this activity that needs to be rediscovered. Unfortunately, no definitive elements remain in this regard. It is true that we can cite the revelations made by Brother Clement Stretton and Brother John Yarker between 1908 and 1913, which were published in a variety of Masonic magazines such as *The Freemason* and *The Co-Mason* in London and *The American Freemason* in Iowa. Their information was then reprinted in a series of articles by the English magazine *The Speculative Mason* between 1950 and 1957. René Guénon mentioned his interest in it a number of times in *Etudes Traditionnelles.*

Clemont Stretton said he had established contact with a lodge that was still operating under the principles of the former operative masonry that had survived beyond 1717 in Leicester County. He declared that similar lodges remained in existence at this time, lodges that had never recognized as authentic or legitimate the modern Freemasonry of the Grand Lodge of London. All of these lodges would have vanished during the period of World War I, 1914–1918. Stretton provided information on the organization, seven-degree hierarchy, and rituals of this operative masonry but unfortunately failed to supply any proof. A number of the revelations made here are so obviously interpolations, such as the seven-degree hierarchy, that it casts a shadow on the veracity of his entire claim.

So it is clear that another approach entirely is required to seek out the operative tradition, which is what we have attempted here. An approach that is based on the study of the authentic elements and some of the rites, symbols, and practices of this operative tradition should enable us to grasp and then renew these principles by reconnecting with the eternal truths that are their constituent elements.

Conclusion

Here, at the end of this study, one conclusion stands out regarding history. A lesson should also be drawn for contemporary Freemasonry, which views itself as the heir to the masons of the past and for all men striving to place human destiny within the sacred value of its essence.

In fashioning here an objective study based strictly on facts, we may understand that today's widespread opinions concerning the historical and spiritual origins of Freemasonry are merely conjectural if not tendentious. The facts, however, can speak clearly enough on their own to require no interpretation at all. It is necessary, of course, to connect them to the social structures of the past, but only the way we think has the power to distort how we see them.

By its very nature and purpose, the art of masonry was never a strictly operative or purely local phenomenon. The millennia-old concept of craft that blossomed in the Christian world viewed it as inseparable from the Divine creative work. The worker could stake no claim to performing his job well without the help of the Lord, and thus, by placing his activity on the path of perfection, he might raise himself to the Kingdom of God. An individual's fine craftsmanship implied that he was a good servant of the All Powerful Deity, who in return granted the worker the grace of approaching him. This grace also required an implicit obedience to all moral commandments. The whole of life was placed in a convergence of the sacred and the necessity to heed the demands of the Divine. The initiatory ritual of death and resurrection is the ascetic reflection of the model of Christ's Passion. More than any other profession, that of construction illustrated this concept perfectly through the different kinds of knowledge it required and the conjunction of science and beauty in its art, and by its purpose, whose grandest and most testimonies are God's dwellings on earth: churches and cathedrals.

The art and learning that finds expression in the smallest detail of every work is based on intangible foundations as they are touching on Perfection. This thereby establishes the tradition as well as the path to which a person must necessarily be initiated in order to take part in the Work.

On the practical and social plane, Freemasonry innately tends to speculative and universal teaching. Although its fundamental values were faithfully handed down, the tradition of masonry was ceaselessly enriched in its formulation by experience and the constant desire to do better. As an itinerant art that established contacts between men from different places and brought different techniques together, the universalist attitude within masonry led to the quest for everything that could bring together everything from the four corners of the world and make of them One through all the generations.

When this coming together took place outside of the exclusivity of dogmas to establish relations between the different religions, it ran the risk of becoming embroiled in conflict with these dogmas, which led to the growth of rationalism in the order's philosophy, allowing room and space for these differences. Does this mean that such antagonism was inevitable and impossible to resolve? This does not appear to be the case. Reason and faith are not mutually exclusive. They occupy different but complementary planes. The precedence we should assign either one is fuel for endless debate by philosophers and theologians and is a delicate question indeed. The answer depends in fact on what should be attributed to discursive thought and intuitive thought—two poles of one mind whose parameters are beyond measure and impossible to determine.

In fact, all authentic traditional paths can intersect only as they are connected to the Absolute, which is One. Forms are merely different; they do not diverge. It is interesting to note that there was never any conflict in the art of building—that is, in the art of serving and expressing the Sacred—among the Christian religion and Islam either in Spain or the Holy Lands at the time of the Crusades. Quite the contrary, their relationship was one of mutual teaching and reciprocal enrichment.

The tragedy of operative masonry was the Reformation and Counter-Reformation. Rather than being a case of opposition between two different religions, it embodied the opposition of different forms of worship within the same religion. This manifested in differente liturgical forms, which are simply circumstancial products of human sensibility—but these forms ceased to be seen as anything more than what they were, an abstraction of the Transcendent Reality they expressed. What resulted was the rule of the iconoclasts.

Freemasonry survived despite this critical blow. It survived through those elements within it that were undying: its iniatory path and its mode of expression: symbolism.

In one country especially, Great Britan, long divided and torn by religious and political conflicts, it succeeded through an adaptation of its mode of thinking and a transposition of its ability to act, to unite men of separate conviction, who, without Freemasonry, would have remained strangers to each other. This provided Freemasonry with a new point of departure. But this transformation did not occur without upheaval, especially concerning the essential: the spiritual transmission, the tradition, that ceased to be seen without an effort to intellectualize it.

This is where our historical record concerning the origins of this tradition comes to a close. Above the vested interests, beliefs, and opinions, and across the centuries and many nations, Freemasonry, loyal to its origins, however hazy, maintained its perennial tradition of an initiatory path that has made it the reflection of humanity's eternal aspiration toward the Beautiful, the Good, and the Perfect.

For a contemporary Freemasonry that still declares itself to be an initiatory society despite the inevitable adaptations that have been made, it is most important to grasp the simple and sublime, clear and profound lesson offered to it by history. It is a valuable lesson for all those who wonder about the essential questions of both their origins and their destiny. The initiatory way from which traditional freemasonry emerged is of a sacred nature. Embodying a quest for the transcendent, a bond with the sacred, it is humanism in its complete and existential acceptance. At the same time this *existentialism* is *essentialism*. It erases any duality between subject and object, between the path and the finality.

In order to grasp these things, which touch on the Absolute, there is no need to employ the abstract vocabulary of philosophers. Such things do exist because they can be felt and experienced. No other iniatory path has managed to better express the inexpressible. The medieval freemason, the builder of the cathedrals, never viewed himself as anything more than the *imagier* of an infinitely more elevated work: the Temple of the Eternal One who dwells within Man, the Heavenly Jerusalem, symbol of the universality of all men belonging to all times and races, temples of Immortality and Perfection.

This Great Work involves Consciousness, another aspect of Infinity. Humans can lay claim to this perfection because they possess it as something virtual, a sacred trust of which we must become aware. The great lesson to be drawn from this by all humanity is found in the words of the good Jeremiah: "Behold the days come, oracle of the Eternal . . . I will set my law within them and write it on their hearts . . . Behold the days come that city shall be built." The apostles Paul and James in turn stressed the divine truth of the indestructible unity and reciprocal demands of faith and works in order to aspire to transcendence.

The key to the Holy of Holies promised to all is Love, the major factor of the comprehensive illumination: Love for everything in Creation that is an immanent sign of the Light from Above; Love for all beings, who are all brothers by virtue of the sublime grace of this Love, which is the presence within them of the Absolute and the ability to perceive this presence. This Love, which is Conciousness, has nothing to do with science, learning, degrees, individual distinctions, and fragile and sometimes deceptive assumptions based on circumstance.

We can recall some other words of Jeremiah heralding the New Jerusalem: "And they shall teach no more every man his neighbour, and every man his brother, saying, Know the Lord: for they shall all know me, from the least of them unto the greatest of them" (Jeremiah 31:34).

The effort required by implementation, the path that must be taken, is the application to acquit ourselves well of every task to which our human condition makes us heir. This is the Work conceived by all and on every plane as a sacred gesture, the co-participation in the perpetual creation of the Great Work of the Absolute. The convergence within man of the finite and the infinite, the simultaneous awareness of humility and grandeur, were regarded by the operative masons as the best foundation for morality and social life: humility and grandeur made liberty, equality, and fraternity primary values.

But what heavy demands are made upon us to attain these! The intelligence of a Saint Thomas Acquinas and the sensibility of a Saint Francis of Assisi while possessing the prescience of Christ's message: These lead to no more exploitation of man by man, no more domination and humiliation based on social distinctions, no more scorn for the weak, no more vainglory, no more baseless enrichment, and no more of anything that degrades the image of the Perfect One from whom the essence of human beings are crafted.

This in brief is the spiritual, moral, and cultural patrimony of operative freemasonry in its constitutive tradition. We can of course be fully aware that all of this never existed either as a whole or as a consequence of this tradition. But we do know, even if it might appear surprising from a contemporary perspective with eyes only for material progress, that all of this was perceived by those who lived during the Middle Ages—and by the masons better than anyone else. In the facts we know, touching upon work and human relations, we find no trace of a failure among them to advance the notions of "fair salaries" and "fair prices" or to condemn profit or to ignore the rule of fraternity.

Today this has all been forgotten and lost. For those very people who claim to best speak on behalf of these values as the foundation of a civilization they ceaselessly invoke, these principles are ignored and the precepts that arise from them are nothing but empty words that have no actual effect on behavior. The more attentive individuals regard these principles only as the historical souvenir of a bygone society that believed in God's presence among men. They view its precepts as lacking any rational support and bolstered by the eternal dream of a leftist Utopia. For them, Freemasonry is a conjunction of this dead past and this lifeless dream that shapes the nostalgic refuge of a few sensitive but faded souls.

It is true that when compared with the ideal aspect of humanism, the realities of our world are quite removed from this ideal. Who still speaks of the sacred value of man and his creative activity, Work? Isn't work all too often a painful and odious constraint from which we should be liberated? Do today's Freemasons, concerned with the problems of the hour and the next day, still know how to decipher the secrets they have in storage? Finally, are these secrets from the small, motionless world of the artisan for whom time and eternity did not matter have any usefulness for our large industrial societies, so complex and overwhelmed by a rhythm that is ceaselessly accelerating? Under these conditions, wouldn't it be better for those still smitten with spirituality to attempt to reinvigorate Freemasonry with a traditional contribution from external sources, and for those whose feet remain firmly planted on the ground to utilize their abilities on a new path that is more rational, useful, and sure?

Some might subsequently believe that, confronted by historical assumptions and objective analysis, Freemasonry will be reduced to either an illusory record or a dilemma requiring abnegation or innovation. In either case, the danger for Freemasonry will be enormous. Cut from its original sources, stripped of the support of the higher order it once held, it will soon be nothing but a mask of good conscience over vague impulses, egotistical actions, and constraints.

Let us not speak of the well-meaning men who introduce themselves into the most reliable lodges with the expressed desire to share with brothers of good will the pure and laudable tradition, but who conceal their true desire to destroy the institution by deforming it, opening it up to unjustified attacks, emptying it of its historical and initiatory content. These infiltrations are not new. We have already seen the distortion of major symbols, displayed before public opinion like trophies.

Without a healthy reaction on its behalf, Freemasonry will leave itself open, without most of its brothers even grasping why, to some fairly rude shocks before being consigned to the museum of history.

For our part, let us remain hopeful. Hope, in fact, is inseparable from faith and love. Only form is mortal; truth remains. It is knowledge and consciousness; it is life. Because the incomparable history of Freemasonry touches the Absolute—that is to say, the truth—it is reasonable to think that the Freemasons will figure out a way to rediscover it beneath the antiquated veil now covering it and will discover a way to restore it with enthusiastic force and vigor.

Those who have faith in God don't see him with the eyes of children, enthroned on top of a mountain of sugar between blessed rivers of honey. We refrain from talking of him too much and seeking to define him. It is preferable to envision the itinerary that allows us to approach him and to think that God constructed himself in such a way that man's gravitation to the Spirit is, by virtue of *reason,* the best proof of God's existence. Those of increasing number who do not believe in God or who turn him into an abstraction out of a concern for tolerance, base what they deem to be just, good, and desirable on the good use of *reason,* on their trust in intelligence, and on the infinite perfectability of humanity.

The difference between these two attitudes is essentially dependent on the value given to the origin of reason: God, still unknown to the believer; or the unknown, for the nonbeliever another cause for natural laws that govern life. In one case or the other, if we use our ability to reason as best we can, to work with the certitude of the goal yet to be attained, what are we doing if not working under the auspices of and for the glory of this Unknown? And what better symbol for this Unknown than that of the Great Architect of the Universe?

The sound use of reason, the goal to be attained, and the rule of conduct to follow still remain to be set. The common denominator to which all is reduced and which encompasses everything in accordance with the initiatory tradition is the human being in whom all virtual states are immanent. The goal is the flowering and fullness of human destiny. The conduct to be upheld is love—the love that permits this flowering through what we receive and, even more, through the complete gift of self to the Absolute. The key to happiness is nowhere else.

The vast chain of union formed by Freemasons remains relevant and full of promise. In the permanence of their order they continue, within the scale of our world and according to its receptivity and needs, the immense but interrupted undertaking of the cathedral builders for both the unity of civilization and that universal nature imagined by the Templars: a peaceful establishment of welcoming and fecund ties with all religions and traditions—the common patrimony of humanity.

Notes

Part 1: The Origins of Freemasonry from Ancient Times to the Middle Ages

Chapter 1—The Ancient Corporations: The Colleges of Builders in Rome

1. O. Wirth, *Les Mystères de l'Art Royal* (Paris: self-published, 1947), 34–35.

2. Mircea Eliade, *Le Sacré et le Profane* (Paris: Gallimard, 1965), 52 ff.

3. L. Hautcoeur, "La Profession d'architecte à travers les ages," *Bulletin de l'Académie de l'Architecture,* no. 60, 1971.

4. Strabo, *Geographia,* L, IV; Aulu Gelle, *Noctium atticarum commentarii,* L, VIII.

5. Emile Durkheim, *Les formes élémentaire de la vie religieuse* (Paris: Felix Alcan, 1912), 480 ff. F. Challaye, *Petite histoire des grandes religions* (Paris: P.U.F., 1947), 21–22.

6. Plutarch, *Vie de Numa Pompilius,* trans. by D'Amyot (Paris: 1559), 496.

7. *La Loi de Hammourabi,* trans. by V. Scheil (articles 228, 229, and 274).

8. Titus-Livy, LI, c. 43.

9. A. Esmein, *Histoire du droit français,* 4th ed. (Paris: Librairie du Recueil Sirey, 1892), 2 ff.; Martin Saint-Léon, *Histoire des corporations des métiers* (Paris: P.U.F., 1941), 13 ff.; J. Ellul, *Histoire des institutions* (Paris: P.U.F., 1957), 2, 530.

10. *Freemasons Magazine* 1862; E. Rebold, *Histoire des trois Grandes Loges de Franc-Maçon en France* (Paris: Franck, 1864), 670; Lionel Vibert, *La Franc-Maçonnerie avant l'existence des Grandes Loges* (Paris: Gloton, 1950), 33.

11. Ernest Renan, *Les Apôtres* (Paris: Calmann-Levy, n.d.), 299.

12. Ibid.

13. Ibid., 359–60.

14. Saint-Léon, *Histoire des corporations des métiers*, 18.

Chapter 2—The Collegia and the Barbarian Invasions

1. Gregory of Tours, *Historia Francorum*, III, 34.

2. Anthyme Saint-Paul, *Histoire monumentale de la France* (Paris: Éditions Hachette, 1932), 51.

3. Bede, *Historia ecclesiastica*, L, IV, c. II.

4. Daniel Ramée, *Histoire générale de l'Architecture* (Paris: Aymot, 1860), 1057; Etienne Gilson, *La Philosophie au Moyen Age* (Paris: Payot, 1925), 184–85.

5. Emile Malé, *L'Art Roman, Histoire générale de l'Art*, vol. 1 (Paris: Flammarion, 1950), 286–87.

6. F. Vercauteren, *La vie urbaine entre Meuse et Loire du VIe au IXe siècle;* J. Hubert, "Evolution de topographie et de l'aspect des villes en Gaule (Ve–Xe siècle)," *Settimane del studio del Centro Italiano, di studi sull'alto medioevo* 6 (1959).

7. Troya, *Observations sur l'Edit de Rothari et sur la Lombardie;* Carl Hegal, *Städte und Gilden* (Leipzig: Duncker-Humbolt, 1891), part 1, chapter 3.

8. F. Brunetti, *Codice diplomatico toscano*, no. 31 (Florence: 1806–1833).

9. Hofmeister, *Monumenta germaniae historica*, vol. 30, part 2 (Leipzig, 1933).

10. F. Olivier-Martin, *L'Organisation corporative de la France d'Anceint Régime* (Paris: Librairie de Recueil Sirey, 1938), 84.

11. Fantuzzi, *Monuments de Ravenne du Moyen Age* (Venice: 1801–1804), 133, 149, 228, 385.

12. Muratori, *Rer. Italic* 12 (1723–1751).

13. Jean Mabillon, *Musei Italic*, vol. 2 (Paris: Billaine, 1668–1701), 19.

14. Jean Mabillon, *Acta SS. Ben.*, vol. 3 (Paris: Billaine, 1668–1701), 2.

15. Eginhard, *De vita et gesti Caroli Magni*, 130.

16. Gobelini Personae, *Cosmodromium*, quoted by D. Ramée, *Histoire Générale de l'Architecture*, 800.

Chapter 3—Ecclesiastical and Monastic Associations

1. Mabillon, *Acta Sanct. Ord. Bened* 25, no. 28.

2. See Caumont, *Essais sur l'architecture religieuse du Moyen Age* (Caen: Imprimerie de A. Hardel, 1841), 66; *L'intermédiaire des chercheurs et curieux* (1904), col. 809.

3. Saint-Paul, *Histoire monumentale de la France.*

4. Louis Hourticq, *Encyclopédie des Beaux-Arts,* vol. 1 (Paris: Hachette, 1925), 233.

5. Louis Gonse, *Le Musée d'Art,* vol. 1 (Paris: Larousse, n.d.), 76.

6. Emile Malé, *Musée d'Art,* vol. 1, 63.

7. Gonse, *Le Musée d'art,* 78.

8. Gregory, former bishop of Blois, *Recherches historiques sur les Congrégations hospitalières des frères pontifes* (1818); Dugange Glossary, under the words *Fratres pontis.*

9. L. Lachat, *La Franc-Maçonnerie operative* (Lyon: Derain-Raclet, 1934), 57.

10. H. Focillon, *Art d'Occident, Le Moyen Age roman,* vol. 1 (Paris: Librairie Armand Colin, 1971), 323; Françoise Henry, *Art Irlandais* (Dublin: A l'Enseigne des Trois Flambeaux,1964), a book which, through its devotion to ornamental art, has shed a remarkable light upon such art's spirit, themes, and techniques.

Chapter 4—Secular Brotherhoods: The Germanic and Anglo-Saxon Guilds

1. Springer, *De artificibus monachus et laicis Medii Aevi* (Bonn: 1861).

2. For more on this subject see especially Saint-Leon, *Histoire des corporations des métiers,* 31 ff.

3. Lujo Brentano, *Essay on the History and Development of Gilds* (London: 1870), quoted by Saint-Leon, *Histoire des corporations des métiers,* 38.

4. Saint-Leon, *Histoire des corporations des métiers,* 39-40.

5. Ibid.

6. *Recueil des Sacrés Conciles,* vol. 25, col. 763–64.

Chapter 5—The Crusades and the Templars

1. René Grousset, *Histoire des Croisades,* vol. 1 (Paris: Plon, 1936), 154.

2. Guillaume de Tyr, *Histoire des Croisades*, vol. 2, 270.

3. Ibid., 277.

4. Grousset, *Histoire des Croisades*, vol. 2, 155.

5. de Tyr, *Histoire des Croisades*, 423; vol. 3, 451.

6. Ibid., vol. 2, 439.

7. Ibid., vol. 3, 27.

8. Rohricht, *Geschicte des Konigreichs Jerusalem 1100–1291* (Innsbruck, 1898).

9. Grousset, *Histoire des Croisades*, vol. 3, 387–88.

10. Ibid., 408.

11. F. T. B. Clavel, *Histoire pittoresque de la Franc-Maçonnerie* (Paris: Pagnerre, 1843), 85.

12. Abbe Lebeuf, *Histoire de la Ville et de tout le Diocese de Paris*, vol. 2 (Paris: Éditions Cocheris, 1887), 467.

13. Grousset, *Histoire des Croisades*, vol. 1, 68–70.

14. de Tyr and his continuers, *Histoire des Croisades*, vol. 4, 229.

15. Ibid., 551.

16. Ibid., vol. 2, 380.

17. T. E. Lawrence, *Crusader Castles* (London: Golden Cockerel Press, 1936), 84.

18. Robert Charles de Lasteyrie, *L'architecture religieuse en France a l'epoque romane* (Paris: Alphonse Picard et Fils, 1912), 279–80.

19. Esmein, *Histoire du droit français*, 336–37.

20. Grousset, *Histoire des Croisades*, vol. 1, 140–44.

21. de Tyr, *Histoire des Croisades*, vol. 4, 406.

22. John Charpentier, *L'ordre des Templiers* (Paris: La Colombe, 1944), 148.

23. de Tyr, *Histoire des Croisades*, vol. 3, 192, 238.

24. Grousset, *Histoire des Croisades*, vol. 2, 807 ff.

25. Ibid., vol. 3, 408–10.

26. Louis Massignon, *Les corps de métiers et la cité islamique;* Louis Gardet, *Les Hommes de l'Islam* (Paris: Éditions Hachette, 1977), 156 ff.

27. Gardet, *Les Hommes de l'Islam*, 273.

28. J. H. Probst-Biraben, *Les Mystères des Templiers* (Paris: Omnium Litteraire, 1973), 116.

29. T. H. Lewis, *Masonry and Masons' Marks*, A.Q.C. 3 (1890), 65–76.

30. Ramée, *Histoire générale de l'Architecture*, 898.

31. Malé, *L'Art Carolingien, Histoire générale de l'Art*, vol. I (Paris: Flammarion, 1950), 308.

32. de Tyr, *Histoire des Croisades*, vol. 3, 154.

33. Charpentier, *L'ordre des Templiers*, 154.

34. Ibid., 166.

Chapter 6—The Templars, the Francs Métiers, and Freemasonry

1. La Curne de Saint-Palaye, *Dict. hist. de l'ancien langage francais* (1879).

2. Hurtaut de Magny, *Dictionnaire Historique de la Ville de Paris et ses environs*, vol. 3 (1779), 103.

3. de Thou, *Histoire de mon temps*, vol. 8, 115.

4. R. de Lespinasse and F. Bonnardot, *Le Livre des Métiers d'Etienne Boileau* (Paris: Imprimerie Nationale, 1879), 18.

5. de Duc de Levis Mirepoix, *Saint Louis, roi de France* (Paris: Albin Michel, 1970), 278.

6. de Lespinasse and Bonnardot, *Le Livre des Métiers d'Etienne Boileau*, 333.

7. Robert Freke Gould, *A Concise History of Freemasonry* (London: Gale and Polden, 1903).

8. For more, see Beatrice Lees, *Records of the Templars in England* (London: British Academy, 1935).

9. Bernard Picard, *Ceremonies Religieuses* (Amsterdam: Chez Laporte, 1789), 385; Thory, *Acta Latomorum*, vol. 1, 5.

10. Gould, *A Concise History of Freemasonry*, 186.

11. de Tyr, *Histoire des Croisades*, vol. 4, 209.

12. Emile Coornaert, *Les Corporations en France* (Paris: Éditions Ouvrières, 1966), 70.

13. Renouvier and Ricard, *Des maitres et autres artistes gothiques de Montpellier* (Paris: J. Martel, 1844).

14. A. Teulet, *Layettes du Tresor des Chartres*, vol. 1, no. 237, 100b; no. 722, 255–66.

15. Grousset, *Histoire des Croisades*, vol. 2, 23.

16. F. X. Kraus, *Kunst und Alterthum in Elsass Lothringen*, vol. 3

(Strassburg: 1889), 770–71; Jean Schneider, *La Ville de Metz aux XIIIe et XIVe siecles* (Nancy, 1950), 233; Eugene Voltz, *La Chapelle des Templiers de Metz,* rev. *L'Acheologie* (1973).

17. A. du Chesne, *Les Antiquités et Recherches des Villes de France* (Paris: 1647), 714.

18. Cadet de Gassicourt, *Les Iniliés Anciens et Modernes, suite du Tombeau de Jacques Molai* (Paris). This theory was first presented in a French manuscript of 1742 or 1743 that was rediscovered in Strasbourg; see also Schiffmann, *Die Entstehung der Rittergrade in der Freimaurerei um die Mitte des XVIII and Jahrhunderts* (Leipzig, 1882). This text is reproduced *in extenso* in A. Lantoine, *La Franc-Maçonnerie chez elle* (Paris: Emile Nourry, 1925), 137 ff.

19. Cited by Ragon, *Orthodoxie Maçonnique* (Paris: Éditions Dentu, 1853), 223–24.

20. Probst-Biraben, *Les Mystères des Templiers,* 155.

21. E. Rebold, *Histoire générale de la Franc-Maçonnerie,* 116; Jean-Pierre-Simon Boubee, *Souvenirs Maçonniques* (Geneva: Honore Champion, n.d.), 22-23.

Chapter 7—The Templars and the Parisian Builders

1. Nesle Archives, Manuscript MM, 128.

2. Esmein, *Histoire du droit français,* 251; J. Ellul, *Histoire des Institutions,* vol. 3 (Paris: P.U.F., 1976), 162 ff.

3. H. de Curzon, *Le maison du Temple de Paris* (Paris: 1888), 117.

4. A. Berty, L. M. Tisserand, and C. Platon, *Topographique historique du vieux Paris, region centrale de l'Université* (Paris: Imprimerie nationale, 1897), 349 ff.

5. See also L. Lambeau, *Histoire de l'orme Saint Gervais,* Appendix to the minutes of the session of March 2, 1912 of the Commission de Vieux Paris.

6. de Lespinasse and Bonnardot, *Le Livre des Métiers d'E. Boilleau,* viii.

7. de Curzon, *Le maison du Temple de Paris,* 276–77.

8. Ibid., 238 ff.

9. V. E. Michelet, *Le Secret de la Chevalerie* (Paris: Brosse, 1928).

10. Abbe Lebeuf, *Histoire de la Ville et de tout le Diocese de Paris,* vol. 2, 517.

11. de Lespinasse and Bonnardot, *Le Livre des Métiers d'E. Boilleau.*

12. de Curzon, *Le maison du Temple de Paris,* 68.

13. Boislisle, *Bulletin de la Société de l'Histoire de Paris,* vol. 8 (Paris, 1881), 115.

14. Dulaire, *Histoire de Paris,* vol. 5 (Paris: Guillaume and Co., 1821–1822), 265 ff.

15. Lebeuf, *Histoire de la Ville et de tout le Diocese de Paris,* vol. 2, 103.

16. Delamare, *Traité de la Police,* vol. 4 (Paris, 1705–1738), 83.

17. de Lespinasse and Bonnardot, *Le Livre des Métiers d'E. Boilleau,* cxlv.

18. de Curzon, *Le maison du Temple de Paris,* 88.

19. de Lespinasse and Bonnardot, *Le Livre des Métiers d'E. Boilleau,* iv.

20. de Curzon, *Le maison du Temple de Paris,* 70, 98.

21. A. Freidman, *Paris, ses rues, ses paroisses* (Paris: Plon, 1959), 79.

22. Lebeuf, *Histoire de la Ville et de tout le Diocese de Paris,* vol. 2, 315, 464.

23. National Archives, S 3454, suppl.; Lebeuf, *Histoire de la Ville et de tout le Diocese de Paris,* vol. 2, 434.

24. Desmaze, *Les Métiers de Paris,* 172.

25. Léon Mirot, "Les hotels de Rohan Soubise" (report from the Commission du Vieux Paris, session of June 30, 1923). Note in particular the name of Quatre Fils Aymon.

26. R. de Lespinasse, *Les Métiers et Corporations de la ville de Paris,* vol. 2, 600.

27. *Revue universelle des Arts,* 1 (1855).

28. For more on the Trinity Hospital and the Confederation of the Passion, see Pierre Bonfons, *Les Antiquités de Paris,* with additions by Jacques de Breuil (Paris: 1608), 227–29; Dom Michel Felibien, *Histoire de la Ville de Paris,* vol. 4, revised and expanded edition by Dom Guy-Alexis Lobineau (Paris: 1725), 743; Delamarre, *Traité de la Police,* vol. 4, 469; Hurtault, *Dictionnaire Historique de la Ville de Paris,* vol. 2 and vol. 3 (Paris: 1779), 2: 543, 3: 242–43; Lebeuf, *Histoire de la Ville et de tout le Diocese de Paris,* vol. 1, 273.

29. de Lespinasse and Bonnardot, *Les métiers et corporations de la ville de Paris,* vol. 2, 600.

30. F. Husson, *Les Maçons et Tailleurs de Pierre,* 247.

31. Lebeuf, *Histoire de la Ville et de tout le Diocese de Paris,* vol. 1, 137.

32. See the text of these acts in Husson, *Les Maçons et Tailleurs de Pierre,* 159 ff.

33. Collin-Danton, known as Collin de Plancy, *Jacquemin le Franc-Maçon,* 364.

34. Lebeuf, *Histoire de la Ville et de tout le Diocese de Paris,* vol. 2, 193, 196.

35. Serge Hutin, *Les Sociétés sécretes* (Paris: P.U.F., 1960), 44.

36. Lebeuf, *Histoire de la Ville et de tout le Diocese de Paris,* vol. 2, 244.

37. Ibid., 241–42.

38. Ibid., vol. 1, 316; Dulaure, *Histoire des environs de Paris,* vol. 2, 2nd edition, 92.

39. Lebeuf, *Histoire de la Ville et de tout le Diocese de Paris,* vol. 2, 463.

40. L. Lambeau, "Report on the rue de la Mortellerie Made to the Commission Municipale du Vieux, Paris, on April 24, 1917," *Bulletin municipal official* (January 24, 1918), 384.

41. Lebeuf, *Histoire de la Ville et de tout le Diocese de Paris,* vol. 2, 464.

42. Lebeuf, *Histoire de la Ville et de tout le Diocese de Paris,* vol. 1, 323, 351; vol. 2, 308; Dulaure, *Histoire des environs de Paris,* vol. 1, 411.

43. J. B. Denisart, *Collection de décisions nouvelles et de notions relatives à la jurisprudence actuelle: Declaration of February 5, 1731, Article 1,* vol. 4 (Paris: Chez la Veuve Desaint, 1771), 785.

44. La Poix de Freminville, *Dictionnaire de la Police Générale,* 505.

45. J. B. Denisart, *Collection de décisions nouvelles et de notions relatives à la jurisprudence actuelle: Declaration of February 5, 1731, Article 1,* vol. 3, 307.

46. A. Bernet, *Joli-Coeur de Pouyastruc, Compagnon du Devoir,* 197.

47. C. H. Simon, *Etude historique et morale sur le Compagnonnage* (Paris, 1853).

48. Sauval, *Histoire et recherches des Antiquités de la ville de Paris,* vol. 1 (1724), 152; Jaillot, *Recherches sur Paris,* vol. 3 (1775), 40.

49. Rochegude, *Promenade dans toutes les rues de Paris* (Paris: Denoël, 1958); G. Pessard, *Nouveau dictionnaire historique de Paris* (Paris: Eugene Rey, 1904).

50. Desmaze, *Les Métiers de Paris*, 11.

51. *Bibliothèque Historique de la Ville de Paris*, ms 11 479 A, 507.

52. See also my book, *La Tradition et la Conaissance Primordiale dans la spiritualité de l'Occident. Les Silènes de Rabelais*, (Paris: Éditions Dervy, 1973).

53. J. B. Le Masson, *Calendriers des Confréries de Paris*, 31.

54. Berty, Tisserand, and Platon, *Topographie historique du vieux Paris (region centrale de l'Universite)* (Paris: Imprimerie Nationale, 1897), 366, 367, 370.

55. It is mentioned in Guillot's *Dit des rues de Paris, 1310-1315* (Paris: Éditions Mareuse, 6.

56. Lebeuf, *Histoire de la Ville et de tout le Diocese de Paris*, vol. 2, 82.

57. Lefeuve, *Histoire de Paris, rue par rue, maison par maison*, vol 2 (Paris: C. Reinwald, 1875), 205.

58. Lebeuf, *Histoire de la Ville et de tout le Diocese de Paris*, vol. 1, 388; J. Hillairet, *Evocation du vieux Paris*, 545.

59. J. du Breul, *Le Theatre des Antiquites de Paris* (1612), 588.

60. J. B. le Masson, *Le Livre des Confreries*, 31.

61. L. Tesson, *Report to the Commission du Vieux Paris, December 22, 1916* (Paris: P.V. 1916), 293.

62. L. Lambeau, "Report on the rue de la Mortellerie Made to the Commission Municipale du Vieux, Paris, on April 24, 1917," 375.

63. Berty and Tisserand, *Topographie historique du vieux Paris (region du Bourg Saint Germain)*, 2.

64. *Paris et ses environs reproduits par le Daguerréotype* (Paris: Aubert et Cie, 1840).

65. G. Pessard, *Nouveau dictionnaire historique de Paris*.

Part 2: From the Art of Building to the Art of Thinking

Chapter 8—Mason Corporations in France

1. Coornaert, *Les Corporations en France avant 1789*, 24.

2. Desmaze, *Les Métiers de Paris*, 210.

3. *Layettes du trésor des Chartres*, 1, no. 350.

4. F. Olivier-Martin, *L'Organisation corporative de la France d'Anceint Régime*, 89 ff.

5. de Lespinasse and Bonnardot, *Le Livre des Métiers d'Etienne*

Boileau. See also Saint-Léon, *Histoire des corporations de métiers,* and Coornaert, *Les Corporations en France avant 1789.*

6. de Lespinasse and Bonnardot, *Le Livre des Métiers d'Etienne Boileau,* cxv.

7. Lantoine, *La Franc-Maçonnerie chez elle,* 2nd ed. (Paris: Emile Noury, 1927), 33.

8. Saint-Léon, *Histoire des corporations de métiers,*102.

9. Luc Benoist, *Le Compagnnonage et les Metiers* (Paris: P.U.F., 1966), 67.

10. de Lespinasse and Bonnardot, *Le Livre des Métiers d'Etienne Boileau,* lxxxix.

11. L. Hautcoeur, "La Profession d'architecte à travers les âges," 4.

12. de Lespinasse, *Les Métiers et Corporations de la ville de Paris,* vol. 2, 597, 600.

13. Lebeuf, *Histoire de la Ville et de tout le Diocese de Paris,* vol. 2, 242.

14. de Curzon, *Le maison du Temple de Paris,* 69.

15. Saint-Léon, *Histoire des corporations de métiers,* 296.

16. Ibid., 392.

17. Abbe Migne, Introduction to *Dictionnaire des Confréries,* vol. 50 of *Encyclopédie théologique,* 26.

18. Saint-Léon, *Histoire des corporations de métiers,* 393.

19. Coonaert, *Les Corporations en France avant 1789,* 204.

Chapter 9—Builders Corporations in Italy, Germany, and Switzerland

1. Onclair, *La Franc-Maçonnerie dans se origins,* 174.

2. C. Hegel, *Geschicte der Städtenverfassung von Italien.*

3. G. Villani, *Histoire de Florence,* L. VII, chapter 13.

4. Statutes of Parma (1255); Onclair, *La Franc-Maçonnerie dans se origins,* 180.

5. Ibid., 187.

6. Carl Hegal, *Städte und Gilden* (Leipzig: Duncker-Humbolt, 1891), Appendix: "Origin of the Municipal Council in Germany."

7. Rebold, *Histoire des trois Grandes Loges,* 30, 672, 676.

8. Ibid., 30; F. T. B. Clavel, *Histoire pittoresque de la Franc-Maçonnerie* (Paris: Pagnerre, 1843), 87.

9. Heldmann, *Die drei ältesten geschichtlichen Denkmäler der deutschen Freimaurer-Brüderschaft* (Aarau: 1819).

10. Gould, *A Concise History of Freemasonry.*

11. Clavel, *Histoire pittoresque de la Franc-Maçonnerie,* 123; Findel, *Histoire de la Franc-Maçonneries,* vol. 2, 478.

12. *Der Steinmetzen Brüderschaft, Ordnungen und Articul. Ernewert auf dem Tag zu Strassburg auf der Haupthütten, auf Michaëlis* (s. 1), 1563, in folio.

13. Rebold, *Histoire des trois Grandes Loges,* 677.

14. Findel, *Histoire de la Franc-Maçonneries,* vol. 2, 429 ff.

15. Gould, *A Concise History of Freemasonry.*

16. Clavel, *Histoire pittoresque de la Franc-Maçonnerie,* 87.

17. Findel, *Histoire de la Franc-Maçonneries,* vol. 1, 71–72.

Chapter 10—The Corporative Masonry of Great Britain

1. Vibert, *La Franc-Maçonnerie avant l'existence des Grandes Loges,* 29 ff.

2. Findel, *Histoire de la Franc-Maçonneries,* vol. 1, 81; Gould, *A Concise History of Freemasonry,* 124–30; Vibert, *La Franc-Maçonnerie avant l'existence des Grandes Loges,* 75.

3. Knoop and Jones, *The Medieval Mason,* 84.

4. Gould, *A Concise History of Freemasonry.*

5. Ordinances reprinted in the anthology *Fabrics Rolls of York Minster* (1859), 171 ff.

6. The Articles of London are analyzed in Jouin, *Le Livre des constitutions maçonnoques,* 27.

7. The text of these ordinances is reproduced in T. Smith, *English Gilds* (London: 1870).

8. J. O. Halliwell, *The Early History of Freemasonry in England,* 1840. A meticulous analysis of this text in French can be found in Findel, *Histoire de la Franc-Maçonneries,* vol. 1, 86–96, and in Jouin, *Le Livre des constitutions maçonnoques,* 28–32. A very beautiful facsimile edition of this venerable work, followed by a commentary by J. F. Smith, a version in modern English by R. H. Baxter, and a glossary by Speth was published by the Masonic Book Club of Bloomington, Illinois in 1970.

9. Regarding their classification and for a critical examination of their texts, see W. Begemann, *Vorgeschichte und Anfänge der Freimaurerei in England* and *Ars Quatour Coronatorum,* vol. 1, 152–61.

10. J. P. Berger, "Le Ms Dunfries," no. 4, translated and annotated, in *Le Symbolisme* 377, October–December, 1966.

11. Findel, *Histoire de la Franc-Maçonneries*, vol. 1, 40 ff; Gould, *A Concise History of Freemasonry*, 208 ff; Vibert, *La Franc-Maçonnerie avant l'existence des Grandes Loges*, 53 ff; F. L. Pick and G. Norman Knight, *The Pocket History of Freemasonry* (London: Muller, 1990), 30 ff.

12. Vibert, *La Franc-Maçonnerie avant l'existence des Grandes Loges*, 62.

13. *The Old Constitutions Belonging to the Ancient and Honorable Society of Free and Accepted Masons*, 4 volumes (London: J. Roberts, 1722).

14. Rebold, *Histoire des trois Grandes Loges*, 673. Findel consistently challenges the veracity of Rebold's information—see Findel, *Histoire de la Franc-Maçonnerie*, vol. 1, 115, ff.

15. Clavel, *Histoire pittoresque de la Franc-Maçonnerie*, 91.

16. Onclair, *La Franc-Maçonnerie dans se origins*, 123.

17. Preston, *Illustrations of Masonry* (London: G and T Wilkie, 1795), 136–37.

18. Clavel, *Histoire pittoresque de la Franc-Maçonnerie*, 90.

19. Gould, *A Concise History of Freemasonry*, 190.

20. Rebold, *Histoire des trois Grandes Loges*, 673.

21. Vibert, *La Franc-Maçonnerie avant l'existence des Grandes Loges*, 88.

22. Le Forestier, *L'occultisme et la Franc-Maçonnerie Ecossaise*, 148.

23. Preston, *Illustrations of Masonry*, 136–37.

24. Rebold, *Histoire des trois Grandes Loges*, 674, 681; Bord, *La Franc-Maçonneries en France, des origins à 1815*, 55–56.

25. Rebold, *Histoire des trois Grandes Loges*, 673-74; Gould, *A Concise History of Freemasonry*.

Chapter 11—Universal Freemasonry

1. Marc Rucart, from a Conference given at the Grand Orient of France, March 1, 1933.

2. Lacordaire, Toulouse Conference, 1854.

3. Lantoine, *La Franc-Maçonnerie chez elle*, 2nd ed., 7.

4. Camille Enlart, *Manuel d'Archéologie Française*, part 1 (Paris: A. Picard, 1902). For more on this rivalry between science and art, see

Louis Hautecoeur, *Histoire de l'Art,* vol. 1 (Paris: Flammarion, 1959), 166 ff.

5. Clavel, *Histoire pittoresque de la Franc-Maçonnerie,* 83; Berteloot, *Les Franc-Maçons devant l'Histoire* (Paris: Éditions du Monde Nouveau, 1949), 20.

6. Malé, *L'Art Religieux du XIII Siecle en France,* vol. 1, 12.

7. Gould, *A Concise History of Freemasonry.*

8. Sauval, *Histoire et recherches des Antiquités de la ville de Paris,* vol. 1 (Paris: Charles Moette, 1724), 361.

9. Abbe Villain, *Essai d'une histoire de la paroisee Saint Jacques de la Boucherie* (1758), 65.

10. Desmaze, *Les Métiers de Paris* (Paris: Leroux, 1874), 211.

11. Quoted by Gould, *A Concise History of Freemasonry.*

12. Péladan, *La clé de Rabelais. Le langage des métiers* (Paris: Rumeur des Ages, 1995), 41.

13. Ibid., 85-86.

14. Douet D'Arco, *Collection des sceaux des Archives Nationales* (Paris: Plon, 1867); Desmaze, *Les Métiers de Paris,* 172.

Chapter 12—Speculative Freemasonry

1. A. Horne, "The Masonic Tradition of King Solomon's Temple," *Ars Quatour Coronatorum* 80 (1967), 8 ff.

2. *The Early Masonic Catechisms,* new ed., 50 ff.

3. Vibert, *La Franc-Maçonnerie avant l'existence des Grandes Loges,* 137.

4. Rebold, *Histoire des Trois Grandes Loges,* 673.

5. Berteloot, *Les Franc-Maçons devant l'Histoire,* 42.

6. P. Bloch, *Travaux de la Loge Villard de Honnecourt,* vol. 2, no. 5, 68.

7. L. Vibert, *La Franc-Maçonnerie avant l'existence des Grandes Loges,* 89.

8. François Rabelais, trans., *Gargantua and Pantagruel* (London: J. M. Cohen/ Penguin, 1955), 159. For more on Rabelais, Freemason, see my book *La Tradition et la Connaissance Primordiale dans la spiritualité de l'Occident. Les Silènes de Rabelais.* (Paris: Éditions Dervy, 1973.)

9. See also Charles Renouvier, *Manuel de Philosophie Moderne* (1842), 12–13.

10. Clavel, *Histoire pittoresque de la Franc-Maçonnerie,* 85; B. E. Jones, 446.

11. Gould, *A Concise History of Freemasonry.*

12. S. Hutin, *Les disciples de Jacob Boehme,* 241 ff.

13. Bord, *La Franc-Maçonneries en France, des origins à 1815,* 53 ff.

14. Ibid., 57.

Chapter 13—The Grand Lodges and Modern Freemasonry

1. For more, see my books *La Franc-Maçonnerie* (Paris: P.U.F., 1990) and *Histoire Générale de la Franc-Maçonnerie* (Paris: P.U.F., 1987).

2. M. Paillard, *Les Trois Franc-Maçonneries.*

3. *Ars Quatour Coronatorum* 56 (1943).

4. *Ars Quatour Coronatorum* 78, (1965).

5. *Ars Quatour Coronatorum* 80 (1967), 42.

6. Ibid., 36 ff. On this question, more interesting reading can be found in Reverend N. Barjer Cryer's long study *The De-Christianization of the Craft,* in *Ars Quatour Coronatorum* 97 (1984), 34–60, and in the same journal, in the response by F. Christopher Haffner (65-68), who follows my own line of argument.

7. *The Old Constitutions belonging to the Ancient and Honourable Society of Free and Accepted Masons* (London: J. Roberts, 1722).

8. *Annales Maçonniques des Pays-Bas,* vol. 4 (Brussels, 1822–1823), 372.

9. Berteloot, *Les Franc-Maçons devant l'Histoire,* 43–44. Most of the historians of Freemasonry in France have always been in agreement on this point. See also N. de Bonneville, Thory, Rebold, and, from the present era, A. Lantoine. In English, see Chalmers I. Paton, *The Origin of Freemasonry* (London: 1871), 34–35.

10. For more on Louise de Keroualle and her intrigues, see H. Forneron, *Louise de Keroualle, duchesse de Portsmouth, 1649–1734* (1866) and A. Lantoine, *Le Rite Ecossais ancien et accepté.*

11. Letter discovered by Miss Françoise Weill and published by her in the *Revue historique et littérraire de la France,* no. 2 (April-June, 1963), 276–78. Reprinted in P. Chevallier, *Les Ducs sous l'Acacia* (Paris: J. Vrin, 1964), 215–26.

12. Refers to a separate printing of the article "Franche-Maçonnerie" in the *Encyclopedia* (1773).

13. *Ars Quatour Coronatorum* 47 (1938), 41–89. This theory was the subject of an interesting analysis that appeared in *Cahier* no. 24 (December 1952), house organ of the Grand Lodge of France.

14. P. Chevallier, *Les Ducs sous l'Acacia* (Oxford: Bodleian Library, Carte ms no. 226 folio), 152–53.

15. Onclair, *Histoire, rituals et tuiler des hauts grades maçonniques* (Paris: Dervy, 1984) and *La Franc-Maçonnerie chrétienne.*

16. See also S. J. Ferrer-Benimelli, *Historia de la Masoneria española en el siglo XVIII. Relations entre la Iglesia Catolica y la Masoneria* (Saragossa, 1971).

17. This manuscript is part of the collection of the Bibliothèque Nationale in Paris (F.M. 4146).

18. *Histoire, obligations et Statuts de la Confraternité des Franc-Maçons* (Frankfurt am Main, 1742), 142.

19. A. Le Bihan, *Loges et Chapitres de la Grande Loge et du Grand Orient de France* (Paris: Bibliothèque Nationale,1967), 176.

20. A. Compigny Des Bordes de Villiers de L'Isle Adam, G. Gleize, and A. Prenat, *Les Entretiens de Cambrai. Fénelon et le Chevalier de Ramsay* (V. Rasmussen, 1929), 38, 137.

21. See my books, *Histoire, Rituels et Tuileur des Hauts Grades Maçonniques* and *La Franc-Maçonnerie chrétienne.*

22. Minutes of the Philalethan Congress, *Le Monde Maçonnique*, vols. 14 and 15 (1872–1873, 1873–1874).

23. *Etudes Traditionnelles* (November 1939).

Index